void if detached

void if detached

SEEKING MODERN SPIRITUALITY
THROUGH MY FATHER'S OLD SERMONS

SARAH BOWEN
BASED ON THE WRITINGS
OF RICHARD MURDOCH

Illustrations by Sean Bowen
Afterword by Amy Murdoch

teras
PUBLISHING

Rhinebeck, NY

teras
PUBLISHING

Void if detached © 2016 Sarah Bowen
ISBN 978-0-615-75548-9
Library of Congress Control Number: 2016960595
First edition 2016

Published by Teras Publishing
Distributed by Epigraph Publishing
www.voidifdetachedbook.com

To my father
(who art in heaven)

Contents

If cobblers' kids have no shoes...

...then do preachers' kids have no religion? That question launched the idea for this book.

For me, being a Preacher's Kid (PK) is often a surreal experience. When someone finds out I am a PK, they usually envision me growing up in a stark, fire-and-brimstone household, and thus solemnly offer me their condolences, combined with looks of subtle pity. Or—having seen *Footloose* one too many times—they ask me if I have red cowboy boots. Or they smile mysteriously and say, "Now *that* explains it."

I try to ward off most of these responses by quickly explaining that my father was not your typical preacher. That our house was not filled with spooky religious paintings. That, yes, my dad loved to dance, and drank vodka tonics.

Oh, and that, most importantly, I am not a bastard. You see, during our elementary school years, my sister Amy and I lived in a neighborhood that felt half Jewish/half Catholic, with us being members of a strange group called Protestant. My Catholic classmates pulled me aside quietly and whispered that I really shouldn't have been born because priests aren't supposed to have wives or kids. Dad further confused this issue by reading Hebrew in my first grade show-and-tell. Now my Jewish classmates were stumped. However, because my father would patiently answer their questions, he became known affectionately as The Rev by our friends of all faiths.

✡ ✝ ☪ ☯ ✺ ॐ

When I was very young, I never questioned whether the Bible stories were true. I felt a sense of awe thinking of Noah's ark or Jonah being swallowed by a whale. Bible stories were just other versions of bedtime stories, in which cats wearing hats spoke, and girls could become princesses of other lands. God was a given and I knew that he loved me.

I loved being at the church with my Dad—and of course I loved the specialness (or entitlement!) that I thought came from being the "boss's" daughter. Christmas brought the yearly Advent musical, and summer brought Vacation Bible School. I sang in the choir, and performed in church musicals.

Sometimes my sister Amy and I would skip church school and run our own club in Dad's office. We'd round up a couple of other kids and play church—all putting our donation offerings in my Dad's velvet-lined pipe box. Once at home we even performed a marriage ceremony for the kids in the neighborhood—dressed in a neighbor's lingerie. Amy gave a rousing speech in a black-and-white peignoir. A neighborhood girl and I dressed in pastel camisoles and fluttered around as butter-flies. (All the best weddings have butterflies, of course.)

We'd raid the church supply closets and make artistic concoctions from colored construction paper, bendy pipe cleaners, and ridiculous amounts of paste. One such project marked the first time I questioned what I learned in church. On the side of our church's property was a large, wooded area we played in with the other curious kids. Affection-ately named the Bunny Woods, it held a special place in the hearts and minds of our group, and served as the backdrop for most of our play.

So imagine our confusion when immense yellow construction ve-hicles showed up in this area and the trees began showing up on the ground! Extremely upset, Amy and I asked Dad what was going on. To us, this was "God's land" and how dare anyone hurt it, taking the homes away from our prized bunnies.

We then got an introduction to real estate development. But fear not, we had the answer. Raiding the church supply closet again with our assembled child warriors, my sister and I created oak tag and construction paper signs (pulling out all the stops by using the extremely precious glitter) demanding, "Save the Bunny Woods" and proclaiming, "Jesus Loves Bunnies!" (My heart goes out now to the construction workers who showed up to work the following day. Sorry.)

Of course, the real estate development machine continued, and we lost the Bunny Woods. This had a profound effect on me. "How could God let this happen?" I cried.

This nagging thought popped up again a few months later on a warm summer day at the Jewish Community Center (JCC). To us kids, the JCC was the ultimate place on Earth—two pools, a youth lounge (with video games!), a hot dog stand, an ice cream shop, and on and on. We spent as much time there as possible.

Dad would take us there, and then spend his time in the adult steam room. When we ran out of quarters for the video games or had some sort of other important crisis, we'd open up the door to the steam room (ignoring the "No Kids Allowed" sign) and yell, "Dad? Dick Murdoch?" to summon him. Sometimes we'd get a glimpse of some random old man in a towel and run off giggling.

One day, I noticed that one of the men in the steam room had a bunch of numbers drawn on his wrist. In my house, drawing on yourself (or on your sister) with markers was forbidden, so I asked my father what that was all about. The answer greatly overshadowed my previous lesson in real estate development. Dad took me to the museum area of the JCC and explained the Holocaust. Again, I asked, "Why would God let this happen?" No answer he gave me would I accept.

✡ ✞ ☪ ☯ ✴ ॐ

As I grew up, I began to develop my own answers to my religious questions, with the infallible wisdom of kids in their elementary school years: "Catholic families have the most kids." "Jewish kids are lucky because they get more presents." My sister followed suit by demanding at dinner one night, "Give me my daily bread!"

We practiced dressing up with neighbors for a First Communion we wouldn't have, then spent the next day eating mini-bagels at a Bar Mitzvah. During the winter holidays, we lit the Menorah and played dreidel with friends down the street, then came home to trim our own Christmas tree.

And all of this seemed normal. My father explained to me that there were many ways to experience God, and never gave me the feeling that our religious denomination was better than those of any of my friends, or that their beliefs were less than mine. And this was all good by me.

But then came puberty. This was the time in our church that kids were asked to dive a little deeper into religion. I attended Sunday evening Confirmation classes where we were supposed to learn about our church's faith, traditions, and practices. I must confess I was more interested in staring at the cute blond boy in my class and wondering if he liked me. Or if he thought I was too tall. Or too short. I worried incessantly about my looks and what other people thought about me.

The strong confident child I had been turned into a nervous gangly girl who felt ugly, poor, and not good enough.

So, needless to say, I certainly didn't learn what our teacher hoped I would. I do remember learning that during ancient times if someone was caught stealing, then his hand was cut off. Our teacher explained how truly awful this was by explaining to us that toilet paper did not exist then, and so one hand was used for eating, and one for "wiping." So having one of your hands cut off was the ultimate humiliation.

I also remember somehow passing the class test—complete with an ordered list of all of the books of the Bible—so that I could stand in front of the entire church congregation and be confirmed—right next to the cute blond boy.

The following year, my father accepted a position as minister of a church in another state. I was now entering ninth grade, and was not thrilled. At all. But after a few rough months at a new school—and a new church—I began to find my way. The hip teen activity in my new church was the bell choir. (No, I am not kidding.) I joined it and must say we had some crazy times in that bell choir. Through it, I found my first serious high school boyfriend and my first fake ID.

I also began to realize that in some crowds being a preacher's kid was a serious liability. Living in a Midwestern college town in the 1980s, the last thing I wanted to be known for was being a square who would rat out a party. So I made sure my appearance didn't give people that idea.

Want to spot a PK at a youth retreat? Look for the one with the spiked hair. Or the blue hair. Or the black leather punk rock jacket. Luckily, since I continued to excel in school and on the swim team I was given a lot of liberty by my parents for self-expression.

Spiritually, I was beginning to question everything. I remained skeptical about whether Jesus truly was born of a virgin as the Son of God. I'd agree that he did seem like a cool dude, but I couldn't buy into him being any more a son of God than I was a daughter of God. And I didn't want to be a hypocrite, so I went through a period where I wouldn't say the word "Jesus" in prayers or take communion.

While my father was always willing to help me with my questions, my self-absorption was growing to a colossal size. Eventually, my questioning spirituality took a back seat to my self-seeking. A large void began to grow inside.

Probably the oddest thing I did was to buy a copy of *The Satanic Bible* by Anton LaVey, founder of the Church of Satan. Now, before you go thinking I was crazy, let me assure you that there was a reason for this madness. The book had been banned at a local bookstore with a lot of media fanfare. Being a curious kid, I wanted to see what all the noise was about, so I tracked down a copy.

Dad saw the book in my room one day and casually asked, "So what do you think of it?" I had certainly been expecting (or seeking?) a different reaction. "Haven't read it yet," I replied. "Well, once you finish it, let me know and we can discuss it," he said.

Well, I never finished that book, so we never did get around to discussing it, but I did come to understand something from the experience. Most people need to believe in something. Or at least they want to believe in something. That book had changed the common perception of Satan and created a religion around it. And that religion wasn't for me.

But I wasn't sure the religion I had was for me either.

✡ ✟ ☪ ☯ ✴ ॐ

After high school, I went to the local college and continued to attend my father's church. But I have to admit that many late Saturday nights led to less frequent attendance at Sunday morning services. Fortunately, the church had a college group that met in the evenings. I loved the community service aspect, including working in soup kitchens and teaching children's sermons, and yet I didn't have a strong connection to any higher power other than community. Slowly I began to drift away from attending church services other than Christmas, Easter, and of course, Mother's Day (an unofficial church holiday requirement).

So it is no surprise that when I graduated and moved to New York I did not find a new church to attend. I was off and running with my new religion—working. Anticipating a move into a beautiful, light-filled SoHo loft, I had instead landed in a small Jersey City studio (roaches at no extra cost!). My new higher power was money. And my apartment became littered with self-help books on finding balance as I tried to fill the hole I had created when I turned my back on belief.

Over the next ten years, my apartments improved, as did my jobs. And it certainly wasn't a bad life. I traveled extensively on business and vacationed in foreign countries. I accumulated stuff. I had success and I made money. From the outside everything appeared to be going as planned. Yet I made many mistakes. The void was growing inside me.

My parents had moved to the East Coast, so I was able to spend time with them, and occasionally attend my father's new church. Whenever I did, I felt *something,* but not enough to seek out what it was.

Then in 2004, I received a call from my sister, asking me to come to the hospital ASAP. My parents had just returned from vacation and my father was sick. An excruciating six weeks later, his body gave out.

The day he died, I had woken up and dressed for battle in black steel-toe boots, ripped jeans, and a Superman t-shirt. As I walked across the city to the hospital, I passed a group of schoolchildren. A little boy pointed at me and declared, "Superman!" A little girl looked at him with disdain and corrected, "Super... girl!"

But I had never felt less super.

When I arrived at the hospital, our family held hands in a circle and said a prayer in my father's room. My mind screamed, "Need... to... get... out... of here!" I had felt my father's soul leave his body the day before, and I had no desire to stay in the room with the body.

I stormed out, crying, through the hospital's huge glass doors and marched up First Avenue with no other direction than away, which happened to be north. Angry, with tears streaming down my face, I had never felt more helpless and hopeless.

Twenty blocks later, I spotted a church across the street. I remembered all the times that my father had been called away from us for an emergency at the church. Or at the hospital. Or the nursing home. I decided now was my emergency. I tried the doors. Locked.

Angrier, I continued up the street and spotted a synagogue. Locked. A cathedral. Locked. Finally, I saw a church with the doors open. I burst in and yelled, "I need clergy!" I was told to sit down in a pew and wait. A few minutes later, a man appeared and sat down in front of me. He quietly asked me what was going on.

And out spouted my anger at God. "Why would he take his best employee? It's not fair! It's too soon! He's only 65. I didn't get to say goodbye right!" was the gist of my twenty-minute tirade. The minister questioned, "Do you have a Bible?" I looked at him blankly. Really?

What good would a Bible do me now? My father was dead. Hadn't this man heard me?

As he handed me a Bible and told me to take it with me, I somehow muttered, "Thanks," and quickly left. I clearly was not going to get the answer I wanted. I walked further north to Central Park and sat with my new Bible in the grass. I have no idea how long I sat there, but somehow I eventually made it back to my apartment.

✡ ✝ ☪ ☯ ☸ ॐ

When a minister dies, it feels as if the entire congregation mourns with you. During the visiting hours, I heard story after story of how important my father had been in each person's life. Cards arrived by the boxful. Flowers by the tableful.

Both my sister Amy and I spoke at the funeral service while my father's urn of ashes sat on a table draped in our family's tartan plaid.

I remember feeling numb.

After a death, there is an endless list of to-dos to close a person's earthly life. My sister, mother, and I divided and conquered the tasks with help from people in the congregation. So many people stepped up and I am truly grateful for their help.

As the list wound down, I tried to get back to some semblance of normal, but the God-sized hole I had been ignoring for years now became a gigantic God-and-dad-sized hole.

I stayed angry for two years.

Then one day I decided I'd had enough. With the help of my husband and some close friends, I realized I had become spiritually bankrupt. And I embarked upon a spiritual recovery.

First, I had to deal with my God issue. So I decided I needed a little more information. Actually a lot more information. I spent a few months pouring over library books about all of the world's great religions and wisdom traditions. I thought that if I could decide what religion worked for me, then I'd know which interpretation of God would work.

The result? I got myself all twisted up. Finally, a friend asked me simply, "Hey, Sarah, can you make trees?" I looked at her as if she had rocks in her head and replied, "Of course not." Her answer—"Well, someone or something can"—gave me the foundation for my faith. I realized that nailing down exactly what God is wasn't the point. I just needed to realize that there was a force working in the world—and it wasn't me alone.

Soon, instead of bristling, when I heard people utter the words of the Lord's Prayer—"Our father, who art in heaven"—I started to hear: "*My* father, who art in heaven." I remembered he always told me it wasn't important that I know exactly what I believed, only that I seek to believe.

I dove into Buddhist writings and started to learn a little more about my suffering. I learned how to meditate. And I started to learn about acceptance. About not having to fight every thought or action that happened in my life. I was fortunate to find a local meditation center in the Catskill Mountains that has since become a spiritual home for me. Through that work, my faith in a power greater than myself grew.

Then one day—amazingly—I heard the word God and did not react with anger. I sought out more spiritual books and retreats. And then finally, I started to read my father's sermons. I began to see the beauty in all faiths. My bookshelf overflowed with sacred writings including the Torah, Christian Bible, Book of Mormon, *Tao Te Ching*, Dhammapada, *Bhagavad Gita*, Zohar, Quran, and on. I sought out theologians, scholars, and writers that my father quoted. I voraciously read the books he had read. I tried to leave no stone (or page) unturned.

And I thought, "These sermons need to be a book." I called my sister Amy, described my idea, and asked tentatively, "What do you think?" Always undaunted, Amy instantly replied, "Go for it!"

In the beginning

"Can you point me towards the Bible section?" I quietly asked the librarian. She looked me up and down, came out from behind the massive desk, and said, "Follow me."

Past the towering book stacks and down a small elevator to the basement there was a room full of old paperback books—mostly romance novels—that were being priced for a community book sale. The librarian stopped directly in front of a shelf of Bibles and asked, "Which one are you looking for?"

"I have no idea," I admitted. "I'm writing a book about my Dad's sermons, and I can't understand the King James Version I have at home. I was hoping you had a copy of that hippy-dippy youth Bible I remember from church in the '70s."

The librarian laughed and gave me a good education about a few of the over three dozen translations of the Bible available at that library alone. Driving home with five of them in the back seat of my Jeep, I called Amy and said, "If Dad could see me now..."

✝✝✝

That day began the process of writing this book. It took me six years to feel strong enough to start the process, and another six to create it. In the process, I felt like I was stealing years of my father's life back.

I started with our inheritance of fifteen hundred sermons. Dad kept typed copies of the majority of his sermons from 1967 through 2004. I quickly realized I had some catching up to do on my theology. (Hence the library trip to stock up on Bibles.)

That being said, Dad taught me that faith was not about religion, church was not about exclusivity, and life was about values. When I asked myself if I could learn from Gandhi even if I wasn't a Hindu, the answer was yes. Could I learn from the writings of the Buddha without being a Buddhist? Again, yes. And from a book on modern physics, even if I am not a physicist? Yes. So could I also learn from the stories about Jesus even if I wasn't sure I was a Christian? You betcha. So I set off in the direction of simply trying to learn something new about myself and the world I live in.

But first I had to get over my fear of the Bible. I was so nervous that someone might see the pile of Bibles in my car and assume that I had become some sort of religious fanatic that I covered the Bibles up with a sweater. But then I remembered having heard something in childhood about not putting anything on top of the Bible or letting it touch the ground. Or was that the American flag?

I started to feel a bit anxious. Could I just write the book without the Bible? Did I really need to dive in? Throughout history, the Bible had been used to justify things I didn't believe in... slavery, homophobia, misogyny, and so on. Was it actually relevant for me?

Then I happened upon the following statement by the British philosopher, William Paley, which hit me like a brick: "Contempt prior to examination is an intellectual vice, from which the greatest faculties of mind are not free."

I realized that by rejecting the Bible in its entirety, I was figuratively cutting off my nose to spite my face. Actually, it was highly likely that there was something of value in there for me, and it was time for a little examination and a lot less contempt.

When I took out my stack of Bibles, though, I realized they were all significantly different. But when I went looking for the "real" Bible, I discovered that, well, there actually isn't a single Bible we can go back to as the "original."

The Bible was written over a time span of more than fifteen hundred years, by dozens of authors from different backgrounds, so it isn't a book in the traditional form. It's a collection of writings that have been bound together. Most versions trace back to manuscripts that were written starting from 1500 BCE. But they've been edited, translated, recompiled, and changed extensively (sometimes on purpose, and sometimes through mistakes) over the years. In fact, until 1551 CE, there were no chapters or verses—each book was a continuous writing.

The actual writings that appear in each version of the Bible are based on something called the canon. A canon, named for the Greek word meaning "rule," is a list of the writings that are considered scripture (i.e. sacred and authoritative) by a particular group of people.

Canons were often decided by meetings of the authority figures of a certain religion, and have been fiercely debated for centuries. So the books found in the Hebrew scriptures vary from those in a Catholic Bible, which will in turn vary from the Protestant version, the Greek Orthodox version, and so on. Also, the canons for particular versions have varied through time.

It can get very confusing rather quickly, but the end takeaway is there really is not a single authoritative Bible. And the Bible isn't a book in the traditional sense of the word anyway. Most books start with a beginning that moves logically to the end, but the Bible isn't like this. Over the years, it's been described by people in various ways: as a divine manual for finding happiness, a handbook for life, the literal word of God, and the most important piece of literature ever written. And, of course, there are some people who will tell you the entire book is hogwash.

So how does someone decide which Bible to use? I'm not going to tell you which one is the best or which one you should read from, because I believe that is a personal choice. But, here's how I went about it: First, I had to decide whether I wanted a word-for-word, idea-for-idea, or paraphrased translation. (Christian Bibles are usually compared on a continuum of these three types.)

I noticed that Dad usually used the word-for-word style King James Version (KJV) for his sermons. (Of course, he also was well known for going back to read original Hebrew and Greek manuscripts. But I simply didn't have time to learn new languages and still keep my day job, although I have learned some key words that seem to come up on *Jeopardy* occasionally!)

I found the KJV a little hard to read, so I realized I might be better off starting with something that was more in the thought-for-thought category. After trying out a few types, I decided to use the New Revised Standard Version (NRSV). The first NRSV was published in 1989 and is on the more literal side of the thought-for-thought translations. Mine also has charts, diagrams, and extra stuff to help me feel less like a theological novice. (I'm fine with admitting I need extra guidance.)

It's amazing how many different versions of Bibles there are to choose from. If you check out your local bookstore, you'll find Yearly Bibles that divide the readings into three hundred and sixty-five days,

Parallel Bibles that have translations side by side, and a wide range of other specialty Bibles. I even found a children's version designed like a large comic book where all of the illustrations were photos of scenes created with Legos.

✞ ✞ ✞

What you'll find before each sermon in this book, for the most part, are verses from the New Revised Standard Version. (In places where my father drilled down specifically into words from a particular translation, I used that version.) If you want to reference your preferred version instead, go for it.

Ultimately, it is all interpretation. I kept looking for what was the "absolute truth" or "right" interpretation of each verse. And the truth is... there isn't *one*. It depends on the person reading the verse. The words are just words until we apply meaning to them—and that meaning is based on our own personal history. So the meaning I place on the ancient words is inherently from my modern view.

These meanings also may change over time. My childhood interpretations of things are rarely going to be the same as my adult interpretations. So, in many ways, I need to adopt an open "beginner's mind," to borrow a phrase from Buddhism.

As I began to learn about the Bible, I realized its writings are more than a collection of simple stories I learned in Sunday school. There are complex moral conflicts and ambitions of the people within the stories that I can learn from. And questions of whether those people were "real" or not was not a critical point for understanding my father's sermons. Although digging into the specific details of each character's life was interesting (I apparently share my father's interest in history), I quickly realized that I didn't need to get bogged down in the debate over the discrepancies that often appear in dates, places, and numbers to get some benefit.

I began to learn specific ways to read the Bible. Historical criticism can help me try to take the primary meaning of what it would have meant to people in the original ancient context. Or, through textual criticism, I can see how certain words were used in other non-biblical writings of the time, to try to understand the meaning of words more fully.

But in the end, I have to realize that the Bible was not written in a vacuum—nor is it read in a vacuum. And of course, this isn't the case just for the Bible. The same thing happens when we read other books or interpret a piece of art. I create meaning. You create meaning. And often, those meanings are not going to be the same.

Does that mean I should throw out the whole thing because of my disagreements with how some Christians have interpreted these words? No. I have to explore the possible meanings and see which makes sense to me. Likewise, I need to allow others their interpretations—no matter how tempted I might be to label them as wrong.

So, this book contains one person's view of scripture (my father's) that has then been interpreted through context by another person (me) and then another (you while reading). And you might interpret it yet again if you talk with someone else about what you read.

To me, these interpretations are part of the spiritual path. Seeking answers of the infinite beyond is a personal experience that, at the same time, is shared with others. And I think knowing that we *don't know* is what makes the shared journey possible.

The "G" word

"There are almost 5,000 gods
being worshipped by humanity.
But don't worry, only yours is right."
—Facebook post

This attitude is exactly what I think leads so many people to say, **"I'm spiritual, not religious."** Or "I don't believe in *organized* religion." And sometimes those words come out of my mouth as well.

But since the sermons in this book are based on the Bible, you can pretty much guess that the words "religion" and "God" are going to come up. And both words may make some folks a little uncomfortable. That's okay.

If you are one of these uncomfortable folks, try not to throw the proverbial baby out with the bathwater. Your nervous response may be because you've experienced religious trauma, you simply don't connect with your birth religion, or perhaps you are an atheist or agnostic. No worries: I don't think you need to believe anything specific to get value from the sermons in this book.

What I think many people mean when they say they're spiritual but not religious, or that they have no organized religion is that they don't want to be told to believe in something specific. They don't want a limited God, and they think that religion can limit God. And it certainly can.

It's interesting to me that prior to Latin (and the Romans' desire to be documenting anthropologists) there was not a specific word for religion. Sure, there were words for specific gods, rituals, sects, etc. But religion was such an inherent part of life that there was no actual word for it. It was like white on rice. There was no need for a word to separate what we now call religion from life itself.

So what does religion mean? The etymology, or source, of the word religion has been debated for centuries. The suggested Latin roots include *relegere* (to reread or go over a text), *religare* (to bind), and *re-eligere* (to choose again).

Webster's Dictionary uses this simple definition: "a cause, principle, or system of beliefs held to with ardor and faith." But it's not that simple, is it? I propose that it is language that limits us, and limits God. Words—and the meanings we apply to them—create inadvertent boundaries. And the meaning many of us apply to the word "religion" is what can cause us to see it as a negative concept to be avoided. We're unable to get beyond our own limited definition of what religion is. One definition I found—and can get behind—is this one:

> *True religion begins with the quest for meaning and value beyond self-centeredness. It renounces the ego's claim to finality.*[1]

If I look at it that way, I can start to work with the word "religion." I can see each religion has universal principles to which it adds cultural ideas. Regardless of the scripture or other text I'm reading, I can identify with the universal principles, and then take what I want and leave the rest, as they say in twelve-step spirituality. Or I can follow Krishna's advice in the *Bhagavad Gita*: "I give you these precious words of wisdom; reflect on them and then do as you choose."

But what about the word "God" then? Why do we hang on to the idea that there is only one way to describe God? Or even one name for that/he/she/it?

We have different personalities, haircuts, and preferences for pets. We can choose from an almost limitless array of favorite ice cream flavors. My cable provider gives me over eight hundred channels to choose from. Such freedom of choice extends to almost everything in our world.

So it makes sense that there is almost an unlimited number of names to describe that thing which is greater than us: God, El, Allah, Brahman, Jehovah, Waheguru, Ahuru Mazda, Creator, Infinite Being, Creative Source, All Wise, The One, HaShem, the Beyond that is Within, Father, Mother, Higher Power, True Self, or even That Which Makes Trees—and the list goes on, ad infinitum.

Have you ever thought about what it must be like on the flipside? Bestselling author Huston Smith challenges us to think about this:

> *What a strange fellowship this is, the God-seekers in every land, lifting their voices in the most disparate ways imaginable to the God of all life. How does it sound from above? Like bedlam, or do*

the strains blend in strange, ethereal harmony? Does one faith car-
ry the lead, or do the parts share in counterpoint and antiphony
where not in full-throated chorus? We cannot know. All we can do is
try to listen carefully and with full attention to each voice in turn as
it addresses the divine.[2]

By understanding that we refer to the divine using different names, and describe it in different ways, can we learn about God through other's beliefs? As often happens when learning foreign languages, can't each description be a description that doesn't negate another's? I think the answer is resoundingly yes.

So, you do not need to be religious to read this book. You don't need to be a Christian. In fact, you don't even need to believe in God. This may sound strange for a book based on Christian sermons. But it's not if you consider this book is about more than theology.

This book deals with my father's language as a Presbyterian minister. And if I listen closely, I find some words that are the same in my language too. I expect you might as well—regardless of your specific brand of spirituality, tradition, or religion.

[1 and 2] from *The World's Religions*, Huston Smith, pages 2 and 19 respectively

My father
(who art in heaven)

I was sitting in a coffee shop surrounded by manila sermon folders one day when a woman inquired what I was working on. (I stood out, of course, since most of the other people in the coffee shop were instead working with digital folders on their laptops.)

After I explained the book project, the woman replied, "Why? Was your dad famous?"

✝ ✝ ✝

No, my father was not famous. But he did affect the lives of thousands of people. According to this biography, culled from his various obituaries, here are some highlights of what my father accomplished in his life:

> *Born June 29, 1939 in Upper Darby, Pennsylvania, Rev. Dr. Richard Murdoch, better known as Dick, spent his childhood there and in Baltimore and Annapolis, Maryland; and Washington, D.C.; and his teens in South Carolina, graduating in 1957 from Abbeville High School, where his classmates named him "Most Likely to Succeed."*
>
> *In 1961, he graduated with honors from Furman University with a Bachelor of Arts in history and a minor in English. He was president of the Joint Legislature, and a member of the honorary ROTC leadership group, Scabbard and Blade, and the honorary society Quaternion.*
>
> *He then attended Colgate Rochester Divinity School. As a student, he assisted two parishes. During a summer internship at Boston City Hospital, he studied at Andover Newton Theological School and Harvard Divinity School. Dick received his Masters of Divinity in 1964 and in June of that year was ordained in the Genesee Valley Presbytery in New York State. In June of 1966, he married Judith Anne Strange.*
>
> *His first pastorate was at Pluckemin Presbyterian Church in New Jersey. Then followed nine years as pastor of the historic Corfu*

Presbyterian Church between Rochester and Buffalo, New York. In his early ministry, he was active in the Civil Rights Movement, Fair Housing Movement, and helped start a ministry at Attica Prison.

In 1971, his daughter Sarah was born. Dick began studies again in 1972, this time at the Rochester Center for Theological Studies and the Graduate Theological School at Berkeley, California, receiving his Doctorate of Ministry and Theology in 1976.

His daughter Amy was born in 1974. From 1977 to 1984 he served the pastorate of Presbyterian Church of the Cross in Omaha, Nebraska. Then, from 1984 to 1994, he served at Peoples Church in East Lansing, Michigan, where he also was a member of the Board of Ethics at Michigan State University.

Over the years, Dick served on numerous Presbytery committees and was well known for his skills and wise counsel. He was a charter and clinical member of the American Association of Marriage and Family Therapists, helping many families and individuals with personal needs.

In 1994, he and his wife Judy (then "empty nesters") moved to Rye, New York and the Rye Presbyterian Church. His extensive community group involvement continued, including the Rye Youth Council, the United Hospital chaplaincy, and the Sing Sing Prison Ministry. The multi-denominational Impact Youth Group was started by Dick and his wife to provide fun and fellowship through faith-based projects such as Habitat for Humanity. He also served as a multi-faith chaplain on cruises to Turkey, Greece, and South America.

Dick excelled in combining his love of history with theology. He enjoyed every aspect of life, traveling anywhere, dancing, gardening, and listening to music. He was active in each of the communities in which he lived.

He died after a brief but courageous battle with cancer on September 24, 2004 at NYU Medical Center with his family at his side.

Dr. Murdoch's constant love, wry wit, spontaneity, generous spirit, and joie de vivre are greatly missed by his wife of 38 years, Judith, and his daughters Sarah and Amy.

But that biography feels a bit dry, and only describes part of the incredible man that my father was. So here are the words a past congregation member spoke during my father's installation at his final church:

> Dick is a creative, intellectually minded, positive, and forward-looking historian. (It is possible to have a forward-looking historian and it's a great combo!) Listen, open your mind and heart, and you will be enlightened.
>
> He has an idea or thought concerning just about everything under the sun. And despite the fact that most of his ideas are pretty good, he rarely takes full credit and always listens to yours, for he recognizes that no matter how impressive the idea, it can never be successfully executed without the nurturing support of many.
>
> Let me share a few tidbits—in no particular order. His favorite cereal is Grape-Nuts—we are convinced that's what keeps him running and able to be in five places at one time. He is fiercely proud of his Scottish heritage. Dick is an avid gardener partial to lilies, hostas, and his grandmother's tree peony—though he loves all kinds of flowers. He and his wife Judy are devotees of the arts and literature and both enjoy traveling. Dick can be silly at times—imagine him dressed as a pumpkin last October reading a book to the church's kids while perched on the stage. He is vocal at sporting events! He enjoys racquetball, skiing, golf, and swimming.
>
> When you talk with him and share deeply with him, you are likely to feel him embrace you with his thoughts, his words, and his deeds more often than his arms, but when his hugs come, they are wonderful. His mind is working all the time (sometimes on several things at once) and his heart is receiving all the time.
>
> We were not excited to say goodbye to Dick Murdoch as our senior pastor. We miss him as you would a dear friend. But we praise God for him and are thankful to God for guiding him to us. We are a stronger, more unified church now. He taught us, counseled us, fed us spiritually, and helped us minister to each other and do things for ourselves to serve God. Be nice to him and take care of him, and guided by God, he will help you to take care of you.

About the sermons

ser·mon ('sərmən)
informal:
a long or tedious piece of admonition or reproof; a lecture.
synonyms: lecture, tirade, harangue, diatribe
—*Dictionary.com*

Unfortunately, that is many people's definition of a sermon. For others, a sermon means it's time to take a nap, scribble on their program, or check their email. If you've been in this camp, then you haven't heard my father's sermons. I promise you will find no fire and brimstone here. You will not be lectured on sin, or harangued.

I like to think of my father's sermons as short stories. In that spirit, each section follows this format:

- Context for the section (written by me)
- Verses from the scripture that the sermon is about
  (most from the New Revised Standard Version of the Bible)
- Sermon (written by my father)

So, you can read this book any way you like. If you consider yourself one of the "religious light," then you can just read the sermons and try to apply the lessons to your life. It is well worth the time.

For the spiritually curious, read the scripture verses before the sermons and the context sections. You might find that you learn much more than you would expect—about history, culture, people, and yes, a bit of theology. Expert Christians may find this book is a way to go deeper into their faith. And it may raise thought-provoking questions to be discussed with their own clergy.

As previously mentioned, religious denominations differ on the books included in their official scriptures, and the way the books are categorized (remember the canon?). For example, the Jewish faith categorizes its primary scriptures into three divisions: the Law (*Torah*), the Prophets (*Nebi'im*), and the Writings (*Kethubim*).

Traditional Christian Bibles include most of these writings (but not necessarily in the same order) and then add the "New Testament," which includes writings about the life of Jesus, and the development of the Christian faith and the church.

Some Christian Bibles also include a set of books (often called the Apocrypha) between the Jewish and Christian writings, but others omit these books. In some, the Apocrypha are interspersed among the other books somewhat chronologically. Looking at the reasoning behind these exclusions and inclusions is like opening a can of biblical worms, but since I don't have any sermons from those books, I'm taking the easy way out and staying out of that debate. Nonetheless, I've provided a context section to help make the transition.

Growing up at church, I heard sermons in a precise order determined by a lectionary. A lectionary is a list of specific scriptures to be read on specific days for a certain timeframe. Our church's lectionary included four readings from the Bible for each Sunday service. However, reading in this order presumes that you have prior knowledge of other chapters and verses, so it can feel like you are jumping into the middle of a story.

So, I've decided to go somewhat chronologically through the "narrative" of the books of the Bible, starting right at the beginning with the Book of Genesis. So if you are following along in your "pew Bible," so to speak, the order of these sermons will not go linearly through your Bible, because the books were not written in a linear way, and therefore overlap each other in terms of chronological timing.

A bookshelf analogy comes in handy. Move right past any anxious flashbacks of memorizing the Dewey Decimal System. Simply imagine you group books of similar style onto the same shelf, and you line them up roughly chronologically. So on the left side of the top shelf, you have five law books. Next to that, place your history books. On the next shelf, put the books by or about prophets. And if there is enough space left, add your poetry and wisdom writings. If not, put those on the next shelf, no worries. Any apocryphal books can go there as well.

Start a new shelf for the Christian-only scriptures. First, place the four canonical gospels. Then add the books about the history of the Christian church. Next, group all the books that contain letters written back and forth to the churches. And finally, slip in a prophetic ending.

The next page shows my mental bookshelf:

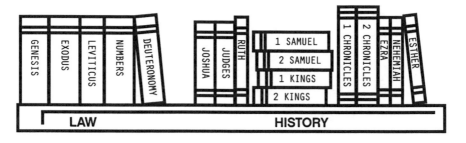

LAW HISTORY

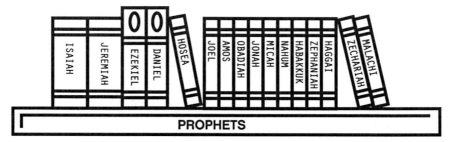

PROPHETS

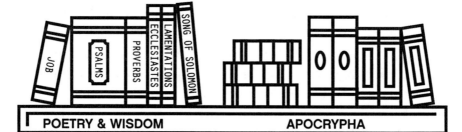

POETRY & WISDOM APOCRYPHA

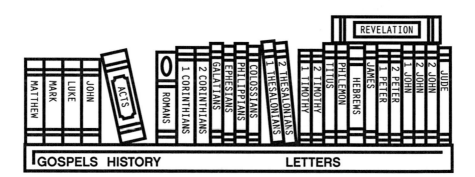

GOSPELS HISTORY LETTERS

Before each set of sermons, I have added a brief explanation of its context. I've written these sections to provide some added help to readers who are new to these scriptures, or rusty on Bible history. When discussing this book project with others, I found that many people have never read the Bible in its entirety, so the context sections will help you keep track of the stories as we go along, as well as provide some context for what was going on in other religions, and lands, at the same time.

You'll also probably notice that I don't have a sermon for every story, chapter, or book in the Bible. Why? Well, my copy of the Bible has two thousand and one hundred and eighty pages (not counting the appendices). It's impossible to cover everything that happened in it within a reasonably sized book. In addition, my father simply didn't write a sermon for every story. And some were a little rough around the edges (almost certainly written during the weeks that my sister or I had a crisis that pulled Dad away from his sermon writing). So I picked what I thought were the cream of the crop.

In the sermons that are included, I corrected any misspellings and grammatical errors I found in the originals (many of these sermons were hand-typed prior to the invention of spellcheck). Sometimes I changed a confusing word or sentence for clarity, but I was careful not to change the meaning of the passage. Likewise, I edited to ensure the chronology of the book as a whole was as seamless as possible. (I'm sure my father would be okay with this, and would consider me akin to the redactors of the Bible, who edited the "divine-ly inspired word," since I think I was "dad-ly inspired" in the process.)

Speaking of spellcheck, there are many alternate spellings for the names of people, places, and things in the Bible. I used the most common contemporary spellings in most cases. But I removed or changed the names of any of the people my father knew and mentioned in his sermons, if I could not contact them to see if it was okay to use their name, especially if there was personally identifiable information. Likewise, I removed information specific to a particular church's business or finances.

So that about covers the who, what, and why. It's time to dig in...

Sermons from the Hebrew scriptures

Context: Genesis

Since the events, traditions, and culture of the Hebrew (and Christian) scriptures did not develop in a vacuum, it is important to view them against the backdrop of the ancient Near East. The scripture stories share significant similarities with other important writings of that time, including *Enuma Elish* and the *Epic of Gilgamesh* (which are both worth reading). Many different religions and cultures share stories of creation, trees of life and knowledge, the fall of man, and a great flood—not just the Bible. And the stories contain a lot of similarities.

Prior to starting the research for this book I had no idea there were over four thousand religions in the world today. Some have written scriptures while many others have oral traditions. Because each tradition's stories were edited (or orally passed on) by many different people over numerous years, there are conflicts in "facts" both between traditions and within individual scriptures. Each storyteller or editor inherently has a particular perspective and intention. Part of what is thought-provoking is learning what these agendas are and what they tell us about the people of that time. Mix in some archeology, history, and a bit of theology and a lot can be learned about the human race.

But let's narrow the focus, and start at the beginning of the Hebrew scriptures.

✡ ✡ ✡

In Judaism, the Books of Genesis, Exodus, Leviticus, Numbers, and Deuteronomy are part of the Torah. Christians often refer to these books as the *Pentateuch* (Greek for "five books").

There is much debate about how these books were written. The traditional view was that Moses authored all five based on receiving the "divine word" from God. Some people still hold this belief.

But in the 1600s, people began to question this view because of the variety of literary styles used, as well as plentiful repetitions, variations, and contradictions. By the 1800s, the Documentary Hypothesis was developed and in wide use. This hypothesis suggested that the five books were actually a conglomeration of four main sources of information, combined into a final form by redactors (editors).

Over the last hundred years, many biblical scholars have proposed other hypotheses. The scholarly debates on the origins of the text—and subsequent edits to the text—are fascinating.

Genesis

In the first portion of Genesis, we are presented with primeval history through two different narratives about the creation of the world, animals, and people. We then move on to some ideas on free will, and "how sin entered the world" with Adam and Eve's choice to eat from the tree of knowledge.

Two brothers, Cain and Abel, have a feud, and we become privy to the story of the first murder. Generations follow, and humans continue to act with corruption, violence, and overall bad behavior.

Next follows Noah and the flood, and then the creation of the post-flood world. God establishes a covenant with Noah, and sets up some new rules for living.

In the second portion of Genesis, we find ancestral history. Noah is said to have three sons—Japheth, Ham, and Shem—who create a lengthy list of descendants that become dispersed via the mysterious language-scrambling Tower of Babel.

At this point, the writings narrow down to focus on one family line, often referred to as the patriarchs and matriarchs. We're introduced to Abram and Sarai (later renamed Abraham and Sarah). The story becomes much more personal, and we start to see clearly the struggle between rebellious humans and their belief in the will of God.

God calls Abram to head out to a new land on faith—actual location TBD. Thus, another covenant is entered into, this time signified physically by circumcision.

Next, we move on to Abraham's sons, Isaac and Ishmael, and through them are introduced to the concept of sacrifice. Isaac's sons, Jacob and Esau, follow (with a lesson on deception), and then Jacob's sons—the heads of the twelve tribes of Israel, according to the Bible's authors.

During this time (also now known as the Bronze Age), the location of the narrative moves from Ur (modern Southern Iraq) to Canaan (coinciding with today's Lebanon, Israel, Palestine, northwestern Jordan, and some of Syria) and then finally to Egypt, where the Hebrews[1] try to escape famine and thrive.

Meanwhile...

The ancient world was experiencing significant development. Populations were increasing, and trade was becoming more important as people developed tastes for things they couldn't find in their own lands. Power struggles abounded, as powerful leaders sought more and more for themselves and their developing empires.

In what would eventually become England, dozens of 26-ton sandstone rocks were laboriously hauled over 20 miles as the construction of Stonehenge began. Its arrangement is thought to be linked to the Summer Solstice, suggesting use as a ritual gathering place.

Egypt unified its Lower and Upper kingdoms, becoming a mighty driving force. The Egyptians developed the complicated process of embalming, and built immense pyramids, designed specifically to assist the pharaohs in the afterlife. Egypt's sophisticated system of hieroglyphics created the beginning of written language.

In Mesopotamia, Hammurabi inherited the throne of Babylon, and built a powerful empire. Although it fell apart shortly after his death, his legacy left the Code of Hammurabi, one of the first written civil codes, which sought to ensure that the strong did not overpower the weak, and that justice, as well as responsibility, should be honored.

[1] Often, there is confusion about the difference between Hebrews, Israelites, and Jews/Jewish people since these terms seem to be used interchangeably within the scriptures. Hebrew is the oldest term and comes from the name "Eber," Abraham's great, great, great, great-grandfather. So technically it applies from Eber down through the time of Abraham and his sons. Around their time, the term Israelite will start to be used (for reasons you'll learn later stemming from Jacob). Jew derives from the tribe of (and then kingdom of) Judah, named for one of Jacob's sons. In modernity, each of the terms has come in and out of favor, with varying levels of offensiveness. Neither my father or I mean any offense by using any of the words. We're simply referencing the people as noted in the scripture. My Jewish friends recommend "Jewish people" over "Jews," so I've tried to keep that in mind.

✡ Genesis 1:1-5 ✡
The Creation of the World

1 [1] In the beginning, God created the heavens and the earth. [2] The earth was without form and void, and darkness was over the face of the deep. And the Spirit of God was hovering over the face of the waters.

[3] And God said, "Let there be light," and there was light. [4] And God saw that the light was good. And God separated the light from the darkness. [5] God called the light Day, and the darkness he called Night. And there was evening and there was morning, the first day.

Bible Version: English Standard Version (ESV)

Why did God make mosquitoes?

Sermon by Richard Murdoch | East Lansing, MI | June 6, 1993

The church school teacher had brought a new children's book to her class, which she was proud to share with her students. She was proud because she had been able to purchase three new books for the small country church's library through a special memorial gift. (The year was 1976 and twenty dollars went a lot further than it does today when it came to buying books!)

One book among the three was a Caldecott Winner, which marked it as a quality children's book, and one in great demand. It was a first-prize book retelling a story from another cultural idiom. Its title was *Why Mosquitoes Buzz in Peoples Ears: A West African Tale,* as retold by Verna Aardema. The teacher invited the class to read it, and one lucky student got to take it home the first week to read. The following week, when the student returned, the librarian-turned-church school teacher asked him how he liked the book. But instead of answering, the child asked his own question: "Why *did* God make mosquitoes?"

If you have ever lived in western New York, you'll appreciate the child's inquiry. The mosquitoes are numerous, aggressive, significantly larger than normal, and seem to live an abnormally long time. I would hazard a guess that at the tender age of nine, the young boy had experienced more mosquito bites and buzzing in his ears, and had more playground picnics ruined than he could endure. He had borrowed the book to find the answer to his misery. What he found instead was not an answer, but a symptom of the problem—some folk wisdom about why mosquitoes make the sound they do before they attack!

The teacher, summoning up her best argument to support God (with characteristic Greek logic), suggested that everything had its good side and its bad side. While humans might suffer from mosquito bites (bad), bats needed mosquitoes for food (good). "Can you imagine," she asked, "that a bat eats three times its weight in mosquitoes every night?" Unimpressed with this logic, the boy replied, "I'm glad I'm not a bat;

mosquitoes taste yucky!" The rest of the class laughed, and the theological discussion that had so quickly begun was just as quickly ended.

It's a pity, really. Mosquitoes are just the tip of the iceberg of theological discovery about how the world works. The real question being asked was the relationship between God and creation. "If the world is supposed to be a good place to live—created by a loving and kind God—then why are there things that can hurt you?"

The teacher had led her class to a truth that many embrace: a loving creator God. As is said in the Book of Genesis, "So it was, and God saw all that he had made, and it was very good." But there was an awakening in the young boy. He was beginning to discern and relate his own experience to a learned truth or belief system: Mosquitoes were a part of God's creation, which was pronounced good. But as far as he had experienced mosquitoes were not good, even as food for bats. His experience contradicted the words of biblical "truth." What should he really believe about God?

While belief is not formed on experience or facts, experience and facts do indeed condition one's belief. It was the experience of being harassed by mosquitoes that caused the young boy's inquiry as to God's good creation. However, the teacher's answer appealed to a fact—that bats need mosquitoes for food—to support her belief that there is a good side and a bad side to everything. She thought that facts would give a wider perspective to belief.

There are a variety of facts she might have given him, such as: There are two and a half thousand kinds of mosquitoes. They are part of the wider fly family. In fact, the word "mosquito" is a Spanish derivation meaning "little fly." Mosquitoes have been observed all over the world, including the Arctic polar region, with one exception—they have not been found yet in Antarctica. They are carriers of at least three deadly diseases: malaria, yellow fever, and encephalitis. The buzzing sound of the mosquito is not designed to do you a favor by announcing its onslaught—its wings beat a thousand times a minute, and the rushing air causes the buzz.

All these facts leave us well versed in biological facts, but no further ahead in theology. So, why did God create mosquitoes—which apparently have inflicted more trouble than helpfulness? And to go further, if creation was intended to be good, why is there evil?

Some people point to the second and third chapters of Genesis, where a second story of creation appears. This second story includes a subsequent story of the "disobedience" in the Garden of Eden. This account personifies the undoing of divine good by our first humanity. Here, humanity is reminded of its disobedience in the figure of a snake, which turns from being friend to foe. Likewise, parts of creation are turned from friend to foe—including, no doubt, mosquitoes—as a kind of divine judgment. Those who point to this story in Genesis remind us that we are cursed with the discomforts of snakes and mosquitoes because humanity disobeyed God.

The acceptance of this story—commonly called "The Fall of Man"—again calls into question the logic of a loving creator God. Why would such a God want to inflict countless generations with misery simply because someone disobeyed ten thousand years ago? It is as if you refused to buy a dog for your child, because your great-grandfather had abused a dog. Why would you punish your child for a mistake made three generations ago?

Well, the teacher didn't take this road. Her explanations about perspectives of good and bad showed a sensitivity to the boy's inquiry—but stopped just short of engaging him beyond presenting a fact which justified her belief system. She could have led her class into seeking the beginnings of their own belief systems. She had done a successful job of providing them with the foundation assumption, but now they needed to build upon that foundation a house worthy of the many blows that their future would bring.

Children need to be engaged in conversation that recognizes their awakening of belief, and how the experiences and facts they have learned come together to mature that belief. What is it about the mosquitoes of life that we believe? Are the inequities, tragedies, hurts, and disappointments that we experience a reflection of God's incomplete creation? Or are they the result of some ancient story of disobedience still being played out? Has God created the world to allow for the evolving of the species, allowing free will to help us manipulate it? Or are we characters in some grand theater called life, in which battles of good and evil, light and dark are given to challenge us?

Being able to perceive the place of mosquitoes in creation is in some measure an indication about how we perceive life. Mosquitoes are real insects—that's a fact about creation. Mosquitoes hurt—that's a lesson from experience. Mosquitoes can be managed—that's a belief that the insecticide, a screen door, or chosen repellent can help minimize their effect. Belief requires some action on our part to accommodate the fact of mosquitoes and our experience of them. Whether mosquitoes are good or bad, as the teacher stated, depends on one's perspective.

Perhaps mosquitoes started out inherently good millions of years ago, but the fact remains that while the bat's experience with them is still good, our experience is negative. So if we believe that creation is ultimately good, we have to commit ourselves to be in partnership with it. For those parts that we experience as hurtful, we must look closely at our perspective and believe that with our creative freedom, we can continue the path of good.

The Covenant with Noah

9 [8] Then God said to Noah and to his sons with him, [9] "As for me, I am establishing my covenant with you and your descendants after you, [10] and with every living creature that is with you, the birds, the domestic animals, and every animal of the earth with you, as many as came out of the ark.

[11] I establish my covenant with you, that never again shall all flesh be cut off by the waters of a flood, and never again shall there be a flood to destroy the earth." [12] God said, "This is the sign of the covenant that I make between me and you and every living creature that is with you, for all future generations:

[13] I have set my bow in the clouds, and it shall be a sign of the covenant between me and the earth. [14] When I bring clouds over the earth and the bow is seen in the clouds, [15] I will remember my covenant that is between me and you and every living creature of all flesh; and the waters shall never again become a flood to destroy all flesh. [16] When the bow is in the clouds, I will see it and remember the everlasting covenant between God and every living creature of all flesh that is on the earth."

[17] God said to Noah, "This is the sign of the covenant that I have established between me and all flesh that is on the earth."

Covenant through Noah: Grace

Sermon by Richard Murdoch | Omaha, NE | June 8, 1980

When I reread the story of Noah, I was reminded of a previous discussion with one of you. We were discussing Protestant denominations and their peculiar religious doctrines. When I mentioned that my heritage was not Presbyterian, but Baptist, the person related that many times she thought Baptists did things and thought things closer to their own religious beliefs than Presbyterians did. "Why did you ever change?" came the question. While my answer was a bit more lengthy, in essence it was focused on the Reformation doctrine of John Calvin, whose interpretation of the scripture led him to write, "Once we are saved, we are always saved." Simply put, Calvin did not believe that we could fall from grace. Regardless of how much you may rebel against God, no matter how deaf an ear you might turn to him, I believe he does not abandon you.

While there are multitudes of scripture passages that support this doctrine of grace, few passages portray it as vividly and as directly as the story of Noah. Every child can tell you something of the story of the flood. We seem to learn it by osmosis, regardless of our religious tradition. We all know the story. Whether we are children or adults, we can recall some of the details of the story as well as we can remember "Goldilocks and the Three Bears" and "Little Red Riding Hood." The flood is a part of our heritage: The last "righteous" family builds an ark that boards the animals two by two, swaying for forty days and nights in a flood, and is finally delivered on a hilltop, alive and dry, after a dove brings a branch as a signal. God provides a rainbow to remind his people in the future of this grace. Every generation replays the story in artistic and dramatic ways to indicate the perennial battle between good and evil.

The geological event of the flood is well known to archaeologists, who confirm that enormous passages of water occurred in that part of the world in that era. Other religions take note of the significance of the event as indicated in the great story of Tiamat, which is a confirmed event in history. The question is, however, what significance does it have to us beyond being a biblical story?

I will attempt to answer this with three points: First, it is a saga, which is a special literary form. Second, it is a covenant, which is a special legal form. Third, it is a token, which is a special sign.

The Saga

If you read the complete saga of Noah, you'll find that it is through his sons that the world is re-peopled. In Genesis, chapter 10, no less than three sons and sixteen grandsons are responsible for the multiplicity of nations that grow after the flood. However, in true saga form, the story is not concerned with this small detail: If the entire world was flooded, and all people destroyed except Noah's, where did the grandsons find wives by which to have the great grandsons who are named?

A saga sings the achievements of a hero. The hero is Noah. He is saved by God from the flood by a special revelation because he had been elected by God to continue the true people. All other people shall be punished for their blasphemy and unrighteousness. If you read just the saga, then the message is clear, as some church schoolchildren learn, that God rewards the righteous. However, that is not the whole story. God doesn't give Noah a reward. He gives Noah a commission. Righteousness leads to a special privilege, not a special reward. The privilege is clear: to establish a new people for God, not to bask in his own accomplishments. It is not primarily by his own accomplishments that Noah earns his, it is more of being chosen by God to be an agent of salvation for other people.

The Covenant

When you visit a physician's office, you'll sometimes notice a small framed picture of the Hippocratic Oath of the medical profession. The very date of the oath shows medicine as one of the world's oldest professions. The legal profession is likewise ancient, although probably much older, beginning in a formalized way with Hammurabi's Code in 1754 BCE.[1] Covenants were a legal form in which people made contracts rather than verbal agreements. One of those legal tools was to cut a covenant. *Berith* is the Hebrew word for "to cut." A common berith was made by first speaking a vow to each party, and then producing a sign that would seal it. Normally, that sign involved the cutting of a sacrificial animal in two, after which both parties to the covenant would walk through the bloody mess. The meaning being, "If you break the covenant, I will destroy you." Later on, berith came to mean "to cut the letters into a clay tablet," which was something that was done by lawyers. But in the time of Noah, a covenant meant having the right to destroy, if the covenant was broken. And this is the background of the covenant with Noah. The people had broken the covenant that God had first cut with Adam; and now the failure to keep the covenant meant the destruction of the people.

In the story of Noah, God commits himself in the New Covenant with his people, to hang his bow in the sky. He will never again use the full power of a covenant to achieve his will. Even though Israel may falter, even though she may stumble, even though she may worship other Gods, this drastic destructive step will never be taken again. The image is one of an archer who rests his bow against the flat earth with the arrow facing upwards to the heaven, but never again to the earth. A second part of the covenant states that it is made with *all* living flesh, which includes not only people, but also the animals.

The Token

In every covenant, there is a token that stands as a sign of remembrance. You can find this biblical idea repeated each time you attend a wedding. Contrary to popular thinking, the giving of the rings is not the binding part of the marriage service. The vows spoken are the binding act of the service. A verbal covenant is made between two people. In fact, it is the only contract in our legal structure in which the parties to it do not sign the marriage certificate; only the witnesses and the officiant sign it. The rings proceed immediately after as the token, the sign of remembrance. In no way are the rings legally or religiously necessary for a marriage. But they provide a constant reminder of the covenant.

In the covenant of grace that God enters into with Noah, his human and "fleshy" descendants are given a token. The token, the physical sign of remembrance, is the archer's bow that appears when the sun shines forth after the rainstorm. It is to be an everlasting sign by which we remember that God will keep his covenant. It should constantly remind us with thankful hearts of God's gracious steadfast love.

The covenant of grace then becomes a word of hope to all peoples of God's great love and concern. So different is God from the vengeful and wrathful parent who punishes at the slight disobedience. So different is he from the parent who can never accept anything except perfection from a child. And so different is God from the permissive parent who, in avoiding all conflict, provides no direction for children in which to grow as adults. God's acceptance and love for us is as permanent and irreversible as the rainbow. We cannot prevent the rainbow, can we? Neither can we prevent God from removing us from his presence, merely because of some act on our part. We may break his covenant and his laws, but that does not lessen his desire and ability to accept us back into his presence.

[1] Hammurabi, the sixth king of Babylonia, had his code copied onto clay tablets and large stone stele about three hundred years before the Ten Commandments are usually dated. The two hundred and eighty-two laws covered everything from contract law to economic matters to family behavior. However, it does not include the key concept of "one God" that is found in the Ten Commandments. There has been speculation that Moses was influenced by the code, but that is unlikely, according to most scholars.

The Sign of the Covenant

17 [1] When Abram was ninety-nine years old, the Lord appeared to Abram, and said to him, "I am God Almighty; walk before me, and be blameless. [2] And I will make my covenant between me and you, and will make you exceedingly numerous." [3] Then Abram fell on his face; and God said to him, [4] "As for me, this is my covenant with you: You shall be the ancestor of a multitude of nations. [5] No longer shall your name be Abram, but your name shall be Abraham; for I have made you the ancestor of a multitude of nations. [6] I will make you exceedingly fruitful; and I will make nations of you, and kings shall come from you. [7] I will establish my covenant between me and you, and your offspring after you throughout their generations, for an everlasting covenant, to be God to you and to your offspring after you. [8] And I will give to you, and to your offspring after you, the land where you are now an alien, all the land of Canaan, for a perpetual holding; and I will be their God."

[9] God said to Abraham, "As for you, you shall keep my covenant, you and your offspring after you throughout their generations. [10] This is my covenant, which you shall keep, between me and you and your offspring after you: Every male among you shall be circumcised. [11] You shall circumcise the flesh of your foreskins, and it shall be a sign of the covenant between me and you.

[12] Throughout your generations every male among you shall be circumcised when he is eight days old, including the slave born in your house and the one bought with your money from any foreigner who is not of your offspring. [13] Both the slave born in your house and the one bought with your money must be circumcised. So shall my covenant be in your flesh an everlasting covenant. [14] Any uncircumcised male who is not circumcised in the flesh of his foreskin shall be cut off from his people; he has broken my covenant."

[15] God said to Abraham, "As for Sarai, your wife, you shall not call her Sarai, but Sarah shall be her name. [16] I will bless her, and moreover I will give you a son by her. I will bless her, and she shall give rise to nations; kings of peoples shall come from her." [17] Then Abraham fell on his face and laughed, and said to himself, "Can a child be born to a man who is a hundred years old? Can Sarah, who is ninety years old, bear a child?" [18] And Abraham said to God, "O that Ishmael might live in your sight!" [19] God said, "No, but your wife Sarah shall bear you a son, and you shall name him Isaac. I will establish my covenant with him as an everlasting covenant for his offspring after him."

How lasting is everlasting?

Sermon by Richard Murdoch | East Lansing, MI | February 28, 1988

As a child, I was always mystified by two framed picture cases that hung on the parlor wall in my great-grandmother's farmhouse. My great Aunt Onie referred to these as the "everlasting" pictures. As a youth, it was eerie enough just to be in the same room with the everlastings! One contained a wreath of waxed flowers in the shape of a horseshoe. It had been a funeral wreath at some ancestor's service, the name of whom I never seemed to have learned. The other picture box contained another wreath, but it was made of strands of human hair woven around wires in curled shapes resembling flowers. This was not a funeral memento, but it might well have been, since the hair belonged to two generations of great-great aunts and great-great grandmothers who had proudly deposited their brushed hair into some dish-like affair called a "hair receiver," as demonstrated to us curious children by my step-great-grandmother Ella. You can be assured that we didn't ask any more questions about the everlastings after that demonstration.

When we had family dinners and picnics, the everlastings were a topic of "peek and gossip" among my first and second cousins. We spun many a tale about those mysterious *objets d'art* hanging there. Quite a few years later, when both my great-aunt and my step-great-grandmother died, there was a simple auction for the family members to divide the family possessions for posterity. I looked for the everlastings in the piles of things. But they had lost their everlasting appearance (as well as their mystery and glamour) in their tarnished state. The strands of hair were dried and falling off the wire. The wax was misshapen from excessive summer heat or freezing winters when the unoccupied house was abandoned. The everlastings had lasted about as long as they could without the tender attention they had been used to receiving at the hands of two maiden ladies.

The reading from the Book of Genesis today states that God made an everlasting covenant with Abraham. The everlasting nature of this relationship provided (and still provides) some lively discussions among Jewish and Christian people. Let me illustrate with this story told to me by a Jewish friend:

A young and enthusiastic son of a Jewish family returned home from college. His family's Judaism being a bit lukewarm, the son found himself receptive to the persuasions of his girlfriend to consider Christianity. At the end of the third semester, their relationship reached the point that some accommodation about religion had to be made, so he converted.

When he appeared at home, he waited for the appropriate time to announce that he would not be at Passover. He was expected to be with his girlfriend's family in Florida for Easter. He expected some distraught parents and braced himself. Instead, the son was caught off guard for the response he received from his father.

"My son, now that you are of the Christian persuasion, did you have to state your belief that the scriptures—not only the Torah but what you call the New Testament—are true?" the father asked. "Yes, I did," replied the son.

"And do you believe that when the Lord God speaks, he does not tell lies?" asked the father. "Yes, I do," replied the son.

"And do you believe that the Lord God made an everlasting covenant with our father, Abraham?" continued the father. "Yes, I do," replied the son once again.

"Since by definition an everlasting covenant can never end; and since you believe that the Lord God does not lie, then how can there be a new covenant?" asked the father. "Because," stated his son, "the covenant with our fathers became tarnished, worn, and faded; our people did not honor it in its entirety; it became useless and no longer operative."

"Then," said his father, "you believe the Lord God lies, because a covenant is not everlasting, it lasts just as long as we keep it. It is clear that it depends not upon God, but upon us. An everlasting covenant becomes as lasting as long as we kept it. Since it is not an everlasting covenant, what the Lord God promises in scripture, you cannot believe!"

Well, the son was stumped. His father had bested him in theology, a discipline that he had no idea his father had known a thing about, since he rarely went to temple or synagogue. Intrigued by this exchange, the son decided to pursue it a bit further. "Dad, tell me, I had no idea that you knew enough Christian or Jewish theology to argue this way. Where did you learn this?"

The father replied, "My mother—your grandmother who died when you were but a child—was a Christian convert to Judaism when I was a child. She converted after my father, your grandfather, used the same argument I have given you!"

We more often than not perceive God's everlasting covenants as everlasting—but only up to a point. They are like the everlasting pictures that hung in my great-grandmother's parlor. Once their awe and mystery has worn off by neglect, they lose their appeal. As long as I was a child, and as long as the two maiden ladies tended the everlastings, the power was there in their appearance.

It was a common interpretation in the early church (and even in the twentieth century) that the covenant made by God to Abraham is really not everlasting at all. It was everlasting as long as the Hebrews were faithful to the covenant. Their unfaithfulness—like worshipping a golden calf—negated the covenant, putting outside the covenant of salvation. Abraham's covenant is not valid in their eyes.

Or consider the everlasting promise made through God's covenant to Noah. "As long as the rainbow is in the sky, I will never destroy the earth again!" And yet some Christians welcome Armageddon in which the whole earth is destroyed, because they believe Jesus cannot come again until a new kingdom is established.

An everlasting covenant is one of the distinctive marks of the Judeo-Christian tradition. It takes a special kind of a deity to make everlasting covenants without knowing the outcome, doesn't it? It takes a special kind of human to believe such without guaranteed evidence. Consider Abraham. He had been promised enough heirs to make him the father of many nations, but nothing seemed to come of it.

He was ninety-nine years of age and had no legitimate heir. His only consolation was a son born to his concubine, Hagar. The scripture states that Ishmael was born when Abraham was eighty-six, and that both father and son were circumcised at their ages of ninety-nine and thirteen. It took a lot of nurturing by Sarah and Abraham to hold onto the promise, to hold on for hope without letting life be tarnished by their inadequacies and unfulfilled promises. Who could believe in a God who waited until both father and mother were beyond their normal childbearing ages to parent an infant? A God that does not consider time as we do! Time is not of essence, the event is.

That is troublesome for us. We are a people who live by calendars. Time is money! We want it done yesterday, and if not yesterday at least today. We are not willing to wait much beyond our own time clocks. An everlasting covenant has no time constraints. If God does not lie, and if covenants are everlasting, then Jewish, Christian, and Muslim people will one day meet within Abraham's covenant to worship the same God—not in our time, but in God's time. God does not make timely covenants to match our goals, but instead he makes timeless covenants.

Or does an everlasting covenant mean that God never gives up on us? Regardless of what we do, the relationship can't be broken by us? Jesus's stories in the Christian Bible, such as the Prodigal Son or the Loving Father, come to mind. He definitely taught contradictory to the current Jewish theology of his day and the current Christianity today. What he taught was no matter how much you sin, God would take you back. That's not an easy metaphor to accept, either in the past or in this age. It smacks of permissiveness; it seems to deny responsibility. There are myriad families in which the role of the prodigal son or daughter has been played to the destruction of parents and siblings.

But there are shortcomings in assigning human metaphors to God. Parenting roles such as father or mother are not adequate metaphors to speak completely of God's activity; neither female nor male metaphors alone will do God justice. The story of the Loving Father or the Prodigal Son was never intended to be a model for parenting; it was a story about how God's activity is different from the usual human level of parenting. No father in his right mind would have done what the prodigal son's father did—but God transcends human activity. God's everlasting covenant is made with Abraham to ensure humanity that our relationship cannot be terminated by us—only by God. We may terminate relationships with each other: wife and husband, father and son, mother and daughter, brother and brother, sister and sister. But God won't quit us. God believes in us when all others fail.

Or does everlasting mean that the relationship with God is endless? At this time of the year, those returning from warmer climates share worship bulletins with me. In reading one, I noticed a list of people to be *prayed for*, a list of people who *were ill*, and then another list of people *in transition*. Maybe you can figure it out before me, but it took me several minutes. At first, I surmised this latter description was for people who were moving, but there were no towns following their names. Then, I thought, maybe they were names of people who were divorcing, but that seemed a bit tacky. Then, my eye caught the clue—a date. These were deaths. My first reaction was one of disbelief! Living in a state where drive-up funeral homes are a part of the scene, I thought we had gotten over the Victorian taboo of speaking about death in plain words. But on reflection, I realized that death was not being denied, but something important was being conveyed theologically. An everlasting covenant has no beginning and no end. Just as none of us can remember the day we begin, neither will we remember the day we end—because there is no end, just a transition from one stage to another stage along a continuum.

For humanity, there is nothing everlasting. Even the most precious golden object from an Egyptian pyramid, thousands of years old, nurtured by caring hands of an archaeologist and a museum curator will someday tarnish into dust. But for humanity, God's relationship is everlasting.

Jacob Wrestles at Peniel

32 [24] Jacob was left alone; and a man wrestled with him until daybreak.

Wrestling with God

Sermon by Richard Murdoch | East Lansing, MI | August 8, 1993

He was a determined young man who was not afraid to work hard for life's rewards. He looked young enough to star as a matinee model who soap opera producers would have grabbed up in a minute. He was an astute businessman whom any corporation would have gladly landed for their CEO track. He had a winsome way with people and was in high demand among charity events raising money for a variety of community agencies.

It wasn't so much that he rode the crest of promise and accomplishment, but he did it with a certain kind of easy style and grace, without rancor against his father-in-law. Most knew that his success had been paid with a price. His father-in-law had originally been the start of his business career, but had deceived him and tricked him into a kind of servitude of debt from which he had freed himself, not once but twice. People had admired this young man, who had just a touch of gray at his temples, and was now entering mid-life.

That's why they were totally confused and bewildered when one day he just up and stuck a For Sale sign on his house, turned his business interest over to a blind trust, and hired a fleet of luxury buses not unlike those in which television stars travel. He hired a couple of drivers for his three automobiles and a pickup truck that hauled his favorite possession, a boat. His children were taken out of school; his lawyer, accountant, and banker left their desks with portfolios in hand to join this procession, which made quite a scene as it moved towards the interstate heading west.

As the entourage made its first evening's stop, the man left the overnight parking facility in the National Park on foot, crossing over a stream. An evening walk to clear the cobwebs of travel turned into an all-night affair. He failed to return until the early morning. And when he did so, his sweaty and disheveled appearance was obvious to all. But more obvious was a noticeable limp as he walked. Reflected in his face was not the pain from the limp, but an apprehensiveness, something that no one had ever seen before in this self-made man. When his wife inquired, he said that he had been wrestling all night long. Her eyes peered a bit in a suspicious disbelief. "With whom?" she inquired. "I don't know; he wouldn't tell me his name," he replied.

Unbeknownst to his wife and all others, he was in the midst of expiating an adolescent guilt in his approaching midlife. Years before, he had deceived his father and cheated his brother—not unlike what his father-in-law had done to him. But nobody here knew it because he had fled his childhood home in such a hurry. In fact, nobody knew except his mother, who had aided him in his adolescent deception.

This paragon of moral virtue would never have been suspected of the dastardly deed he had done—that had rendered his father into life-long humiliation and his brother into near poverty. For years, he had planned a homecoming to make things right before his parents died. He did not want this evil deed to blot his conscience before God, and he found it impossible to live with the guilt.

But by that first evening's stop, he was getting cold feet. Was he doing the right thing by his family and friends? Why couldn't he just let sleeping dogs lie? What was the point in bringing this out in the open? Would the bribe work? Or would his brother, still enraged, kill him as he had sworn to do? Would he really feel freed from this painful memory? Would his plan work to protect himself and his family if his brother still sought revenge?

His plan was composed of several parts. First, he would send his lawyer to work out the details of the homecoming so there would be no reprisal. If that were successful, then he would send his banker to show how much of the assets he was willing to reimburse his brother for the years of absence. If his brother was still amiable, then he would send the accountant to show him the actual goods—the cars, the cash, and the bonds. If all of that worked, then he would send his family to meet him; and lastly, he would appear.

As he mulled over his plan on his evening walk in the darkness, someone who he could not see attacked him from behind. He was wrestled to the ground; he tried to pin his opponent, but failed. Then his opponent made his move. At first, it seemed as though it was his brother with whom he was wrestling, but as the night wore on, his adversary seemed to have a divine quality. By morning, the man would no longer be mistaken for a matinee model. His dislocated hip changed his gait permanently; his hair appeared grayer and he had a new name: no longer was it Jacob, it was Israel, which means "the one who wrestled with God."

As the procession exited the interstate near his boyhood home— from which he fled two decades before—he was stunned to see his brother coming out to meet him. He hurriedly organized his four echelons to protect himself against the revenge of his brother: the lawyer and his staff; the banker and his staff; the accountant and his staff; his wives and children. Taking no cognizance of the trapping of Jacob's wealth (which he was prepared to turn over to his brother as a peace offering), Esau walked directly to Jacob and embraced him. Jacob's private nightmare was over; but his limp would always mark him as the one who wrestled with God.

***

Commentators and scholars have offered a variety of interpretations of this story ranging from suggestions of a symbolic interpretation (that Jacob was really wrestling with his conscience) to a very literal suggestion (that God took on human form to show humanity that the spiritual is stronger than the physical). I wonder, though, if the scholarly approach overlooks the human drama that is played out in the heart and not the head.

Few people seeking faith are attracted to a God that wants to wrestle; we more often seek a soothing faith. Our expectation of faith is not to greet the sunrise exhausted and sweaty from wrestling with God. If we do, we are convinced there is something wrong or inadequate with our faith. Our cultural expectation of faith is to greet the sunrise with a confidence of God's care and faith's certitude. That's what real faith is all about we are told in the Good Book!

It's a misnomer to label the Bible the Good Book. It's far from that. In fact, every plot ever conceived in drama, movie, opera, or soap opera can be found in the Bible first. Stories of violence and mayhem, murder, revenge, adultery, incest, deception, and infidelity abound. While the Bible offers a multitude of real, live stories of the failures of human beings to live their lives in the image of God, it recounts the stories, not for entertainment, but to offer encouragement in the midst of lives gone awry yet put back together. Consider Jacob.

Jacob would have difficulty making it to the boardrooms of modern CEOs and would find it almost impossible to be elected or appointed to a public office. His past actions in regards to his brother and father would render him a political liability. Of the Ten Commandments, he had broken at least three when he stole his brother's birthright through the deception of his father (with the help of his mother).

Opponents would be quick to raise doubts about your support of a man who had dishonored his father, borne false witness against his brother, and yet coveted his father's patrimonial blessing. And of course, Jacob's new physical handicap would be a liability as well. "Can you trust such a person to represent you?" the television advertising would scream. Yet Jacob is one of the three most famous persons, held in the highest esteem, in the biblical genealogy. It is the "God of Abraham, Isaac, and Jacob" who calls the "children of Israel" out of Egypt.

But our culture today not only often holds people accountable for their past failings, but also exacts a punishment from which they can never recover. It is not unlike the seventeenth-century Age of Puritanism against which Nathaniel Hawthorne wrote *The Scarlet Letter*. In that novel—which used to be required reading in high school—Hester Pryne has had a love affair with a married man (whom she will not reveal). For this act, she must wear a large red A on her dress to mark her as morally corrupt. In addition, she is shunned for a penitent period of time.

But, as Hawthorne makes clear, Hester is marked for the rest of her life for one lapse of morality, even after her penance has been performed. No one in Salem can let her forget her crime. In fact, some cultural observers suggest that we are now in the Age of New Puritanism because not only is penance exacted from us, but also our careers, as we undergo lifelong punishment for our perceived moral and political incorrectness.

Wrestling with the past and with the dark side of our lives is dangerous. It appears to be the better part of valor to simply not put ourselves at risk unless we are squeaky clean. Jacob could have easily done that: gone about his business as usual in his adopted city, let his mother and father pass away without resolving the heat of adolescent passion, and sent some money to his brother through an anonymous source.

But the pain of his own ego led Jacob to confront his past and repair his relationships. He made his plans, risking his entire financial empire. But that wasn't the greatest risk. Reconciliation is a two-way street. What would happen if Esau wouldn't respond? No matter how carefully Jacob planned, no matter how carefully Jacob manipulated his four echelons of lawyer, banker, accountant, and family, there was no guarantee that his brother would be receptive. Jacob wrestled with an *angel* (the Greek word for "God's messenger"), hoping to exact some certainty that God would prepare the way for successful reconciliation. But the angel was never pinned down. Jacob had to face Esau—risking everything—if he was to repair his past.

The good news brought to the Jacobs of the world needs to be heard in more than just Bible stories. It needs to be heard in the halls of government, the boardrooms of companies, and in our social institutions. Jacob acted upon his conscience: He risked his life to recover a lost innocence with his brother, and moved on to a peaceful life.

Well, that's sort of what happened. As in a soap opera, there is actually another chapter. Later in the story, we find out that Esau welcomed his brother without condition or acceptance of bribes. Jacob inhabited land close by and settled his family again. His parents, Isaac and Rebecca, died and were laid to rest. Then the next installment of Jacob's story unfolds, portraying another drama, one that's centered instead on his adult children.

✡ Genesis 34:30 ✡
Dinah's Brothers Avenge Their Sister

34 [30] Then Jacob said to Simeon and Levi, "You have brought trouble on me by making me stink to the inhabitants of the land, the Canaanites and the Perizzites. My numbers are few, and if they gather themselves against me and attack me, I shall be destroyed, both I and my household."

Bible Version: English Standard Version (ESV)

Wrestling with life

Sermon by Richard Murdoch | East Lansing, MI | August 15, 1993

Betrayal and revenge. These are the plots of great drama, opera, and theater, which have entertained centuries of audiences from ancient Greece to modern cable television. They are also the poison that destroys marriages and families, churches and corporations, communities and nations.

While the Judeo-Christian tradition celebrates the positive characteristics of life portrayed by its heroes, it does not shrink from reporting their flaws. After Jacob wrestled over the reconciliation of his brother, Esau—the outcome of which initiated the hope of a peaceful and successful co-existence—he was plunged into wrestling again, this time with three of his adult children: Dinah, Simeon, and Levi. Once again, he is brought to the brink of despair. But this time, it is not due to Jacob's own behavior.

After Jacob had bought land and resettled in Palestine, near his boyhood home, his troubles began again. A neighboring tribe of people called the Hivites, of whom Hamor was the leader, occupied the city near where Jacob had settled. Dinah, Jacob's very beautiful daughter, ventured into town one day to do some shopping and have lunch, seeking some new friendships. Shechem, son of Hamor, and himself probably a very handsome young man, was bored with the local young women, and thus intrigued by the new beauty he saw in town that day.

At this point in the Genesis text, the Hebrew is somewhat vague and the English translations are quite diverse, depending on a translator's bias. Some say what happened next was rape, some say it was sexual assault, others call it seduction, and yet others say it was a lovers' tryst. But whatever happened, Dinah didn't make it to lunch that day. And the result of that lunchtime encounter between Dinah and Shechem was not an isolated fit of passion. Shechem was smitten with love and asked his father, Hamor, for permission to ask Jacob, Dinah's father, for her hand in marriage.

In the negotiations for this impending marriage, as described in Genesis, some practical aspects emerged. Jacob's tribe had sons who needed wives and Hamor's tribe had daughters who needed husbands. So even though Jacob wanted his sons and daughters to marry their own kind, he couldn't ignore the property and wealth that would come in the deal. Jacob's financial as well as military position would be strengthened by entering into an alliance with another tribe like Hamor's through marriage. Hamor saw a similar military advantage in allying with Jacob if unfriendly invaders would try to take his city. Shechem and his father informed Jacob that no price was too high for the dowry of lovely Dinah.

Only one impediment remained in the negotiations. The Hivite men did not practice circumcision. To the Hebrews, this custom was symbolic of the covenant that God had made with his people through Abraham, Jacob's grandfather. It was a tradition that marked Yahweh's people as different from the people of other gods. While Jacob was willing to overlook this religious custom, his sons Levi and Simeon were not. They were not in agreement with their father, Jacob. They thought he was getting older and a bit weak in the head. They were getting antsy in their twenties and wanted more decision-making power in the family business. They thought he could probably strike a better deal, and harbored some real doubts about their prospective brother-in-law, Shechem. They thought their sister Dinah was being manipulated by this young man their own age. "Love? Ha! All he wanted was sex!" They thought Shechem should have paid dearly for his lunchtime escapade, and here he was, entering their tribe by marriage, after which he could lay claim to Dinah's share of Jacob's property when Jacob died.

Simeon and Levi seized upon this religious custom to hatch a vicious and terrible plot to get revenge, all of which is told in remarkable detail in the Hebrew text of Genesis, but only alluded to in our English translation. Jacob agreed innocently to the logic that his sons put before him. While the Hivites would not be asked to leave their own gods, they would need to be circumcised in order for the children whom they sired with Hebrew wives to be a part of Abraham's covenant. But as the story unfolds, we find that the real reason for the two brothers' demand of circumcision had nothing to do with religion, it had to do with rendering the Hivite men powerless to fight.

While circumcision might be a relatively painless surgery for an infant male, it is exactly the opposite for an adult male. Verse 25 says: "Then two days later, when they were still in great pain, Jacob's two sons, Simeon and Levi, full brothers to Dinah, armed themselves with swords, boldly entered the city and killed every male. They slaughtered Hamor and his son Shechem, took Dinah from his house. Jacob's other sons came in over the dead bodies and plundered the city to avenge their sister's dishonor. They seized flocks of cattle and donkeys and everything inside and outside the city. They also carried off all their possessions, their children, their women and tore down their houses."

And what was Jacob's response? "You have brought disaster upon me and my name *stinks* [a euphuism for feces] among the people of the country, the Canaanites, and the Pezzites. My numbers are few and if they muster against me and attack me, I will be destroyed, our whole household." So Jacob sought God's help. God told him to head for the hills (or Bethel, which is the same place where he had hidden almost twenty years earlier from Esau). Jacob was wrestling again. Is that what life is all about? Starting over again and again and again?

This time it was different. It was about the inability of Jacob's children to learn from their father's mistake. What is it about humanity whose memory is so short from generation to generation? I watch with fear as representatives of NATO meeting in Belgium this week argued their positions for offensive aerial bombing of Sarajevo. The quagmire of the Balkan history is intimately known to historians. What kind of madness is it for the State Department to issue its opinion that the defense of that Balkan city is "in our national interest?" Those same words were echoed seventy years ago to give credence to Mr. Wilson's War, as some called World War I, which was the so-called "war to make the world safe for democracy." As we all know, democracy is no safer today than it was then. The problem is not so much to pay blind homage to the historian's edict that "Those who don't know their past are doomed to repeat it." The problem is our ability to discern the human emotion of revenge that continues to drive not only national and world histories, but also our personal histories.

In some ways, the real hero of the Jacob epic in the Bible is Esau, who first sought revenge upon Jacob. But as time passed, Esau realized that revenge would continue the cycle of destruction. So he gave up on revenge and accepted the outstretched olive branch, as imperfect as it was, with Jacob's elaborate bribes, which we heard about last Sunday. The outcome was peaceful co-existence. Everybody could get on with their future lives and leave the past be.

But that experience didn't soak in with Jacob's kids. Why? Was it a case of Jacob protecting his children from the difficult lessons of life? Or was it their sibling jealousy that blinded them from the consequences? Their self-righteous judgment upon Hamor claimed that as an uncircumcised man (or a non-Hebrew), he had violated their sister as a common whore. But there is no scriptural evidence until five hundred years later in Deuteronomy that such a sexual encounter would call for vengeance. In that day, women were the property of their father, not their brothers. And Jacob was ready to give his full approval without revenge. Jacob knew what his kids did not: Revenge is in all of us; it's part of the human given. The cycle is broken only when we refuse to act upon that emotion.

The scenario is played out in country after country that demands our military and economic support. Whether it is Somalia, South Africa, Palestine, or Bosnia[1], we are asked to support this side or that side in their quest for revenge buried in histories so old, the real reasons have been forgotten. Or the scenario is played out in our cities; whether it is one drug gang against another; one political party or another; one candidate or another. It is played out in businesses and boardrooms of educational institutions—one corporate buy-out against another or one philosophy winning over another philosophy. Or played out in our families, with spouses avenging love affairs or parents avenging their children's attacker.

What makes revenge so appealing? It is immediate gratification. It cleanses the anger and brings satisfaction, now. It's punishment that people can see, right in front of them. It's instant justice. But as the Bible knows, revenge is deceptive. Once unleashed, it is contagious. It has no ending until it has destroyed everyone and everything in sight. Like the once beautiful Winter Olympic resort city of Sarajevo or like Beirut (called the Paris of the East) the result of revenge is ruin upon ruin of lives, families, property, and nations from which it takes generations to recover.

But ancient words can contain the compulsion to act upon our desire to avenge whatever wrong. "Revenge is mine, says the Lord; and I will repay." Esau knew that, Jacob learned that, yet generations of their adult children refuse still to listen and to learn. But we must not give up. We—like Jacob—must continue to wrestle with life, until our revenge has been given up to God. Only then will the cycle be broken and our lives safe.

[1] Or current issues in Israel, Iraq, Pakistan, Syria, and Afghanistan!

Context:
Exodus & Leviticus

Enter Moses, possibly the most important man of the Hebrew scriptures. And although he himself is quoted as saying "I am not eloquent," his actions provide strong examples of both hope and faith.

Exodus

At the end of Genesis, Jacob dies after seventeen years with his family in Egypt (thanks to his son Joseph's political prowess). Upon Jacob's death, under Joseph's lead, life continues comfortably. But after the death of the current pharaoh, a new one rises to power who "did not know Joseph." The Israelites suffer under the Egyptians until they are led by Moses (after he gets some guidance from the burning bush) out of Egypt (after a series of nasty plagues) to a mountain in Sinai.

This is not an easy trip, and along the way, they are subject to hunger, thirst, and violence from others. But they prevail with God's help and receive a covenant with God—the infamous Ten Commandments—as well as myriad other rules and regulations to help the Israelites change from a family to a nation.

Finally, they follow very specific directions to construct the tabernacle, a portable shrine to serve as an earthly home for God and the Ark of the Covenant (an elaborate chest for the Ten Commandments).

Leviticus

Named after one of the tribes of Israel (the Levites), Leviticus is filled primarily with religious ritual and law, including the governance of offerings to God, dietary restrictions, purification rites, and the setting aside of holy days (such as the Sabbath, Passover, and Yom Kippur). The laws resemble those of many other ancient Near Eastern cultures: part danger avoidance, part societal need, and part rich symbolism.

If these laws are followed, then it is believed that God will stay among the Israelites. If the laws are not, it is believed God will leave the tabernacle and the Israelites. Simply put, although they believe there is a divine will, they believe humans are ultimately in control of their own destiny. The actions of the individual will influence the society as a whole, so collective responsibility begins to be very important.

In Leviticus, Moses's brother Aaron and his family were ordained officially as the formal priesthood.

Meanwhile...

Everywhere, civilizations were flourishing.

The Pacific Islands were finally inhabited, as seamen headed out farther out into the Pacific in double-hulled outrigger canoes. A rich Polynesian culture spread as a trade network spanned the vast ocean.

Life in China was becoming more urban, as the Shang Dynasty came into power and brought with it the beginnings of the area's recorded history. In addition to ancestor worship, the people worshiped Shang Ti (literally "lord on high") who was believed to be the divine link between heaven and earth.

In India the seeds of Hinduism were spreading. The evolving customs would influence the Samhitas, the oldest scriptures in the Hindu tradition and the precursors to the Vedas.

States were organizing in South America, and the 100-foot tall Huaca La Florida ceremonial center was built in central Peru, capable of accommodating over 100,000 worshippers. Farther north, the first known urban center in North America developed along the Mississippi River. The inhabitants constructed a complex ceremonial structure of earth mounds and ridges.

The Old Babylonian Empire came to an end, as the Hittites traveled through northern Syria and the Levant, then set their sights on sacking Babylon. But their victory would be short-lived, as Assyria regained its independence after four hundred years of foreign rule, and began gaining in power in Mesopotamia.

✡ Exodus 12:29-36 ✡

The Tenth Plague: Death of the Firstborn

12 ²⁹ At midnight, the Lord struck down all the firstborn in the land of
Egypt, from the firstborn of Pharaoh who sat on his throne to the firstborn
of the prisoner who was in the dungeon, and all the firstborn of the livestock.
³⁰ Pharaoh arose in the night, he and all his officials and all the Egyptians;
and there was a loud cry in Egypt, for there was not a house without someone dead. ³¹ Then he summoned Moses and Aaron in the night, and said,
"Rise up, go away from my people, both you and the Israelites! Go, worship
the Lord, as you said. ³² Take your flocks and your herds, as you said, and be
gone. And bring a blessing on me too!"

³³ The Egyptians urged the people to hasten their departure from the land,
for they said, "We shall all be dead." ³⁴ So the people took their dough before
it was leavened, with their kneading bowls wrapped up in their cloaks on
their shoulders. ³⁵ The Israelites had done as Moses told them; they had
asked the Egyptians for jewelry of silver and gold, and for clothing, ³⁶ and the
Lord had given the people favor in the sight of the Egyptians, so that they let
them have what they asked. And so they plundered the Egyptians.

Israel's golden parachute

Sermon by Richard Murdoch | East Lansing, MI | July 12, 1987

Do you know people who ante up the count after you thought the last card had been played? Moses, for all his saintliness and righteousness, exhibited such shrewd behavior that it is difficult to blame Pharaoh for all of Israel's troubles. If you want a modern-day parallel to the current nuclear reduction negotiations between the Soviet Union and the United States, you won't have to look far. The Book of Exodus will give you an example of how to play one-upmanship to your advantage, whether it is between Moses and Pharaoh or Gorbachev and Reagan.

The vision, which God gave the Israelites through Moses, was simply being freed from their economic bondage in Egypt so they might resume the search begun by Abraham for a "land filled with milk and honey." But the odds were great. Egyptians had close to a half million people, Israel about four thousand. That's a ratio of one hundred to one—not very good odds. Egypt had a standing army that included six hundred chariots; Israel had no army and not one chariot. The Egyptians were the masters; the Israelites were the slaves. The Egyptians were rich; the Israelites had sunk into poverty. The call to lead the people of Israel in making their vision become reality was not given in a formula to Moses. He knew who he was to lead (the Israelites) and where (out of Egypt) and why (economics and security), but he did not know how. No instructions were given. In fact, he was such a poor public speaker that his brother Aaron was appointed his spokesperson.

But as the story in Exodus slowly unfolds in chapters 3 through 12, we note the strategy by which the vision is going to become reality. Moses made a simple, initial request to Pharaoh. "We need a three-day holiday from making bricks in order that we may have a great sacrificial feast in the wilderness for our God!" Now Pharaoh was no fool. He managed a large empire. He knew you couldn't get to the wilderness in one day, have a feast with four thousand people the next day, and return the third day! Not only was it impractical, it was costly to his production plans. Three days might not be all that long, but he knew these Israelites. They counted differently: Three days would stretch into weeks once they got into the wilderness. While his advisors suggested that it might not be all that bad of an idea, simple as the request was, Pharaoh was a man of principles. "No dice" is the response Moses received from his hard-earned audience with Pharaoh. To reward Moses for his effort, Pharaoh decreed to the Israelite brick-makers' union, "Double your brick production and gather your own straw!" Moses lost a lot of popular support for his vision.

Moses's second attempt was not in an audience, but was a chance meeting as the Pharaoh went down to the river to bathe one morning. Moses was standing down the bank at a safe distance. As Pharaoh was about to enter the Nile River, Moses shouted to him: "My God still wants you to let his people go have a feast in the wilderness!" Then he stuck a rod into the water, and the Nile turned red as blood and all the fish died. "Take that," cried Moses as he stomped away. "Yahweh is no puny god whom you can avoid!"

That night, Egyptian and Israelite alike had no fish for food, nor water to drink. The Egyptians were awed; the Israelites were angry. Moses lost more popular support for his cause among his people.

This episode affected nothing. Next came the frogs. Seven days after the red river episode, Moses and Aaron suggested to Pharaoh that it might be wise to let Israel go or something like a plague of frogs might appear. And they might be just everywhere—in your house, in your bedroom, in your bed, in your kitchens, and in your bread bowls! Pharaoh laughed at them. The next day frogs were jumping everywhere. Moses was summoned. He would get his request. The people could go for a holy day—but first they had to clean up the stinking mess. One squashed frog on a summer road is one thing, a city full of them is another, especially when they were in the Israelites' homes also. A few more of Moses's loyal supporters left him. The Israelites didn't like these plagues any more than the Egyptians did. It was beginning to be difficult to figure out who was the friend and who was the foe.

Pharaoh reneged on his promise. So they were hit with another plague—one of gnats or horse flies, depending on how you translate the word. But something changed. This time they didn't invade Goshen. (This was the Israelite quarter of town, so now they were making a little progress: Moses's supporters were spared the gnat-flies!) The succeeding plagues of boils on human skin, death of the livestock, hail, locusts, and, finally, the mysterious death of all first-born humans and animals were alternated with Pharaoh promising to let the people have a religious feast in the wilderness. Each time Moses added another condition. The initial request was a three-day feast for the men in the wilderness, but as the suspense built, the list of conditions grew. Now Moses decreed that all the people must go to the feast—the sons and daughters with their herds of animals accompanying them, and taking all their possessions with them since they didn't know how long the feast would last—only God knew! Really! And finally, Moses suggested that Pharaoh really wouldn't even have to give permission, he would instead invite them to leave and shower them with gifts of gold, silver, and fine clothing as they went!

What an audacious strategy. With the odds at 100:1, the Israelite slaves would be invited to leave for a holy day with all their possessions and showered with gifts by their masters, the Egyptians. Not a shot would be fired, not a bow raised, not a single act of struggle would occur! No wonder God didn't reveal the strategy to Moses—Moses would have never believed it. There was no master plan. Instead, it unfolded in stages.

How many of us become frustrated when our plans cannot be mastered and fit into a grand scheme? We have entered an era of business, of education, of politics, of culture, and of religion, in which we are always expected to be able to see ahead, years down the road, instead of day by day. Anyone who plans day by day or even month by month is often considered a poor planner. Instead of letting the plan fit the process, we make the process fit the plan. Instead of letting our plans fit our lives' needs, we make our lives fit our plan.

It is a bit like this story of an old table, which a family passed from generation to generation: It started as a great-grandmother's canning table. It showed the character of an eighty-year-old maple piece, which had been lovingly refurbished and promoted from the back porch to the formal living room. But one thing stood out: The legs were not all the same height. Nobody knew why. The table needed a couple of shims under two legs to level it—always had and always would. One member of the family surmised that it was probably easier for canning that way.

Another offered that through the years, the wood probably had dried and shrunk a bit. Yet another offered the explanation that since it was just a back porch table, its maker didn't really care how it looked. But the recently married couple to whom the table had been given was not satisfied. They desired to know the truth about their odd table.

The great-grandmother was in her nineties, residing in a retirement apartment. Upon a visit, the couple inquired about this lovely antique with its odd characteristic. When the couple told her of the various explanations they had heard, the great-grandmother, whose name was Roselle, threw back her head and laughed heartily. "Lawsy me! There's not an ounce of truth in any of that! Carl, your great-grandfather, discovered after he made the table for me, that the back porch sloped a bit, and the table wasn't level. He reckoned it was easier to make the table fit the porch than to make the porch fit the table, so he cut off about an inch on two legs!"

The Israelites and Moses experienced the same thing. They were trying to fit God's strategy into their own plans, rather than fitting their plans into God's strategy. This was tested finally by God's strategy that each Israelite slave should ask his or her Egyptian master for gold, silver, and fine clothing. This was ridiculous and outrageous. What kind of fools did Moses think the Israelites were, by asking their very masters for the most precious things in their household? For the Israelites, this was the golden parachute.

I know that golden parachutes have tarnished a bit in the last several years. But in the not-too-distant past, an executive or public official in a significant place of leadership might be asked to leave that position either because the philosophy of a board had changed or his objectives had not been reached as far or as efficiently as they might have been. There would be several years on a contract left. The executive's contract would be bought out or some substantial financial arrangements would be made which could not be refused. To let the executive down easy, a golden parachute could cushion the potential lawsuits from termination of contracts. Theoretically, the recipient could live in the style that was customary until another position could be secured, which could take several years.

Theoretically, the Egyptians' gift of gold, silver, and fine clothing was a final gesture to get these Israelites into the wilderness to do their religious duty for a couple of days (or weeks) and get this new and powerful God called Yahweh off the Egyptians' backs so they could get on with their lives. And it worked for both the Egyptians and the Israelites. The Egyptians got the Israelites into the wilderness, while the Israelites got their golden parachute. The golden parachute lasted for forty years as the Israelites slowly sold their gold, silver, and clothing to the wandering Bedouins in order to finance their sojourn. Without their golden parachute, they would surely have had trouble surviving on just manna and quail.

Each time that Israel restricted God, God would break out in a new direction, seeking to demonstrate that God is more than majority opinion or a success formula.

That's hard to take in our objective-laden world. Popular self-help books will sell you foolproof strategies for your lives. Many preachers will do the same. Often educators, health professionals, and businesses will. This is not to say there is no truth in any formula given to you for problem solving, but it is to say there is always more room for other possibilities. There is always room to re-adjust the goals. There is always more time to leave a bit of planning to the sometimes unpredictable.

That's hard advice to take in an era when planning is necessary years in advance to prepare for the future. We all sit in meetings and hear that old adage: "No one plans to fail, but one fails to plan." But no plan is foolproof. We cannot mold everyone into our plans. Like the Israelites, we have at times been captive to our own ways, and other times we have wandered around in a wilderness. Like the Israelites, we have made our plans and expected God to fit into them. And then when God didn't fit in, we just went along with our plans anyway. It's hard to fit ourselves into God's strategy. We are such take-charge people. We want to shape our own destiny. We want to control what we want in life. It's what has made us a great civilization; it should be so. But is there not room to let God challenge us and speak to us? Is there not room to fit into divine plans instead of human plans? I hope so and pray so!

As we move into our tomorrows, let us expect God to lead us in ways that will enhance our service to others, rather than ways in which we expect God always to enhance us. We may be surprised to find that in the most hopeless days of our life, we can expect (if we allow it) a golden parachute from God so that we might survive the wildernesses in our lives. We can allow our plans to unfold day to day, week to week, month to month, and year to year. Let's stop expecting God to fit our plans. Let's learn from Moses. Let's fit into God's plans.

The Ten Commandments

20 [7] You shall not make wrongful use of the name of the Lord your God, for the Lord will not acquit anyone who misuses his name.

When is vulgar vain?

Sermon by Richard Murdoch | Rye, NY | July 14, 1990

> *I was sitting in a row just behind some teens. The advertising slides were sliding along on the screen. A theater is never quiet then. There is a din of crunching popcorn and the slurping of sodas accented with lively conversation. But from the row in front of me, every other word was cursing or profanity relating to mothers, women, or homosexuals. After a while, I was fed up. I said nicely to the young men of my race, "I'm sorry, but there's not much other choice of seats, otherwise I would move. But do you think your mothers and your sisters and your brothers do what you say they do in those words you are using?" I expected of course to hear a retort in much the same language. But I was surprised. In fact, I was stunned. They apologized. "Sorry, lady. Nobody said it's bothered them before. Sorry."*

So wrote Betty DeMaaus, a columnist for the *Detroit News*, illustrating the low estate of slang and vulgar language.

Testing boundaries moves youth to the adult world. Testing the boundaries of language is part of that transition. And it starts early. In my college days, when I was a summer youth counselor in the Poconos, I found that first graders from the Lower East Side of New York City had by far a more extensive vocabulary than I had had even as a junior high student. Swear words and cuss words—as they were called—were simply not acceptable then in front of adults, even though we teens knew that adults used them when we weren't around. There was a code of conduct in those days in the South that required genteel substitutes for swear and cuss words when in the mixed company of men and women or youth and adults, or any combination thereof.

As I reflect upon it today, the substitute words sound arcane; but the principle behind them had been carefully thought out generations before in Southern society, which adhered strictly (at least publicly) to its particular religious interpretation. My Southern uncles and aunts used expressions like "Oh Law!" as a substitute for "Oh Lord!" As a child who had grown up in the North, I used to wonder whether "Law" was just a drawn-out pronunciation of "Lawd" for "Lord," dropping the "d" in Southern dialect and coming up with "Law," or whether "Law" was referring to the Bible.

Biblical words seemed to be used most frequently when people were trying to find a substitute for the expression "My God!" My uncle liked "Jumping Jehoshaphat!"[1] and my aunt favored "Oh Methuselah!"[2] In the Southern society of my youth, these substitutes allowed one to express the emotion of joy, sorrow, pleasure, or pain without taking the Lord's name in vain—so we could avoid violating the third of the Ten Commandments, which we teens recited annually at Sunday school Rally Day.

As Betty DeMaaus pointed out in her column, one does not have to go very far these days to observe the decline of civility in language. What she heard from young moviegoers may not have differed much from what she may have heard from the language in the actual film. The boundaries of acceptable language in our culture have been greatly widened—and not necessarily for the best. But as Ms. DeMaaus noted, does anybody care?

The breakdown of the civility of our words parallels a breakdown in our perception of the boundaries between human and divine. The Third Commandment is based upon an ancient perception, which is greatly diminished in our technological society. It was believed by many ancient religions—not only Judaism—that the very pronouncement of the name of the divine by a human diminished the respect for divine power. To this day, in Orthodox Judaism, when the reader of the Torah comes to the name of God—which is an unpronounceable tetragram (four letters)—the silver reading pencil is lifted over the word, the reader remaining silent.

Ancient peoples considered the gods powerful enough to intervene at any time to change the course of individuals' lives or a nation's history, given the right combination of rituals enhanced with the perfect accompanying words. Ancient Judaism had an annual festival that lay blessings and curses for the coming year before Yahweh. But the Levites, who led two groups of worshippers on either side of the valley in a litany described in the Book of Deuteronomy, were careful not to usurp Yahweh's divine power by using his name.

The ancients would have told you that when you willfully consigned damnation of another's action in God's name you took for yourself the place of God. You used the precious power of the divine name in vain, because in reality, you alone cannot be God.

The Third Commandment protects the power of God and the power of God's creation, which is introduced in the first two commandments. There is but one God. None of God's power can be usurped by an idol created from nature, nor can God's power be taken over by a human being. Now all of this may seem like a far trip around the horn to understand the prohibition of taking God's name in vain, but I believe that it helps explain that the breakdown of civility in language is really not so much a cultural issue as it is a theological one. Much of what we have come to accept as human progress in life was once thought to be God's province.

Take for example, modern neonatal medicine. In a small church cemetery in South Carolina, three infants are buried in our family plot beside my grandmother and grandfather. All would be described as premature today. In my grandfather's small pocket diary, there were notations that God saw fit to take them because they were not strong enough to live on their own.

Today, with the assistance of modern medicine, my grandparents would have had eight children (instead of five) growing to maturity. And our family plot is not unique. In almost any older cemetery, there are often as many infants and children as adults buried in a family plot, with grave markers indicating that "God needed a child home in heaven." But today, we would attribute the death not to God's power but to the power of diseases like measles, chicken pox, or scarlet fever, which we have eradicated by human progress.

The looseness with which we treat cursing and profane language is a result of the loss of the fear that God will strike us dead or something disastrous will happen if we exceed the boundaries of civility. Ms. DeMaaus, the columnist, noted that at first she felt a bit unsure about confronting the teenagers in the theater. But once she challenged them about having exceeded a reasonable boundary—by suggesting what they could be implying about those who were special to them—they stopped from profaning fellow human beings and treated each with the respect they were due.

The word "vulgar" has an honorable origin in Latin. The first Bible translated from Greek into Latin was called the Vulgate Bible, meaning it was written in the common language of the people. Today, the word vulgar has come to mean the lowest common language, street or gutter talk. While not directly related to the Third Commandment etiologically, the use of vulgar and profane language in describing another person directly implies that such a person, though created in God's image, is somehow unworthy of God's creation.

Vulgar is vain because the power that is implied by it is really no power. It speaks more of the speaker than the one spoken about. Its accusatory finger-pointing is not unlike a visual symbol of a gun. The accusing finger points the barrel at the one spoken about, but three fingers remain pointed backward (as if they were the handle of the gun), accusing the speaker.

I don't suppose anyone can truthfully say that he or she has never taken the Lord's name in vain or that a profane word has never come from their lips in their lifetime. But when such words become the backbone of everyday conversation — or are uttered so frequently that they carry no special meaning—not only does it say that we have little respect for those around us, but that we have little understanding of the God who created us. Vain becomes vulgar and vulgar becomes vain when we lose sight of the relationship between the Creator and the created.

The ancients were not so far from the truth, were they? And we can do precious little to improve upon their wisdom. What is different is that in the biblical world the consequence of pushing those boundaries too far was the fear of retribution by God. Some external force was expected to enforce the Third Commandment.

Today, in a secular, democratic republic, we must rely upon an internal force, that of self-discipline. God will not strike us dead and there are hardly enough police to enforce a profanity law. We should be grown up enough to know the boundaries of civility; and if some people are not quite grown up enough, they may need some encouragement, like Ms. DeMaaus gave those young men. It is not a biblical axiom, but it works just as well: "Your freedom ends where my nose begins!" Those several young men can thank Ms. DeMaaus for her encouragement—so could our entire society. The Third Commandment still makes sense to encourage language of civility among us all.

---

[1] Jehoshaphat was a king of Judah. There are myriad suggestions for why the term "jumping" was added from simply good alliteration to a midrashic suggestion that he jumped off his throne when wise men entered his presence (in joyful surprise) to it being a reference to the verse 2 Samuel 22:30: "By my God I can leap over a wall." As to the definitive answer, the world may never know. However, I agree it is a darn good phrase for when I drop something and it breaks on the kitchen floor.

[2] Methuselah, on the other hand, is the man purported to have lived the longest in the Hebrew scriptures... a whopping nine hundred and sixty-nine years. His name also means "his death shall bring judgment." After this research, I'm a bit afraid to use this term anymore when I drop something. I think I'll stick with "Jumping Jehoshaphat."

Context: Numbers & Deuteronomy

Albert Einstein once said, "Learn from yesterday, live for today, hope for tomorrow. The important thing is not to stop questioning." While Albert was obviously not an author or editor of the Bible, this quote could easily be a synopsis of the next two books of the Hebrew scriptures.

Numbers

This book begins with a census (hence the name). The remainder of the book covers another journey for the Israelites, this time from Sinai back to Canaan—the land they believed was "promised to Israel" by God.

Extensive logistics and rules were set up for the journey, including ones for the transportation of the tabernacle. The approximately two hundred-mile journey would take decades to complete.

Along the way, there would be complaining about food and water, rebellion against Moses, and fear about the validity of the new land. Order would transform into disorder. Catastrophes would befall the group. So patience developed as a theme, through Moses's back-and-forth conversations with God along the way.

Numbers ends with the Israelites on the verge of arriving at the "Promised Land."

Deuteronomy

In the Book of Deuteronomy, the Israelites are finally poised to enter the Promised Land. Deuteronomy (meaning "second law") is formatted as three long speeches delivered by Moses. In them, he bridges the distance between the past and present.

Forty years had passed since God handed down the Ten Commandments and made the original covenant, so many of the original group had passed away and a new generation had begun. Moses reminded this new generation of their history, their laws, and the importance of loyalty to God.

At the end of his last speech, he announced that God had told him he would not cross over the Jordan River into the Promised Land. Then Moses "[wrote] down the law" (thus creating the Torah) and passed the leadership to his trusty No. 2, Joshua, to continue.

The book ends with Moses's death, and the Israelites mourning him for thirty days.

Meanwhile...

The center of political and cultural power around the Aegean Sea shifted from Crete to the mainland of Greece. In the city of Eleusis, a temple was built to Demeter and Persephone, and ancient Greek religion began to develop. Soon the city of Troy would be destroyed.

Egypt's greatest era was in full swing. Its city, Thebes, was the largest in the world at this time. Pharaoh Amenhotep introduced a major theological change in Egypt by abandoning polytheism (the worship of many gods) in favor of monotheism. He would change his name to Ikhnaton (in honor of his stated only true god, the god of the sun, Aton). However, his religious influence would last only during his reign. And the infamous King Tut would soon begin his reign, returning Egypt to polytheism.

On the other hand, the Hittite Empire was about to collapse.

The Iron Age began, bringing widespread changes to how the world traveled, farmed, and fought. The drastic changes iron brought to weaponry would reverberate throughout the world, as war chariots no longer had the edge on infantries with stronger weapons.

On the horizon, the Olmecs (the first major civilization in Mexico) would lay the foundation for many Mesoamerican cultures. Very innovative, the Olmecs are often credited with the invention of zero as well as the compass. Surviving stone carvings suggest that they worshiped multiple gods, and though the gods' names have been lost over the ages, the carvings show a rich theology encompassing human, bird, reptile, and feline qualities.

The Seventy Elders

11 ²⁴ So Moses went out and told the people the words of the Lord; and he gathered seventy elders of the people, and placed them all around the tent. ²⁵ Then the Lord came down in the cloud and spoke to him, and took some of the spirit that was on him and put it on the seventy elders; and when the spirit rested upon them, they prophesied. But they did not do so again.

²⁶ Two men remained in the camp, one named Eldad, and the other named Medad, and the spirit rested on them; they were among those registered, but they had not gone out to the tent, and so they prophesied in the camp. ²⁷ And a young man ran and told Moses, "Eldad and Medad are prophesying in the camp." ²⁸ And Joshua, son of Nun, the assistant of Moses, one of his chosen men, said, "My lord Moses, stop them!" ²⁹ But Moses said to him, "Are you jealous for my sake? Would that all the Lord's people were prophets, and that the Lord would put his spirit on them!" ³⁰ And Moses and the elders of Israel returned to the camp.

All stressed up
and nowhere to blow

Sermon by Richard Murdoch | East Lansing, MI | October 10, 1992

There is a story that persists along the Oregon Trail. Contrary to most people's remembrance—Conestoga wagons and ox-carts—there was a caravan of shining black carriages that accompanied at least one of the wagon trains through the ruts and dust of the Oregon Trail. It set out from St. Joe, a virtual parade of conveyances. Inside were French "dandies" dressed in velvet and lace, complete with plumed hats. On the trail, these carriages (drawn by fine horses) out-paced and out-classed the ruddy frontier wagons. Waving their handkerchiefs as they passed, they sped their carriages toward the night's stop, accomplishing in one day what most travelers did in two days. Surely, they would get to the Promised Land first, if speed would help.

However, the French never made it there. They turned back at Kearney, Nebraska. It is said that their wine gave out. If they could not travel with the convenience of the lifestyle to which they were committed, they just wouldn't go to the Promised Land, no matter what lay there for them. The French were accustomed to stopping early for supper, served on fine china and linen. They would not stoop to a frontier supper over the open fire from an iron kettle. It was either first class or nothing at all.

Maybe this can help you understand the scripture reading for the day from the Book of Numbers. The Israelites were tired of going second-class. They remembered what it was like to go first-class, even if they were not free. Too long, they had been gathering that manna and beating it into a paste that they could bake and eat as a bread substitute. As with the human race in general, their first complaint against things not going right came from their stomachs! They complained to Moses—and indirectly to God—that their food had never been worse. How they wanted to go back to Egypt where they could fill their bellies with some meat and fish for a change. Then they remembered the fresh fruit, cucumbers, and melons. Some remembered that leeks and onions were available back in Egypt for soup. Others complained that they had no garlic or cumin with which they might season their food. The rabble began with a palate that had become bored with manna. But that was just the beginning. How gladly would they have traded their freedom for just a bit of food—first-class food, that is. Who cares about the Promised Land on an empty (and bored) stomach?

Rabble is nothing more than a Hebrew word for what most of us do sometimes in our lives: complain. There are numerous other words, not polite enough for church, which describe this human condition of verbalizing. Rabble started with the stomachs of the Israelites, but from there, it went on to several other levels—the first of which turned out to be the inability to trust in the future. As far as they were concerned, there was no future worth living unless they went back to Egypt. For there was at least a secure future in servitude. "Better to have a bird in hand than two in the bush!" they might have said.

Imagine poor Moses! He had staked his life on God's invitation—no, really God's demand—to lead his people to the Promised Land. There really was no reward in it for him. He was not promised anything for his part, except that it was Yahweh's call for him. And he really wasn't very enthusiastic, if you will remember. But each stumbling block Moses put in God's way, Yahweh removed. The final one was that Moses was not a good orator or public speaker, for which Yahweh supplied Aaron. Moses needed this rabble as an iceberg needs the equator. Here he was trying to keep alive Yahweh's vision of the future: a future filled with freedom, justice, and mercy for God's people in their own blessed land, and the Israelites didn't appreciate what he was doing one bit. It was more than he cared to answer, so he sought out God in order to seek his counsel on this rabble.

But before he could get to it, the Israelites went on to complain that not only was their future unsure, but their immediate needs were also not being met. Moses wasn't paying enough attention to their spiritual, emotional, and physical needs. Here they were in the barren Sinai with nothing to do during the day but gather manna and think about their plight. Their minds worked overtime dwelling on how cheated they were in life. Life just wasn't fair, was it? "Moses should be helping us get our lives together," they complained, "and yet he's always gone up there on that mountain or out there on that butte, contemplating Yahweh when he should be helping us." The Israelites were not the first needy-dependent people, but they certainly played their case hard. Moses found that in the tough days, there were lots more takers than there were givers. And whatever the givers failed to give, Moses had to make up if this mission was going to be accomplished and this rabble be stopped from sapping the energy of God's people.

Yahweh had an answer for him: Choose seventy elders from among you and have them go among the people as you have. So seventy people were commissioned to go among the clans to sustain the vision that Moses had received from God. They were also to pass among the people as givers in order to encourage self-esteem. With so many takers, self-esteem had sunk to an all-time low level in Sinai. These seventy would give the personal encouragement that Moses couldn't give to all, in such an abundant form, as they needed. The Israelites had great difficulty reconciling their short-term goals with their long-term goals. Their anxiety and anger grew in direct proportion to their rabble. Today, we might call it stress.

Stress has become the favorite word of the age, hasn't it? We engage in coining the word as if our age was the only one that participated in it. How little is our world to think that the Israelites could not have the same feelings as we? Stress has always been with us, regardless of the age of humanity. But each generation deals with it in a different way. Each generation has a different set of parameters with which to work. And there is hardly an age in which religion has not been a part of the parameters.

We moved out of an age in the last generation in which religion—as a change agent—fostered conflict in order to effect change. To right the injustices of the previous years, it was to religion's credit to get people upset to the point that change was a holy obligation. Religion was not supposed to soothe, it was to convict—if not of personal sin as in the Revivalist Age, then of corporate sin such as war mongering, poverty, and racial injustice. In other words, religion added to the stress level of people in order to effect a change in their lives.

It is an unwritten axiom that people rarely change voluntarily, but more often involuntarily. So hit 'em, sock 'em, beat 'em, until they wake up, convicted of their sins, and change will occur. But, not all people change by being shocked, blamed, and harangued. People were not content to be harangued from pulpits Sunday after Sunday about their negative sinfulness in either the Age of Revivals for personal salvation or the Age of Social Change for their corporate sinfulness.

The story is told of a conversation between a convert from Buddhism and a missionary. A businessman, who had converted from Buddhism, had significant influence in the Asian community. The missionary was pleased that God had rewarded his labors with such a notable convert. But after some months, his zeal had begun to flag. The missionary was concerned. "You were such a great conversion; I am disappointed that your faith has started to wane. Is there any way I might encourage you?" the missionary asked.

"Yes," replied the man, "each time I come to a service, you discover a new sin for which I am to receive penance. I began keeping a little book to help me remember each and every sin from which I am to refrain. The list is growing endlessly. When I accepted Christ as my savior, I was a happy man. I felt great freedom to live in joy. It seemed that even the sun shone brighter, the birds chirped more sweetly, my business became a pleasure. My wife and children abandoned me because of my conversion, but an inner peace kept me well. But now, I don't hear the 'Yes to God for his love and mercy.' From your lips, now, all I hear is, 'No to sins.' Faith has become a list of NOs instead of a life of YES! I feel discouraged. I cannot change all the NOs to a YES again."

So here are a few key thoughts:
- Stress comes to all of us when the NOs outweigh the YESes.
- It comes when there are more takers than givers, and you have to make up the difference.
- It comes when expectations are not realistic.
- It comes when life is lived second-class, and you remember what first-class was.

The Israelites wandering in the wilderness were little different from us. Their stressors were as real as ours are. And as destructive as ours are. To his credit, Moses was able to see that the chastisement of his former days—"You are a stiff-necked people"—did not get the response he wanted-ed. Instead, Yahweh directed him to manage the stress with an action, which would match the problem, whether he acknowledged it or not.

Get seventy people to do what you thought you had to do yourself. Let go, Moses!

There was a bumper sticker not too long ago: "Let Go and Let God!" Do you remember it? It was good psychology, but better theology. Moses had to learn that. We have to learn that. Rattlesnakes know that! In the mountains, during the month of August, rattlesnakes let go of their old skin and then a new one appears. During the time in between, the snake must remain immobile, and it is blind. At the slightest movement near it, the snake strikes out in its blindness, directing its attack by its sense of sound. If some object touches its body, in panic, it strikes the spot that has been struck on its body injecting into itself the very venom that kills another—instead killing itself. If the snake lets go of its skin and waits for the new one, all is well. Otherwise, destruction comes.

Not only Moses had to let go—the people had to let go, too. The Israelites had to let go of going first-class. They had to lower their expectations, trim their needs, and curb their appetites. If they were ever to get to the Promised Land, they would have to concentrate less on the trip and more on the future objective.

The Israelites were all stressed up, but had no place to blow—except in their stomachs. Their homes were gone, their families decimated, their leaders out of reach. So they turned to their food. We Americans are all stressed up, too, and have no place to blow. We lash out at our families if we are unemployed or our business is poor. We "rabble" about how unfair life is to us with our reduced expectations. We project onto others our unhappiness with ourselves. Our rapid technological advances have put us in such a generational conflict that we are like volcanoes, just waiting to blow—some skyward, some sideways. We are so inundated with demands, we just want to find a little calm piece of earth until it all passes. And it won't.

We need to "let go, and let God." Stop and take a deep breath! Stop and treat yourself to a moment of silence away from the haranguing words of government, education, business, and religion. Stop, be still, and remember that God is still God.

✡ Deuteronomy 5:1-7, 28-33 ✡
The Ten Commandments

5 [1] Moses convened all Israel, and said to them:

Hear, O Israel, the statutes and ordinances that I am addressing to you today; you shall learn them and observe them diligently. [2] The Lord our God made a covenant with us at Horeb. [3] Not with our ancestors did the Lord make this covenant, but with us, who are all of us here alive today. [4] The Lord spoke with you face to face at the mountain, out of the fire. [5] (At that time I was standing between the Lord and you to declare to you the words of the Lord; for you were afraid because of the fire and did not go up the mountain.) And he said:

[6] I am the Lord your God, who brought you out of the land of Egypt, out of the house of slavery; [7] you shall have no other gods before me.

....

[28] The Lord heard your words when you spoke to me, and the Lord said to me: "I have heard the words of this people, which they have spoken to you; they are right in all that they have spoken. [29] If only they had such a mind as this, to fear me and to keep all my commandments always, so that it might go well with them and with their children forever! [30] Go say to them, 'Return to your tents.' [31] But you, stand here by me, and I will tell you all the commandments, the statutes and the ordinances, that you shall teach them, so that they may do them in the land that I am giving them to possess."

[32] You must therefore be careful to do as the Lord your God has commanded you; you shall not turn to the right or to the left.

[33] You must follow exactly the path that the Lord your God has commanded you, so that you may live, and that it may go well with you, and that you may live long in the land that you are to possess.

Making dreams come true

Sermon by Richard Murdoch | East Lansing, MI | July 26, 1987

Today's reading comes from the Book of Deuteronomy, literally *deuter*, meaning "second," and *nomos* meaning "law." Moses is long gone by the time King Josiah's hand is seen in this book. Deuteronomy is written from the other side of history. These are words that Moses would have said, if he were here. Moses's sermons to the people gathered in the Temple Square include most of what has already been spoken in the Book of Exodus. Hence, the common name of "Second Law" or Deuteronomy. As an example of this, you can tell from the reading today, here is a another list of the Ten Commandments. (There are already two lists in Exodus.) Numerous other restatements appear.

Around 622 BCE, King Josiah brought about the Deuteronomic Reformation (as it is called in biblical history). The Assyrians had devastated Israel. The strong military might of these intelligent and land-acquiring foreigners had crisscrossed the land flowing with milk and honey. They had pressed Israelites into economic and military service for them. But Josiah—when the Assyrians were at their weakest—renewed the hope of the Israelites by "discovering" the words of Moses. Using an emotional appeal based on the figure of Moses and his vision, they could make the dream come true for them!

One of the most significant theological passages for Christian, as well as Jewish, people appears in our reading today. "The Lord our God made a covenant with us at Horeb. Not with our ancestors did the Lord make this covenant, but with us, who are all of us here alive today."

Now, when we read the English version, we know that part of this verse is untrue. God *did* make a covenant with those whom Moses led out of the wilderness, even though the verse says he did not. As with many translations from one language into another, we need to make some adjustments from the literal words. "Not only" might help us get the sense of this verse: "Not only did God make a covenant with our fathers, but with us here today." Why is this so significant? Because it tells us the Judeo-Christian religions are contemporary faiths. They deal not only with the past, but also more importantly with the here and now.

We know from Exodus and Deuteronomy that Moses did not enter the Promised Land. He was allowed to peep over the ridge to see it, but it was Joshua who led the Israelites into the land "flowing with milk and honey." All his life, Moses had dreamed of the day his vision would be fulfilled. And when the day came, his dream did not come true.

Dreams are complex in the human mind. When we speak about dreams, in a contemporary technical sense, we think about Freud who unlocked dreams for psychology. He began the basis upon which years of inquiry have been spent. Since a hundred years ago when he began, we have learned some things. For example, there are different dreams for different purposes.

Some dreams help us de-role from the day's stress and help us wake up refreshed. Other dreams seem to cause us to wake up exhausted; our minds have worked through the night. Yet other dreams seem to be for pure pleasure with no thought in mind. Sometimes dreams are anticipatory, looking forward to a future date. Then there are the dark dreams—the times of anticipated tragedy and evil. These nightmares cause us to wake up with starts. We dream we are falling, running. We get scared when someone tells us that if we don't wake up before we hit the ground, we really will die! Mythology and fact get all mixed up in dreams as the different levels of our brain interact—without our ability to control them—in our sleep. But we have made a bit of progress. Unlike a hundred years ago, we do consider dreaming a healthy and normal activity today.

While dreaming is an unconscious behavior, visioning is a conscious one. What Moses did for Israel was to transmit or sell a vision (or view) of the future to which they should strive to fulfill, if they wished to be a free people. But along the way, there was a lot of dreaming connected with that vision. Moses undoubtedly had dreams of what the land flowing with milk and honey might be. He would dream of his delight in seeing each family secure in its home and sitting under its big tree. He would dream of their coming to him and calling him father, as they did Father Abraham.

While Moses's vision came true, not all his dreams did. The Israelites did have a land to call their own. And after conquering the Canaanites and others, they made the land flow with milk and honey. But the inclusion of the second law (or Deuteronomy) gives evidence that Israel's vision for itself had dreams that did not come true. Inhabiting the land was not enough, now the people had to defend it. Josiah was convinced that foreigners could only overtake the land if the Israelites were morally bankrupt. As the Israelites traded with other countries, like the Assyrians, there would always be the danger of adapting to the ways of their customers—just as they had in Egypt with their superiors. Josiah suggested that Israel's unfaithfulness to God was the source of moral depravity that let the Assyrians in their land through the back door—and then the front.

This certainly is not a new theme in history, is it? It's been played out many times. But the important part to remember about Deuteronomy's injunction is this: When people center on God, they will take risks beyond themselves for others. When people refuse to center on God, they turn inward, more interested in their own security than the security or aims of the group. To put it another way, they are preoccupied with making all their dreams come true at the expense of the total vision.

As an example, Israel had both regained and lost its land through the centuries to the Assyrians, the Seleucids, the Babylonians, the Turks, the Egyptians, and so forth. It was during the Middle Ages that the Jewish people finally lost their land permanently and were scattered once again to all points on the map—once again an Exodus experience. And the rabbis would point to Josiah's Deuteronomy to name the cause and solution for their plight. "God's covenant is with you. It is yours to live! It is not a past covenant of your grandfathers to be admired from afar, nor worshipped in solemn assemblies. It is a covenant to be lived in the heart!"

How about your vision? Has it become dulled by trying to make every dream come true? We cannot manipulate the world or God to make each dream come true—regardless what the racks of self-help books may promise. Some dreams, yes! Every dream, no. We need to keep sight of the vision in order to judge which dreams need to be worked on and which need to fall by the wayside.

Dreams need to take new forms. As these verses remind us, the covenant is not with the past, but with the present. There is no point in going back and restoring the symbol of the past. The dream is with us who are here today. We are dreaming new dreams as the time begins anew. Some dreams won't be dreamed anymore. Other new dreams need to be dreamed. But we must remember covenants are made by God with the living, here and now. Covenants, which are worshipped from the past and from afar, will not energize us any more than they energized the Israelites.

Context: History

Joshua – Judges – Ruth – 1 Samuel – 2 Samuel – 1 Kings
2 Kings – 1 Chronicles – 2 Chronicles

It's often said that those who don't know history are destined to repeat it. And that's more than evident in this next set of writings.

Many theories have been suggested as to how these books were originally written, collected, and ordered. But in the simplest terms, they include written versions of documents and oral traditions of different ages that were compiled by numerous editors along the way. The common Deuteronomistic history theory proposes that these books were edited together after the fall of Israel and Judah (while the people were in exile in Babylon) to try to explain the tragedy that had happened.

This can make reading these books challenging, as often they are contradictory to related historical facts (from archaeology and non-biblical documents), and other versions of the same stories and events.

In the Hebrew scriptures (*Tanakh*), some of these books are included in the *Nevi'im* (Prophets) and some in the *Ketuvim* (Writings). In most Christian Bibles, they've often been categorized as part of the "Historical Books" since the fourth century CE.

Regardless of how they were put together or ordered, they give a good view into perspectives about the relationship between Israel and her God. As such, they provide a constant theme of the recurring defiance of the people, and the results of that defiance.

An interesting tidbit is that the division of Samuel, Kings, and Chronicles into two separate books each is a tradition that dates back to the Greek Bible (or Septuagint) where they were split in order to make the scrolls each a reasonable size independently.

Joshua

In the Book of Joshua, the extraordinary conquest Moses began to the Promised Land is finally completed. The well-known battle of Jericho (where the walls came tumbling down via trumpets) is covered as well as other battles with the Canaanites. Afterwards, the land is divided among the "twelve tribes of Israel" (sons of Jacob).

(However, it's unlikely things went as smoothly as presented. There is a lot of contradictory evidence archaeologically and in extra-biblical sources for the conquest and subsequent development of Israel. Interesting alternative models include an immigration model, a revolt model, and a model of gradual emergence.)

Judges

The Book of Judges details the approximately two hundred-year cycle of war and peace after Joshua's death. The themes of sin, punishment, suffering, repentance, and salvation play a substantial role in the narrative. Furthermore, the Israelites begin to intermarry with the Canaanites, and practice Canaanite worship, causing new discussions on what it means to be "an Israelite."

The title of the book refers to the series of judges (or rulers) that act during this period—varying from military rulers and warriors to local heroes and priests. They are viewed as temporary rulers, though, since God is viewed as the ultimate king in Israel. However, none is ultimately successful enough to bring lasting peace to the land. Israel slides into chaos and finally a messy civil war.

Included are the familiar stories of Deborah's military victory, Samson and Delilah, and Gideon.

Ruth

Here we find the poignant story of the soon-to-be-great King David's great-grandmother, Ruth. A story full of family heartache, it provides a perspective into the complicated issues arising from intermarriage that were being experienced by many.

Samuel

The Book of Samuel records the transition from the period of the judges to the creation of the monarchy. The book is named after the prophet Samuel (who appears at the beginning of the book, and dies before the end of the first half), but this name is misleading as much of the book centers around the rise of other characters.

Samuel functions as the last judge during a time of crisis. He warns of the tyranny of kings, but the people insist on having a king so that they can be like other nations, and hope to end the current disorder. Pro- and anti-monarchy discussions follow, and ultimately Saul is chosen as the first (human) king of Israel.

We see Saul's rise and fall, leading to the rise of David as the next king. Here we find the fourth covenant in the scriptures—the Davidic covenant—through the prophet Nathan. This "eternal" and "unconditional" covenant (prior covenants—such as the one with Noah—were considered conditional on behavior), creates the foundation for the belief in the dynasty of David and the belief that Israel will ultimately be victorious over its enemies.

At the onset, only one tribe (Judah) recognizes David as king, but ultimately he becomes king over a united kingdom. The story of David is a complex drama full of passion, politics, and poetry.

Kings

The Book of Kings picks up at the death of King David (of natural causes), and continues as his son Solomon becomes king. (This starts a four-hundred-year run of kings from the line of David.)

Prosperity continues under Solomon. The Ark of the Covenant, which had been stolen by the Philistines, is brought to Jerusalem and Solomon completes the creation of a central temple for all of Israel. He also builds a wall around the city to fortify it.

Solomon makes many political alliances, which he seals with marriages (over 700!). With these wives also came foreign religions, and heavy taxation to support his large court and lifestyle.

The prior tribal democracy is increasingly changing to an urban structure, with class distinctions, and forced labor projects. As a result, when Solomon dies in 922 BCE, the ten tribes of the north revolt, and a new structure develops—two kingdoms, Israel (northern) and Judah (southern), each with their own king.

The remainder of the Book of Kings deals with the relationship between the two. For two hundred years, they'll switch between war and alliance, with various kings on either side.

Ultimately, Israel falls to the Assyrians in 722 BCE. Some people flee south to Judah. But many of the residents are taken off to Mesopotamia (and thus become "the ten lost tribes of Israel"). The Assyrians then imported people to repopulate the area as Samaria (which will get a bad rap by the Southern kingdom of Judah).

About a hundred years later, the Assyrians are conquered and the Babylonians come into power. Judah falls to the Babylonians (under King Nebuchadnezzar) in 586 BCE. The temple is destroyed, the walls of Jerusalem come down, and many of the residents will be taken into Exile in Babylonia.

Chronicles

The Book of Chronicles repeats much of the history found in the Books of Samuel and Kings. However, this time it is from a priestly perspective (instead of a prophetic one).

Meanwhile...

Massive migration of Bantu-speaking people was taking place in Africa, spreading southward. The intermingling of groups created rich and complex oral traditions that would be passed from generation to generation. Many focused on a supreme God whose work in the world was supported by numerous deities.

In China, the *I Ching* was compiled. This book of divination provides instructions for interpreting sixty-four hexagrams, each consisting of a combination of six lines. Readers used the interpretations to provide divine guidance for decision making.

Not too far west, another classic was in the making. The Upanishads (translated as "sitting in front of") documented the wise teachings of Indian sages on topics including karma, reincarnation, and the single universal soul, known as Brahman.

The Greek city-states (such as Sparta and Athens) began to organize. Pythagoras derived his famous theorem, the first Olympic Games were held, and Homer wrote *The Iliad*.

Ancient Rome grew from settlements around the river Tiber into the Roman Kingdom, ruled by a series of kings. The Roman Senate was created and a formal political structure developed.

Samuel's Calling

3 [1] Now the boy Samuel was ministering to the Lord under Eli. The word of the Lord was rare in those days; visions were not widespread.

[2] At that time Eli, whose eyesight had begun to grow dim so that he could not see, was lying down in his room; [3] the lamp of God had not yet gone out, and Samuel was lying down in the temple of the Lord, where the ark of God was. [4] Then the Lord called, "Samuel! Samuel!" and he said, "Here I am!" [5] and ran to Eli, and said, "Here I am, for you called me." But he said, "I did not call; lie down again." So he went and lay down. [6] The Lord called again, "Samuel!" Samuel got up and went to Eli, and said, "Here I am, for you called me." But he said, "I did not call, my son; lie down again."

[7] Now Samuel did not yet know the Lord, and the word of the Lord had not yet been revealed to him. [8] The Lord called Samuel again, a third time. And he got up and went to Eli, and said, "Here I am, for you called me." Then Eli perceived that the Lord was calling the boy. [9] Therefore Eli said to Samuel, "Go, lie down; and if he calls you, you shall say, 'Speak, Lord, for your servant is listening.'" So Samuel went and lay down in his place.

[10] Now the Lord came and stood there, calling as before, "Samuel! Samuel!" And Samuel said, "Speak, for your servant is listening." [11] Then the Lord said to Samuel, "See, I am about to do something in Israel that will make both ears of anyone who hears of it tingle. [12] On that day I will fulfill against Eli all that I have spoken concerning his house, from beginning to end. [13] For I have told him that I am about to punish his house forever, for the iniquity that he knew, because his sons were blaspheming God, and he did not restrain them. [14] Therefore I swear to the house of Eli that the iniquity of Eli's house shall not be expiated by sacrifice or offering forever."

[15] Samuel lay there until morning; then he opened the doors of the house of the Lord. Samuel was afraid to tell the vision to Eli. [16] But Eli called Samuel and said, "Samuel, my son." He said, "Here I am." [17] Eli said, "What was it that he told you? Do not hide it from me. May God do so to you and more also, if you hide anything from me of all that he told you." [18] So Samuel told him everything and hid nothing from him. Then he said, "It is the Lord; let him do what seems good to him."

[19] As Samuel grew up, the Lord was with him and let none of his words fall to the ground. [20] And all Israel from Dan to Beer-sheba knew that Samuel was a trustworthy prophet of the Lord.

You have three chances

Sermon by Richard Murdoch | East Lansing, MI | January 17, 1987

When you are in unfamiliar territory, signs become a necessity. Once you are familiar with your surroundings, then signs blend into the background, unnoticed. I am reminded of that when someone arrives at our church for an evening appointment. "Just come in the side door and wind your way around to the far side of the building. There are signs marked 'office' to help you find your way." Invariably, people get lost in a hallway somewhere in the vicinity of the library. When they discover that they haven't gone quite far enough, they say, rather apologetically, "I'm sorry I'm late; it's just such a big place, I got lost looking for the signs!"

When I first came here, I found myself rather sympathetic. I could identify with what visitors might feel. They were in unfamiliar territory. But recently, I have found myself getting a little callous. I even find myself retorting, "Didn't you see the signs?" Now that I am an old-timer, I don't need signs. I forget what it feels like to be in an unfamiliar place.

But there is more to a sign than pointing out a direction. It also may give instructions. Six months ago, we found our behavioral signs were ineffective. They were not as professional as our directional signs. We ordered some new signs to catch people's attention by using a bolder color, and then direct people to assist us in keeping our building clean. We planned to use the new motivational research, which the American Cancer Society introduced to us through: "Thank You for Not Smoking!"

Our new signs arrived this week. One of our staff members remarked: "Why don't we just say it outright? 'Don't throw rice, confetti, or birdseed at weddings.' What is this 'thank you' stuff?" I gave my best motivational speech, including that old saying, "You can catch more flies with honey than you can with vinegar." But this person believed if you said it once, with vigor, that's enough. People ought to change their behavior.

You and I are the subjects of motivational signs each and every day. Soft sell, suggestive, and repetitive advertising build a subtle alliance with a product. Advertisements that use a hard sell commanding a customer to buy or behave in such a manner (merely because the sign says so) will meet with resistance head on. "Who says I can't?" "Who is going to tell me no?" "This is public space, isn't it? I have as much right as anyone else."

From time to time, *Candid Camera* is revived on television. One program included an episode about signs on different tables in a small, liberal arts college cafeteria (that shall remain nameless). One table had a sign that read "Absolutely No Food Throwing at this Table." Another table had a sign that read "Remember Your Laundry Bill, Don't Throw Food." Finally, in another part of the hall, there was a sign reading, "Now That You've Made It to College, Thanks For Not Throwing Food!" You probably know what's coming—and so did the behavioral researchers. While people did not throw food at the first table, their legalistic perspective led them to a neighboring table that had no sign, where they took the suggestion to heart—flipping butter squares off the ends of their forks towards the ceiling. (You remember that, don't you?) At the second signed table, there was a little horseplay because people wanted to get the best of other people's laundry bills. But at the third set of tables, students smiled and went about their business of eating.

Behavioral change can come about by direct confrontation of a command—as long as there is clout to inflict disastrous consequences if the command is not followed. Or behavioral change can come from within, when a person is receptive and gradually owns the suggestion being made towards him or her as meeting a need or desire. The first way is directed by an outside authority; the second way is directed by inner strength or self-will.

The scripture reading this morning is unique among the passages of the Bible for its motivational focus. In the great majority of biblical passages, God is presented as outside authority. God's booming voice commands Moses to take his sandals off, for he is on holy ground. God speaks in thunder and lightning to the Israelites as they wander in the Sinai for forty years. The prophets have explicit visions in which God speaks to them in a chariot of fire, in a whirlwind, in the temple holy place, in a bonfire. God's power and authority is experienced as awesome because in their mind, their Yahweh must compete with the gods of their neighbors, which are strong, mighty, and forthright. Yahweh's majesty, power, and glory inspire a behavioral response befitting a God who has created the universe and everything in it.

Yahweh is no puny wimp! But the story of Samuel introduces a contemporary strain into their understanding about God. Yahweh's calling of Samuel differs from all previous calls. Instead of being a cataclysmic event, it is a quiet, persistent call. It comes in the silence and shadow of the night. It comes not to a seasoned adult, steeped in wisdom; but it comes to a youth in his teens. The call comes to a youth, who had as yet never made an acknowledgement of his faith in Yahweh. The biblical evidence suggests that the equivalent of confirmation—bar mitzvah— had not taken place.

Three incidents occur when Samuel is awakened by a voice that he assumes to be that of his mentor Eli. Three times Eli patiently tells Samuel that his inquiry had awakened him, and then Samuel could not get back to sleep. Samuel was afraid of the information being revealed by Yahweh. Samuel was even more afraid when Eli demanded that he reveal the contents of his call from Yahweh. Can you feel for this young man who revealed to the old sage Eli that his sons (all of whom were older than Samuel) were not fit to succeed him as prophet? Instead, Yahweh told him the job was his when he grew up. Would you have believed Samuel's audacity and his arrogance had you been Eli—or better still, one of his sons? If such were the case, for the call to be credible, we would have demanded more than merely three whispers in the night to a youth who was not even a recognized member of Israel.

We, like the Israelites of old, want our God to act in decisive and powerful ways to indicate direction in our lives or to intervene in a world event. Television ministries and religious crusades reinforce this expectation for us. Dramatic events are popularized. Yet it doesn't always happen that way for us.

We ask God for a path, for a way to be clear. We look for decisive answers, but we wind up like this often-told story: A man was caught in his home as a flooding river caught it up in its turbulent current. At first, his danger was rather temporary, for the water came up to the first-story window. A motorboat came and offered to remove him to the safety of higher ground. He declined, "My God will save me if I need it. I will not leave my home." The waters swirled; the man fled to the second story. Again, a boat offered to rescue him. Again, he declined.

"My God will save me, if things get worse." And things did get worse. The third time the boat made its round, the man was seen hanging onto a furnace flue. He declined again. "God will save me. I don't need your help!" When the boat came around a final time, the house and the man had sunk below. The next morning in the heavenly courts, St. Peter had an angry soul on his hands, pounding upon the gates. "All my life I served God faithfully. I never asked God for a thing. When I really needed a rescue, I was turned down. Three times I put my faith to the test in front of nonbelievers in order to give you an opportunity to show God's power and you blew it!" "Hold on a minute," said St. Peter. "That boat was our answer to your prayer. We even sent it three times!"

How ordinary: three calls in the night to Samuel, three rescue trips by a boat. But most of faith happens in rather ordinary ways. While dramatic events might and do occur—such as conversion experiences, tragedies averted, and diseases healed—these are the few mountaintops among the usual miles of prairies in our ordinary lives. But there on the prairies lie vast, untapped sources of God for us. We are seduced by the psalmist who constantly reminds us that we should "Look to the hills, from whence cometh my strength." We miss the whispers of God in the night that might direct us. We leave the grass unnoticed as we head for the trees.

We need to seek direction from God not only in the thundering voice, but also in the quiet and persistent voice. That's probably more difficult for us than it was for our grandparents. Our world is a world of mega-trends, mega-bucks, and megabytes. We let the seemingly insignificant slip through our awareness. We are intimidated by reports of mega-faith experiences, when all around us God speaks to us in quiet and persistent ways. We hardly ever give God three chances—one chance is enough, we figure! Either we get the answer we want now, or that's it!

Consider the situation of Frances Bone, a French woman of Normandy, in World War II. She was a widow and had one son. He was her dearest treasure. When the war broke out, she did her best to shield him from the patriotic hustling of her village for he was but twelve. But it was to no avail. Against his mother's will, he joined the French underground. More than once the Vichy government raided her home looking for evidence of espionage. Each night, Frances would pray for some sign from God that her son was safe and well. But there was no assurance. There were no contacts, no letters, and no news. At the same time, Frances was asked by her Huguenot pastor if she could care for several young boys whose families had become separated by the conflict.

First, she offered a no. She had to keep her son's room ready for when he came home. But the pastor asked again, saying there was no place for these three boys to go. "Yes, I'll take one." The boys turned out to be young American soldiers who looked hardly older than her son. They were communications experts who were infiltrating the invisible line between the Free French and the Vichy French. Quietly, Frances asked for another young man after the first. At the time, she didn't exactly know why, but it felt right to her.

When American units returned to the Normandy shores for a fortieth reunion, a couple of years ago, Frances was one of those sought for publicity interviews. She is now in her early nineties. Her son never returned to his room. She commented that while she had lost one son, she really had gained a dozen or more. She had hidden a succession of soldiers. Each was treated as though he was her son, in the hopes that someone else was doing the same for her son. Through the years, her "adopted" sons visited, wrote, brought their families, sent her gifts, and even brought her to this country. "What a waste I would have made of my life, had I never listened to the small voice of God. He gave me back what I had lost, and I almost lost it all!" she said.

Who knows what opportunities we are missing as we roll along in our busy lives? Learn to seek the quiet voice of God and you will be begin to notice.

David Mourns for Saul and Jonathan

1 ⁵ Then David asked the young man who was reporting to him, "How do you know that Saul and his son Jonathan died?" ⁶ The young man reporting to him said, "I happened to be on Mount Gilboa"...

¹¹ Then David took hold of his clothes and tore them; and all the men who were with him did the same. ¹² They mourned and wept, and fasted until evening for Saul and for his son Jonathan, and for the army of the Lord and for the house of Israel, because they had fallen by the sword...

¹⁷ David intoned this lamentation over Saul and his son Jonathan.
¹⁸ (He ordered that The Song of the Bow be taught to the people of Judah; it is written in the Book of Jashar.) He said:

¹⁹ Your glory, O Israel, lies slain upon your high places!
    How the mighty have fallen!...

²¹ You mountains of Gilboa,
    let there be no dew or rain upon you,
    nor bounteous fields!
For there the shield of the mighty was defiled,
    the shield of Saul, anointed with oil no more.

²² From the blood of the slain,
    from the fat of the mighty,
the bow of Jonathan did not turn back,
    nor the sword of Saul return empty.

²³ Saul and Jonathan, beloved and lovely!
    In life and in death they were not divided;
they were swifter than eagles,
    they were stronger than lions.

²⁴ O daughters of Israel, weep over Saul,
    who clothed you with crimson, in luxury,
    who put ornaments of gold on your apparel.

²⁵ How the mighty have fallen
    in the midst of the battle!

The toughest thing about being a father

Sermon by Richard Murdoch | Rye, NY | June 18, 1995

The title of this sermon is not intended to be sexist. It could just as well be titled, "The Toughest Thing about Being a Mother." You can easily apply today's scriptural theme to either parent. But Mother's Day is long past; Father's Day is today.

Today's reading focuses on David, King of Israel. David's centrality in Israel's faith is undisputed. But unlike other Bible heroes such as Moses and Abraham, he is equally central in Christianity. The claim of Jesus to be the Messiah is wholly dependent on the title of "Son of David" given to Jesus. To be of the lineage of David not only brought a special privilege and recognition in the secular world, it also brought credibility in the religious world. In the Gospel of Luke, the author is careful to document the physical lineage of Mary through David, so the claim that Jesus is the Son of David is not only a religious title but also a physical reality.

David was the youngest son of Jesse, a shepherd who was asset rich and cash poor. Jesse came from a background that raised more questions than answers. Jesse was the son of a non-Jewish mother, Ruth, and a Hebrew father, Boaz, a friend of her mother-in-law, Naomi. After the death of her first husband, Ruth, who was David's grandmother, was a poor woman gleaning the fields owned by Boaz.

Continuing the family tradition, even David's choice of wives raised a few eyebrows as to his commitment to maintaining a pure Jewish bloodline. King Saul, whom David served in a military capacity, wished to reward him for his faithful service with a marriage to his eldest daughter. However, David had his eyes on Saul's younger daughter Michal. Saul, hoping to discourage such a union, offered Michal to David in marriage only if David would bring one thousand foreskins of the enemy Philistines as evidence of his military prowess. This was an impossible task in King Saul's eyes, so Saul never thought the marriage would take place. However, David successfully completed the task and the arranged marriage did take place—with a rocky start between groom and father-in-law.

But the relationship between David and Saul continued to be an uneasy alliance, because King Saul's son Jonathan was not only David's brother-in-law, but also his best friend. Unknown to Saul, the prophet Samuel had anointed secretly not Jonathan, but David to be the next king. Normal royal succession called for the son, not the son-in-law, to become king. However, Saul sensed what was happening behind his back, and on more than one occasion, Saul began to arrange plots for David's death. In one instance of palace treachery, Saul even used his own daughter in the death trap.

Yet, when the word came that King Saul and three of his sons (including Jonathan) had been killed in battle, our English translation fails to make the scene come alive. In the Hebrew, David's emotional response is searing. Although this very event paves the way for David to assume his kingship and eliminate the influence of his treacherous father-in-law, we are told that David took hold of his princely robes and tore them from top to bottom.

His wails of anguish could be heard for miles, like an echo down a canyon. Our English translation says that he fasted, although literally the Hebrew says he "threw away all the food brought to him." The mourning scene is one of powerful love, exorcized in deep, primitive emotions, culminating in the most eloquent of all eulogies, verses 19-27. And all this love for his father-in-law and employer, who plotted to have him killed on numerous occasions?

While it might seem that David was the unappreciated son-in-law, as king he was hardly an honorable husband and father. Having tired quickly of Michal's charms, David's interest turned to Bathsheba, the wife of his military captain, Uriah. A love affair followed and Uriah was murdered to make a marriage possible for a conveniently widowed Bathsheba, whose love child was stillborn. However, Bathsheba quickly brought forth a second son, Solomon. All in all, David was a prolific father by our contemporary standards. He sired nineteen sons: two by Michal, four by Bathsheba, and thirteen by Abigail, Ahnoan, Macah, Magiith, Abital, and Eglah. (His offspring numbered at least thirty-eight, if we assume that at least an equal number of daughters were born, even though they didn't "count" in those days.)

All of David's nineteen sons had secret wishes to inherit the throne and wealth of their kingly father. It is difficult for us to imagine the family dynamics operating in such a competitive setting. But the scriptures tell us that the first family of Israel was not one that today's political campaigners would claim exhibited family values. First, there was rape and incest. (Amnon feigned illness at an unruly banquet, drew his sister Tamar into a back room, and raped her.) Then there was fratricide. (Absalom avenged his sister's rape by killing Amnon.) And finally, there was rebellion. (Absalom, drawn into a palace rebellion by opponents of his father, was banished to the northern deserts, where he was hanged when his horse encountered a low-hanging tree limb.)

It was through David's relationship with his sons that he found the toughest thing about being a father was that he had been a son. As a son, he had already walked in their shoes. He had experienced the unruliness of sexual passion as Amnon had. And as a consequence of his inappropriate sexual activity with Bathsheba, he had mourned the death of his first son, stillborn. His grief and mourning—publicly proclaimed as the prophet Nathan called for David to repent for his sins of adultery and murder—led to David's authorship of a dozen psalms.

Like Absalom, he too had been approached by opponents of King Saul, who promised a more just society if young David would join with them against the old king. They had energy, vitality, and vision. Now David was old, and the tables were turning against him, just as they had against Saul.

And of course, there was Solomon, the son who had replaced the stillborn love child of Bathsheba. Upon him was visited every jealousy by the other brothers and sisters, for Solomon was the blessed child. Never allowed in battle for fear of his defeat, he was reserved to build the temple as a man of peace. David knew that same jealousy—from his brothers when Elijah singled him out as the future king. David had walked in Amnon's, Absalom's, and Solomon's shoes, yet now he had to be a father.

The toughest thing about being a father (or mother) is that often you have stood in the same place years earlier before your own parents. And you told yourself that you would be more understanding with your children! What a bind to be caught between two generations—the memory of the past and the hope of the future—and you are right in between. How comforting it would be to erase the memory of being a child and just be a parent! Our role as parents would be so much easier and simpler.

Relationships are often marked by the attributes or qualities attached to them. As parents, we have a wealth of life experience that our children do not share, simply by their younger age. It is often difficult to stand by and watch them make mistakes and even fail. It is often times uncomfortable to say no, when we'd like to say yes. We find our parental role to be in conflict with wanting to be able to be a brother or a sister— more in sympathy with a situation. The ideal, of course, is to be able to play God, and be all: father-mother, brother-sister. It is an impossible task even if we were able to pursue it. Instead, with a sense of certain faith, the mistakes which we make as father to son, son to father, mother to daughter, and daughter to mother are forgiven by God's grace.

The story of David can serve as a model regardless of our shortcomings as parents to children and children to parents. David's life was filled with missteps of human behavior—as a son, a husband, and a father. His kingship depended not upon his perfection, but upon his willingness to acknowledge his humanity. His life was not stunted by his imperfection, but was larger than life because he was forgiven and went on. He would not allow himself to be held hostage by his failures or the guilt imposed by others. He trusted in God to forgive, and he, David, would forget. There was always the next morning, fresh and new, to rise again.

Elijah's Triumph over the Priests of Ba'al

18 ²⁰ So Ahab sent to all the Israelites, and assembled the prophets at Mount Carmel. ²¹ Elijah then came near to all the people, and said, "How long will you go limping with two different opinions? If the Lord is God, follow him; but if Ba'al, then follow him." The people did not answer him a word.

²² Then Elijah said to the people, "I, even I only, am left a prophet of the Lord; but Ba'al's prophets number four hundred fifty. ²³ Let two bulls be given to us; ... ²⁴ Then you call on the name of your god and I will call on the name of the Lord; the god who answers by fire is indeed God."

²⁵ Then Elijah said to the prophets of Ba'al, "Choose for yourselves one bull and prepare it first, for you are many; then call on the name of your god, but put no fire to it." ²⁶ So they took the bull that was given them, prepared it, and called on the name of Ba'al from morning until noon, crying, "Ba'al, answer us!" But there was no voice, and no answer. They limped about the altar that they had made.

³¹ Elijah took twelve stones, according to the number of the tribes of the sons of Jacob, to whom the word of the Lord came, saying, "Israel shall be your name"; ³² with the stones he built an altar in the name of the Lord. Then he made a trench around the altar, large enough to contain two measures of seed.

³³ Next he put the wood in order, cut the bull in pieces, and laid it on the wood. He said, "Fill four jars with water and pour it on the burnt offering and on the wood." ³⁴ Then he said, "Do it a second time"; and they did it a second time. Again he said, "Do it a third time"; and they did it a third time, ³⁵ so that the water ran all around the altar, and filled the trench also with water.

³⁶ At the time of the offering of the oblation, the prophet Elijah came near and said, "O Lord, God of Abraham, Isaac, and Israel, let it be known this day that you are God in Israel, that I am your servant, and that I have done all these things at your bidding. ³⁷ Answer me, O Lord, answer me, so that this people may know that you, O Lord, are God, and that you have turned their hearts back."

³⁸ Then the fire of the Lord fell and consumed the burnt offering, the wood, the stones, and the dust, and even licked up the water that was in the trench. ³⁹ When all the people saw it, they fell on their faces and said, "The Lord indeed is God; the Lord indeed is God." ⁴⁰ Elijah said to them, "Seize the prophets of Ba'al; do not let one of them escape." Then they seized them; and Elijah brought them down to the Wadi Kishon, and killed them there.

My dad can beat your dad

Sermon by Richard Murdoch | East Lansing, MI | June 20, 1993

The two little boys were barely six years of age, but they were already very competitive. However, they had few skills with which to express that competitiveness. So, in their primitive frame of reference, they shifted to a higher playing field. Instead of competing on their own playing field, they transferred to the adult playing field: a comparison of their dads. Each claimed his dad was better. Then finally came the challenge in their escalating war of words: "My dad can beat your dad. Any day. With one hand, too!" It was the best they could do. In the heat of the moment, it seemed a natural solution. Might makes right. Victory brings truth. At the very earliest ages, violence stirs in the human heart, which strangely enough is also said to be the locus of love.

A week ago, Hollywood and media moguls were summoned before a Congressional Committee investigating violence in American society. Those entertainment giants who produce movies and television sensed they were on the hot seat, so to speak, because they followed the testimony of L. Rowell Huesmann, a University of Michigan professor who, as author of *Growing Up to Be Violent*, spent twenty years studying how aggressive behavior develops in children.

His thesis posits that violence is a learned behavior. Huesmann states, "The future of our children and society is too precious to leave in the hands of the purveyors of violence any longer. A national rating for television, movies, and cassettes should be mandatory." He goes on to say that "children need desirable heroes with whom to identify. If a boy is surrounded by aggressive family members and peers who solve problems in violent ways he learns a violent script. Similarly, if a boy is constantly exposed to television and film heroes who solve problems aggressively, he will mimic those behaviors. Media violence increases dramatically the level of society's violence."

Huesmann's testimony implied that if Hollywood would clean up its act, then violence in the country would decline. But Jack Valenti, president and CEO of the Motion Picture Association of America, took the Congressional Committee members to task, lest they lose their objectivity. "Long before there were movies, there has been violence in this world. Violence is a given in the very model of human survival. Movies and television didn't invent violence and we won't take the rap for it. Violence is the result of economic, social, political, and family deprivation. Censoring movies won't end violence."

Now, I think there is more to the story—and it is in what Valenti didn't say more than in what he said—but to a degree, history gives Valenti some pretty good examples to throw back at the investigating committee. I've been doing some preparatory reading for a trip to Spain next summer. What good, moral, and upstanding Christians in the fifteenth century did first to the Moors, then to Jewish people, and finally to their own Christian brothers and sisters makes the ethnic cleansing of Bosnia look like a Sunday school picnic! While quoting scripture on the one hand, good Christians with righteous indignation used the other hand to burn, beat, mutilate, and annihilate any and all who did not come to faith—as they interpreted correct faith to be. And the violence was effective. The reign of violence during the Spanish Reconquest and the Spanish Inquisition was powerful enough to convert tens of thousands of Moors and Jewish people to Christianity, and kept countless other Catholics from becoming Protestants.

Violence is no stranger in the scriptures. The contest of Elijah with the followers of Ba'al, which we read today, is typical where violence is permissive because it has a righteous purpose. While we don't have nearly as many examples in the New Testament, the Gospel of Mark is the most familiar (Mark 11:15-18). Jesus, who usually is thought of as a "mild and meek" peacemaker, becomes angry at the injustice of moneychangers in the temple courtyard and overturns their tables.

This is not your simple, little tripping of the table leg. There is wholesale bedlam as coins splash across the paving stone and pigeons squawk as they are buffeted by their falling cages. But this destruction is not condemned because it promotes a righteous or moral result. Violence against property and persons—such as murder, mayhem, hanging, and so on—has been used by state and church alike when the purpose for which they are intended can be cited for an ultimate righteous purpose.

But righteous violence has a flip side to it. Instead of producing a victor, it can result in a victim. Michael Barkun, in the recent article "Reflections After Waco: Religious Millennialists and the State," in the magazine *The Christian Century* [June 2, 1993], calls us to another point—that some people welcome being victims of violence, because it has a purifying and redeeming nature. He cites the Branch Davidians as standing in a long tradition of Christianity dating from the first century.

Millennialists like the Branch Davidians see the essence of Christianity in the "awe-full power of God" to avenge the injustices of the world in a final Armageddon. They welcome violence (natural and manmade) as a means to final redemption. Therefore, any violence is seen as an indication of the beginning of the end of the world, and a welcomed sign of the beginning of the thousand-year epoch. The author cites the failure of the federal authorities to take seriously the theological framework in which the Branch Davidians' religious community saw itself. As he writes:

> *If indeed the fires inside the compound were set, it is evidence of the further working through of the religious script. It's not the first time that vastly outnumbered Millennialists engaged in self-destructive behavior in the conviction that God's will required it. In 1525, during the German Peasant's Revolt, Thomas Munzer led his forces into a battle so hopeless that five thousand of his troops perished compared with six fatalities among the authorities. Just now as then, authorities did not understand the connection between religion and violence under charismatic leadership.*

For those two little six-year-old boys, their solution of truth lay in "who beat who." The dad who beat the other dad in their imaginary boxing match would be the victor, to whom, of course, would go the spoils. Hopefully, socialization of the boys would modify their behavior in the future years—when they could cite more appropriate competitive feats. But the dark fact of human existence remains, violence is both a given and a learned behavior.

The boundaries between the two shift with generations and cultures. Today it is estimated that one in four college women has been the victim of rape or attempted rape. Rape is no longer represented as a crime of passion. It is spoken about as a crime of violence, power, and rage. And usually, the victims are women and the perpetrators men.

Katie Roiphe, a doctoral student at Princeton, writing in the *New York Times Magazine* last Sunday [June 13, 1993], examines the mystique surrounding rape crisis counseling programs on campuses. It leads her to compare male and female perceptions of violence and gender, as well as assumptions of moral rightness. Her calling to task some established feminist assumptions will bring her few accolades from many feminists. Her thesis is that by describing rape in the language of victimization, women will continue to be thought as the "weaker" sex in need of protection against the "stronger" sex. The language of victim encourages the stereotype of power, because the stronger must win.

Victim language leads us back to our two six-year-olds, who unwittingly set up the victor/victim typology. The word "victor" comes directly from the Latin *vincere* (to conquer), while "victim" comes from the Old High German, which means set apart or holy.

In ancient times, a victim was a person offered to the gods as a sacrifice for victory in battle. More often, the best soldier was not sacrificed, but a weaker one was substituted in the stronger one's clothing, thus duping the gods.

Competitiveness is often misread as the play between power and impotency, stronger and weaker, success and failure, winner and loser, or victor and victim. The most well-meaning of society's reformers (Socialists and, later, Communists) have often tried to eliminate competitiveness from a society because they cite its destructiveness. They cite power by violence against person and property. As the young boys illustrate, these patterns begin young by our very nature, and continue later through socialization. The key is harnessing the raw human data into appropriate boundaries suitable for today's world in light of what we believe about the worth of life.

As Christians, we believe that worth of life is defined by our Creator (and that its potential is always for good), yet the dark shadow of the negative must be acknowledged. If families, churches, and communities are successful, these two boys will develop appropriate boundaries and skills to bring out the best of human potential in themselves and others without resorting to skills and language of primitive violence. They will be able to compete with women and men in healthy patterns.

They will make informed choices that will bring them to the goals they have made for themselves.

The task of our families, churches, and society is not to create more laws, but more self-respect. And to always act out of worthy internal goals, not simply react to fear and suspicion.

Elijah Meets God at Horeb

19 [Elijah] got up, and ate and drank; then he went in the strength of that food forty days and forty nights to Horeb the mount of God. [9] At that place he came to a cave, and spent the night there.

Then the word of the Lord came to him, saying, "What are you doing here, Elijah?" [10] He answered, "I have been very zealous for the Lord, the God of hosts; for the Israelites have forsaken your covenant, thrown down your altars, and killed your prophets with the sword. I alone am left, and they are seeking my life, to take it away."

[11] He said, "Go out and stand on the mountain before the Lord, for the Lord is about to pass by." Now there was a great wind, so strong that it was splitting mountains and breaking rocks in pieces before the Lord, but the Lord was not in the wind; and after the wind an earthquake, but the Lord was not in the earthquake; [12] and after the earthquake a fire, but the Lord was not in the fire; and after the fire a sound of sheer silence.

Am I
only left?

Sermon by Richard Murdoch | East Lansing, MI | July 1989

You have heard it said many times: "A picture is worth a thousand words." It is often just as true that not only do pictures communicate more effectively than words, but pictures can also be remembered better.

This week there was another picture that spoke a thousand words and will stand out in our memory. It will join those few pictures that impress our memory, which include pictures from the covers of *LIFE* magazine, such as John-John Kennedy saluting his father's casket or the young Vietnamese girl aflame with napalm. It will join the Biafra starvation picture from the evening news that interrupted us as we enjoyed dinner at our full tables.

I am, of course, speaking about the nameless young Chinese student whom we saw this past week standing before a line of oncoming tanks in Tiananmen Square, China. The president noted it, and we noted it: a lone student against the world of military hardware.

When the tank ground to a halt, he jumped upon it, looked into the turret's view, and yelled something. Then, when the tank resumed its roll, he again stood in front as if in a dance with certain death. The column of tanks stopped a second time. In moments, the lone student's friends came to push him away, trying to signal that he had stood his ground and made his point. When the tank would stop next time, he'd not be that fortunate.

This picture tells us what started—oh so slowly. It was as if a small hairline fracture occurred in the hip of totalitarianism. But the more the Eastern Bloc nations hobbled along, paying no attention to the winds of change, the hairline fracture turned into a crack, and finally it reached Asia. And now it has stumbled and fallen before an outcry of younger citizens, all whose education is paid by the very government they decry. In Marx's classless society, classes did not disappear but merely reestablished themselves in another way. The privileged students challenge the ruling Communist party, which uses the military whose volunteers are from the traditional peasant class.

And for one glorious moment, a nameless and solitary person suspends time against the greatest of odds. Before the might of the world's third-largest army—in the world's most populous nation—he stands and then is pushed from the scene. He disappears, but never can his nation return to normal.

Three thousand years earlier Elijah, a lone prophet, stood before Ahab (the king of Israel) and his infamous spouse, Jezebel (the queen of Tyre). Elijah—a young man of the Hebrew northern kingdom called Israel—represented the winds of change in his century. Jezebel had brought her people and culture from Tyre into the royal house of Israel, displacing the law and culture of the Hebrews.

Her husband, Ahab, had become a closet Yahwehist, unable to stand alone before his people. Someone had to bring sanity back to life, and it fell upon Elijah to challenge Jezebel's disastrous ways, which were economically and morally bankrupting the northern kingdom. The royal family was heavily into debt with the Tyre bankers. Tributes and royalties consumed the majority of the gross national product. The priests of Ba'al had multiplied under Jezebel's sponsorship, receiving a majority of the priestly income. Sanctuaries sacred to Yahweh were shared with the infamous Ba'al, an agricultural god. It was believed that success in crop raising was directly related to human sexuality, calling for religious prostitution that threatened the traditional family structure upon which the Law of Moses rested. Jezebel's informers were legion. Those who threatened her administration were sought out and destroyed as enemies of the state.

Elijah alone stood before Ahab, announcing that neither God nor God's people could continue down this disastrous road of economic and moral doom without some dire consequences. While Ahab worried about hostile attacks from the outside bringing down Israel, Elijah pointed out very clearly that no matter how much military hardware Ahab could buy and employ to defend the country, the real enemy was from within. Israel would crumble under the weight of its own royal household. Such a word was an anathema to Jezebel. When Ahab told her of the prophet's visit, Jezebel sent her men to hunt him down. Her solution was simple: destroy the message by killing the messenger! But Jezebel was unsuccessful in killing the messenger. Wily Elijah escaped time after time from her clutches.

Elijah complained to God that he was alone, that there was none to join with him and to comfort him in his solitary witness for justice and faithfulness. He refused to acknowledge divine care for him, instead complaining that no one ever cared. Yet when he was hungry, God sent food. When he had no shelter, a widow opened up her home. When he was thirsty, water appeared from a roadside cave. Even companionship was offered by Elisha, a young admirer. Yet Elijah's temptation to lapse into self-righteous pity was a constant problem.

While Elijah was hardly a giant like Moses or Abraham, the picture of this prophet lived on in the hearts and minds of Jewish people for generations. (Those sent from Jesus asked John the Baptist if he was Elijah reincarnated. And Jesus—upon the cross of his crucifixion—was heard by the crowd as calling for Elijah to come and deliver him.) The tradition of Elijah is a vibrant word of hope for a better time. Having never experienced death, being assumed into the heavens in a chariot, he was seen as having special and miraculous power not unlike a saint.

But Elijah differed significantly from a saint who, as a martyr, stands unto death. He did not bear the consequences of his words unto the end. Elijah did not declare, as John Hus did against the forces of an imperialistic Roman Pope in the thirteenth century: "I would rather suffer the consequences of the burning stake, than the consequences of a burning hell." He would never be one to say, as the reformer Martin Luther did in the sixteenth century: "Here I stand, I shall not be moved." He would not be one to stand in front of a tank until it finally crushed him in death. Instead, he darted through the countryside, declaring a word of hope for a new age, planting seeds of thought for the next generation, biding his time until when the word would sprout up yielding its fruit.

It is not always necessary to die for one's faith to make a stand. Like Elijah, the young nameless student stood against military might. He spoke a word of hope to the driver of the tank, made his point again, and then disappeared into the faceless crowd. His action—picked up in a picture—conveys a word of hope. The world is changing faster than we had ever dreamed. Communist nations, once feared by us as strong and invincible nations against which we had to keep immense arsenals, are crumbling from within. Their economic and moral cultures are bankrupt. For three generations, they have made promises they cannot keep; expectations that cannot be met; and the masses are calling their leaders to accountability. Israel knew it; China and the Soviets know it. Realistically, repression will dampen for the moment, but the waves of change are set loose. There are Elijahs all over those countries now, darting here and there, planting seeds of hope and change.

But before we become too self-confident with our "I told you so" attitudes, there is as much a lesson from them as there is for us. That's a very disturbing part of the biblical message: "What's good for the goose is also good for the gander!" Winds of change need to blow in this beloved country of ours as well. We are not immune from the same unresponsiveness of our administration and elected representatives. We are fast becoming a country with a permanent underclass that will not have access to the traditional middle-class ladder, due to our housing and employment structures. People without hope of permanent homes raise another generation without regard to other people's possessions and safety. People who have seen their minimum wage jobs buy half the food it did when they started working get angry. People see their children refused from a medical emergency room because they can't get medical insurance.

We need to sow words of hope for our economic and moral system of values. We need some Elijahs too. The world of tomorrow is being ushered into today. We need those who—even though they feel they stand alone—stand before our places of power in the most biblical of traditions, Elijah. Who will they be? From where will they come? We must depend upon them from within; for they are our salvation more than tanks and guns.

When people's expectations are not met—generation after generation—the disappointment turns into seething anger that erupts into if not outright violence, then into passive-aggressive behavior against the perceived enemy. Sociologists point to the economic disenfranchisement of people as the beginning of violence in a society. People's disregard for other people's property and personhood stems from their own low self-esteem. What do I have to lose if I rip a store off? What do I have to lose if I take some medicine for my child? After several generations experience personal violence, we build more jails and arrest more people, yet the rate of crime continues to climb. We are attacking the symptom but not the root. People need to build self-esteem; they need to see that what is promised is received. As expectations are fulfilled, self-esteem is built.

The winds are beginning to blow. Developing new ways to teach and learn social as well as moral values can help us all usher in the world of tomorrow today.

Context: Prophets

Obadiah – Joel – Amos – Jonah – Hosea – Isaiah – Micah
Nahum – Zephaniah – Habakkuk – Jeremiah – Daniel
Ezekiel – Haggai – Zechariah – Malachi

No, this is not just a list of old men with odd names. It's a list of some of the prophets from the Judeo-Christian scriptures covering a span of over 300 years. Mostly, these books are named after the prophet for whom they are attributed.

As mentioned previously, where the specific books of the Prophets fall within the canon or how they are ordered depends upon the particular version. For example, the Hebrew scriptures (*Tanakh*) divide the group into Former and Latter prophets. Some Christian Bibles refer to the Greater/Lesser or Major/Minor prophets. (This is not a judgment on greatness, but rather refers to the physical size of the books.) Most versions of the Catholic and Protestant Bibles divide the books between the Historical Books and Prophets categories.

The timeline of these books overlaps with the books we've already covered, so they could be arranged in numerous ways. Often the order is based on length of book, which was typical in the ancient world.

So, what exactly is a prophet? Prophecy was widespread in the ancient Near East in many cultures, and prophets served a wide variety of purposes, from anointing kings and approving military expeditions to proclaiming messages from God about the present or the future.

Some prophets were simply royal "yes men," while others stood as a moral compass, closely watching over the actions of the king and not being quiet about it when they disagreed with him. Some exhibited seemingly bizarre behavior (such as Ezekiel's eating barley-cakes baked on human dung or Jeremiah burying his underwear in a rock's cleft) while others functioned in a more laidback manner.

Not surprisingly, the prophets tended to be most active during times of crisis. During the Assyrian crisis, right before the fall of Israel (in 722 BCE), we hear from Amos, Hosea, Micah, and Isaiah.

Over a century later, we have the prophets of the Babylonian crisis (before and during the fall of Judah in 586 BCE), including Zephaniah, Habakkuk, and Jeremiah.

During the exile, Ezekiel takes the spotlight. The Book of Daniel, attributed to a Jewish man living in Babylonia during the exile, presents a series of visions and dreams in an apocalyptic genre. After the exile, others will prophesy through the Restoration.

Meanwhile...

The Persian Empire expanded to include increasing portions of the ancient world. At its largest, it would encompass eight million square kilometers, and contain over forty percent of the world's population. Zarathustra began teaching a new monotheistic philosophy, simplifying many Persian gods under one God he called Ahura Mazda ("Wise Lord"). The resulting religion, Zoroastrianism, was widely practiced throughout Persia and is still practiced today. In the dualistic Zoroastrian worldview, an ongoing struggle between the forces of good and evil happens both cosmically (opposing forces within the universe) as well as morally (opposing forces within the mind). Unlike most other cultures of its day, it explicitly forbid slavery.

Over in India, another tradition was growing, termed Jainism. Jains aspire to conquer their inner passions—such as desire, anger, greed, and attachment—through the management of their karma. In contrast to many ancient cultures' practice of animal sacrifices, Jain practices include stringent non-violence in both thoughts and actions, inclusive of vegetarianism. Jainism's unique concept of God regards all living souls as potentially divine. When a soul completely sheds its karmic bonds, it then attains God-consciousness. (Twenty-five hundred years later, Mahatma Gandhi would be significantly influenced by Jain principles in his mission to lead India to independence.)

Nearby in Japan, the roots of Shinto were spreading. Not attributed to any specific founder, nor having any formal doctrine or "official" sacred texts, Shinto has nonetheless had a lasting effect on Japanese culture. Its foundation lies in the belief in *kami*, which can be described as sacred beings or spiritual essences. Shinto followers strive to live in harmony and peace with the kami, nature, and other human beings.

✡ Amos 8:1-4, 7-8, 11-12 ✡
A Basket of Ripe Fruit

8 ¹ This is what the Lord God showed me—a basket of summer fruit.
² He said, "Amos, what do you see?" And I said, "A basket of summer fruit."
Then the Lord said to me,

"The end has come upon my people Israel;
 I will never again pass them by.
³ The songs of the temple shall become wailings in that day,"
says the Lord God;
"The dead bodies shall be many,
 cast out in every place. Be silent!"

⁴ Hear this, you that trample on the needy,
 and bring to ruin the poor of the land, ...

⁷ The Lord has sworn by the pride of Jacob:
Surely I will never forget any of their deeds.
⁸ Shall not the land tremble on this account,
 and everyone mourn who lives in it,
and all of it rise like the Nile,
 and be tossed about and sink again, like the Nile of Egypt? ...

¹¹ The time is surely coming, says the Lord God,
 when I will send a famine on the land;
not a famine of bread, or a thirst for water,
 but of hearing the words of the Lord.
¹² They shall wander from sea to sea,
 and from north to east;
they shall run to and fro, seeking the word of the Lord,
 but they shall not find it.

Summer's spoiled fruit

Sermon by Richard Murdoch | Rye, NY | July 23, 1995

Over the sideboard in the dining room of my great-grandfather's farm-house hung a framed picture of summer fruit. When we sat down for Sunday family dinner, my assigned seat afforded me a clear view of it. And since children finish dinner quicker than adults do, I had lots of time to stare at it. So much time, in fact, that I can still see the faded colors of watermelon, peaches, cherries, and plums bounded by a black frame. In my adult years, I realized that the picture probably was acquired as a giveaway with some farm product, because, in my travels, I have noted a more original likeness hanging in an art museum.

While the picture displayed food, which seems reasonable in a dining room, the sideboard below it never held serving dishes. In retrospect, I am not sure why that was. It could have been because the dining room was not adjacent to the kitchen, meaning that by the time hot dishes had been carried through the house, they were passed immediately. Or it could have been because family style rather than buffet style was the accepted way of dining. Or maybe my great aunt, who was the hostess of the house, preferred to use the sideboard as the display place for her limited artistic skills. Just directly below the picture was a somewhat faithful copy of the same with real fruit in the summer. From the garden and orchard, she harvested the fruit as the rewards of summer.

But regardless of how inviting the fruit basket appeared, nobody but my aunt (that I can remember) actually ate the fruit. "Pretty to look at," my mother would say, "but don't eat it." Just in case we were tempted to disobey, the fruit flies convinced us otherwise. The underside of the fruit spoiled quickly in the hot climate because there was no refrigerator in that house to cool it. Only essentials could be held in the small, old-fashioned icebox. And fruit was not among the essentials that my great aunt felt earned a place in the icebox.

Fresh fruit is a welcome sign of summer—fresh cherries and peaches appear at the farm and market stand beside the road. But summer fruit is deceptive. Enjoy its enhanced flavor quickly; otherwise tree-ripe fruit will spoil without appropriate cooling. And beautiful summer fruit quickly comes to its end.

A vision of summer fruit appeared to Amos, the prophet from which we read today. In the Book of Amos, this is the fourth of the five visions by which God speaks to Amos with words of caution about the course the people of Israel are taking. Biblical scholars point out that a significant play on words is contained in the first two verses of this chapter. The Hebrew words for "summer fruit" and "end" are spelled differently, but pronounced the same. In English, we would call them homonyms.

Amos's audience knew that summer fruit was deceptive, and that without care, it quickly becomes spoiled. So, instead of Amos using summer fruit as the symbol of a bountiful harvest—hope after a winter-weary diet—his audience heard that a basket of summer fruit was the symbol of their end, the destruction of Israel. Who was this shepherd from the little village of Tekoa? And why did he dare lift his voice in a warning on market day in Jerusalem?

* * *

Market day in Turkey's Bergama, ancient Pergamon, is unchanged after many centuries. Sheep, goats, and cattle are clustered in a large field, dotted by shade trees, under which horse carts and pickup trucks are parked side by side. Buyers wander here and there, yanking open the jaws of animals inspecting their teeth to confirm their age, as they bargain with hopeful sellers. Under a row of lean-tos, piles of watermelons and boxes of cherries are protected from the hot summer sun. It is a man's social world, young and old renew friendships over a smoke, a drink, or a story. They sell. They buy. They arrange marriages and they pledge loans. They argue politics and religion. Meanwhile, our modern, air-conditioned coach made its way along the road at the edge of the market field, ascending to the acropolis, where ruins of the once powerful capital of the Province of Mysia shine in white marble. We left the twentieth century and entered a scene reminiscent of Amos's world, the eighth-century BCE prophet of Israel, northern kingdom of the Hebrews.

Amos—sometimes shepherd, sometimes prophet—lived one thousand miles to the east of Pergamon. It was the temple of Yahweh—not the temple of Zeus—that shone on the acropolis above *his* market field.

He could view the homes of the newly rich perched just beneath the acropolis, but high above the market place. Merchants, brokers, and bankers were a new class in Jerusalem and Pergamon, made wealthy when cessation of hostilities between East and West opened up lucrative trade routes providing an opportunity for new merchant wealth. With peace came new and secure trade routes. Both cities boasted of beautiful public buildings and well-appointed places for entertainment with coliseums, fountain piazzas, and boulevards. Fashion in dress and food lost its strict ethnicity as traditional tribal towns were replaced in importance by these new cosmopolitan urban centers.

If the absence of conflict constitutes peace, this was the first world peace the Hebrews had known since the death of the beloved Solomon. But if peace is defined as harmony and tranquility, this was far from it. On the surface, all might be well; but Amos reminded his hearers of what their eyes were seeing but their hearts did not want to believe. Their new peace and wealth was being enjoyed by a favored few. When a poor harvest left little money for next year's seed, bankers were foreclosing immediately instead of extending credit to the small farmer. Instead of donating the wheat chaff with its occasional grain to the less fortunate, grain merchants were selling it. Instead of being honest with scales to weigh produce, they developed two sets of weights: one weight for selling and one weight for buying—sell light and buy heavy.

Merchants were running virtual sweatshops allowing no time for seasonal religious festivals to their workers, yet they themselves dreamed up new festivals to entertain themselves in their idleness. The social fabric of the Hebrews was unraveling before their very eyes in greed and lust for individual power. They were dividing themselves into two peoples: the few rich and powerful vs. the many poor and disenfranchised. Getting ahead—at the expense of each other—tears the fabric of a nation apart. The enemy is not without; it is within. With a house divided, Amos predicted that Israel would not stand against the next enemy. And they didn't. Within fifty years, Israel found itself captive in Babylon. Its great cities laid waste. Its market places empty. The summer fruit spoiled. What had been the hope of peace brought the end of those who had fought expecting peace.

Peace is delicate business whether it is in a family, a society, a nation, or a world—that is, if peace is as Webster defines it: harmony and tranquility. Since harmony and tranquility are not considered self-actualized behaviors of humans by many cultures, social laws have been promulgated and given authority by religion, military, and governments. For example, cheating one's neighbor often results in revenge by the neighbor. As the desire to get even accelerates, individuals lose control and the feud becomes cyclical between families. Then soon the community takes sides. A classic Hatfield and McCoy picture appears. Societies have found it essential to draw boundaries for acceptable social behavior between individuals if a family, a community, or a nation is to function or even survive. When prosperity is the only goal of peace, then peace is spoiled.

Since the fall of the Soviet Union and its Eastern satellites, the world has been engaged in expanding markets and international trade to rebuild what the Iron Curtain had eliminated after World War II. We envisioned that finally peace would come to the world, because no longer would two super powers be drawn into conflict with little nations as pawns. No more Viet Nams. We assumed that the absence of a competing super-power would bring peace because the threat of global warfare was no longer a reality. Harmony and tranquility would be enjoyed.

This is the fiftieth year of the founding of the United Nations. Do you remember the steps and missteps that brought the U.N. into existence? After two disastrous European wars within hardly a generation's interval, few nations had to be convinced that a new way had to be found if the historic cycle of distrust and destruction within the family of nations was to be changed. Words like Amos's have rung true, generation after generation, not only within nations, but also now between nations. Support from religious and secular worlds put their hopes in a lasting world peace through the cooperative efforts of so-called super powers and the average everyday countries.

The summer fruit of peace that was so welcomed has quickly spoiled. The harmony and tranquility sought between some ancient enemies who had ceased to war, has brought the specter of past. In the hurry to right ancient wrongs, revenge again has lifted its head. It is not the common good that is sought, but what is good for *me*. Once again, the specter of man's inhumanity to man lifts its head around the world—Africa, the Middle East, and the Balkans. The first two seemed far away culturally and ethnically; but the third is close to home. The euphemism, "ethnic cleansing" is now in our daily vocabulary. Serbian Christians are driving out Muslims in a land that they have shared for over five hundred years. Displacement and abuse of basic human rights appall the Western Christian world, with little interest from the Middle-Eastern Muslim world. The political intrigue of the Balkans is legend. It took an autocratic Tito to forge Yugoslavia together after the disasters of two world wars. But in the wake of a welcomed disintegration of the Eastern Block, the Serbian rebels claiming the right to wage their own civil war—without interference from abroad—have unloosed the specter of a holocaust, unseen for almost sixty years.

The summer fruit of peace has spoiled, so quickly the wonderful promise of peaceful harmony and tranquility slipped from the world's grasp while we were seeking prosperity. The gauntlet has been thrown down by a tiny country's civil war that impairs the peace of the whole family of nations. What follows in the next weeks, years, and decades is again a test of the resolve of the family of nations to keep peace.

Will peace be an absence of conflict? Or will it be harmony and tranquility? Amos's words are still clear. True peace would be the latter.

✡ Jonah 2 ✡
A Psalm of Thanksgiving

2 [1] Then Jonah prayed to the LORD his God from the belly of the fish, [2] saying,

"I called to the LORD out of my distress,
   and he answered me;
out of the belly of Sheol I cried,
   and you heard my voice.

[3] You cast me into the deep,
   into the heart of the seas,
   and the flood surrounded me;
all your waves and your billows
   passed over me.

[4] Then I said, 'I am driven away
   from your sight;
how shall I look again
   upon your holy temple?'

[5] The waters closed in over me;
   the deep surrounded me;
weeds were wrapped around my head
[6]   at the roots of the mountains.

I went down to the land
   whose bars closed upon me forever;
yet you brought up my life from the pit,
   O LORD my God.

[7] As my life was ebbing away,
   I remembered the LORD;
and my prayer came to you,
   into your holy temple.

[8] Those who worship vain idols
   forsake their true loyalty.
[9] But I with the voice of thanksgiving
   will sacrifice to you;
what I have vowed I will pay.
   Deliverance belongs to the LORD!"

[10] Then the LORD spoke to the fish, and it spewed Jonah out
upon the dry land.

Vows before God

Sermon by Richard Murdoch | Corfu, NY | August 7, 1977

In the early fall of 1965, a plane crossing the Pacific Ocean began to have fuel line trouble. In order to prepare the passengers for a sea landing—and ditching procedures—the pilot announced the fate of the plane. A popular magazine published a blow-by-blow account given by one of the passengers who turned her experience into a profit. She described the individual passengers one by one—what they saw, what they felt, and how they reacted. A priest prayed fervently that the plane would be spared. A mother lamented that her children weren't sent with the husband on an earlier flight. A businessman cursed himself for not forgoing the extra hoopla after the sales talk and making the earlier flight. A young man asked himself why things like this always happened to him. He must be a jinx because everyplace he went, something goofed up. The stewardess remained calm, but wondered who was responsible for this, vowing to set a few things right when and if they landed safely.

Close to three thousand years ago, a ship was sailing in the eastern end of the Great Sea—now known to us as the Mediterranean. A storm was brewing in the west and the ship's crew saw it coming. Storms had a way of taking sailboats and tossing them like toothpicks. The optical illusion created by such a situation looked as though a dragon or sea monster was flapping its tail, stirring water in order to render a few men helpless and corral them into its mouth. Men were afraid. In their hurry to make the ship secure, they had enough warning to stop and pray for their safety at the small figurines placed on the masts and on the railing. Oftentimes, their gods were not enough to work by oneself, so each sailor prayed at each station of the devotional—except one, a Hebrew by the name of Jonah. The sailors suspected him of being up to something; one of them even had the gall to say, "Jonah, give yourself up—you are the cause of this." Meanwhile, Jonah was saying to himself, "If I ever get out of this mess, I'll set some things right."

Unfortunately, Jonah didn't have the chance that the flight attendant on the 1965 flight had. Every child knows the story of Jonah being swallowed by a large fish. In the story, we are told that after a suitable period for Jonah's reflection and repentance, the fish received a stomachache (from all of Jonah's complaining) and spat Jonah up, unwanted, on the shore. When the story first entered Jewish teaching circles, it was meant to be a ridiculous and funny—yet pathetic—example of people who become sour by the virtue of their righteousness. Not even a fish with the simplest digestive system could stomach Jonah.

Jonah really hadn't intended to put himself in this position by any means. He was a prophet, a member of the order of priests in the temple who studied and prophesied. But he was also studied *by* God. Before the fish incident, Jonah was supposed to go to Nineveh, a great city of the East. It had culture, beauty, money, and learning. Jonah was to denounce the people of the city for their false sense of security, false progress, and unconcern for human development. Jonah was not too happy with this mission and decided the best thing was to run away to escape the responsibility—however, he left the door open for his return.

In the prayer that is recorded in the scripture, Jonah puts himself in a very different light. He no longer is the prophet so proud he refused to mix with the Ninevites (who didn't live as he did). Nor is he so unsure of himself (because he didn't really know what to say since his hometown Jerusalem was no different). He says, "How shall I look into thy holy temple after I have done such a thing?" This means he had little sense of self-worth and no longer felt of much use to God. About all he could do was to attempt to renew his vows before God, make a sacrifice, and reflect outwardly what he felt inwardly about this decision.

We make vows as inward commitments and we match them with outward or physical acts. For example, the marriage service involves vows between two people—promises made in the presence of God, their friends, and their church. The physical symbol of these vows is the giving of rings that are worn as an outward sign of an inward commitment.

Often we are similar to Jonah—making a vow, breaking it, then remaking it and giving physical evidence of our sincerity and intent. Baptism falters in vows, because homes cannot always be peaceful, tranquil places. Strong words are said, things are done, but the vow is always remade in forgiveness. Likewise, marriages are not always joyful, pleasant experiences. There are times when things are done and said—things that are expressed in tension and anger—and then resolution and forgiveness bring a peace offering after the battle. Church membership is not always exciting, vibrant, and caring. Words are said, things are done, and people alienate themselves from each other. Some don't get what they want; others are rebuffed for their ideas. Petty jealousies add fuel to the fire. Membership vows need to be remade, reminding us this place belongs to God and not to us, that we worship God and not our own accomplishments, and that we are responsible for a ministry of God's service to humanity—not a social service committee to each other, whom we pick and choose.

Vows are not symbols of perfection or strength; rather they are symbols of intent. Anyone who admits failure publicly or bares himself to people—who dares expose his own weaknesses to others—is considered by most of our culture as a weak person. We lead by putting our best foot forward and keeping our dusty shoe in the background.

But once the strength begins to fail, once the polish of the shoe becomes slightly scuffed, people see through the cheap sheen and quick brushing to the actual shoe beneath. Jonah was a prophet; he didn't want people to know he refused his mission to Nineveh. He couldn't stand to be exposed—his leadership would be jeopardized. He didn't want people to question his reason for a new sacrifice to declare his intent regarding a new promise (after he muffed the first one). So he went off into the belly of the fish to hide. The sailors didn't like him; even the fish spat him up. There he lay on the beach, unwanted by fish, fowl, or human. And God took him up again, challenged him again, and he remade his vows.

It usually takes a crisis or an upheaval to bring out what is underneath the surface in people. And after all is said and done, they find themselves in a position of weakness instead of behind a secure mask of strength. The weakness has always been there, but it has been hidden. We have come to believe people don't lead lives from weakness. But Jonah points out that the opposite is true. You can lead from weakness—for it conveys to others that you too are human and caring.

That is, unless you don't care to be human and caring.

Some people have told me that they cannot participate in the prayer of confession because it is negative instead of positive. Other people are very adept at confessing their neighbors' sins during confession, but wouldn't touch their own sins with a ten-foot pole. Some tell me they enjoy confessing each Sunday and would like to do so more often and more publicly. But the real purpose of confession is a means by which you are made aware of the intent of vows you have made. Confession brings you to the point of renewing your vows, of reviewing your purpose, of asking the question, "Is God passing me by? Or am I passing God by?"

Renewing your vows is not a fun game, but it is a necessary part of living and evaluating your life. But more than that, it is the only way for personal, human growth. You must constantly put before yourself the *why* of living—otherwise you will lose the *what* of living. And you may end up like Jonah—cast upon a shore where neither fish nor fowl wants you. But God does want you. And the best lives are lived from strength in weakness rather than strength from behind masks.

Further Assurances of God's Redeeming Love

3 ¹ The LORD said to [Hosea] again, "Go, love a woman who has a lover and is an adulteress, just as the LORD loves the people of Israel, though they turn to other gods and love raisin cakes."

Sex, marriage, and God

Sermon by Richard Murdoch | East Lansing, MI | September 12, 1993

The young man walked up to the large residence next to the cathedral. He knocked on the door. It opened, and the bishop standing there asked, "Can I help you?" The man replied, "Yes, I heard that you are searching for a rector for a difficult parish. I'm available."

The bishop was intrigued because he did have a difficult parish for which he was looking desperately for a priest. Thinking it was a heaven-sent opportunity, the bishop asked the visitor to come into his office and be seated, continuing, "What qualifications do you have?"

The young man said, "I have answered God's call."

"And just how did you do that?" the bishop asked.

The young cleric continued, "He instructed me to take a wife."

The bishop—expecting an educational or theological answer—thought this answer was a bit unconventional, but continued his inquiry. "I see, but what relevance does that have to God's call?"

"Well, she is a prostitute and leaves me on occasion to live with another lover. But we do have three lovely children as God commanded, and to them I gave names as God instructed me: *Jezreel* ('God shall sow'), *Lo-ruhamah* ('not pitied'), and *Lo-ammi* ('not my people')."

The bishop immediately escorted the cleric to the door and, slamming it, muttered to himself, "Of all the crazy things I have heard, that takes the cake!"

Would you agree with the bishop? It *is* crazy. And it sounded no less crazy when the story was originally told, in the seventh century BCE. And if this story wasn't a part of the scriptures, then we might simply dismiss it as foolishness.

It is crazy to expect that God would deliberately command one to sin to be good, or condone irreligious behavior in order to promote religious behavior. But that's the story of Hosea, who was commanded by God to break the Seventh Commandment: Thou shalt not commit adultery. Or at least that is what Hosea claimed. Some fastidious scholars argue that, technically, Hosea did not break the law because Gomer was the adulteress, not Hosea. But the point is really moot, because no self-respecting member of the clergy would go near a temple prostitute of the god Ba'al and risk his reputation, much less take a known prostitute for a wife.

Some more fundamentalist scholars argue that since Gomer's marriage to Hosea led her to respectability, adultery was the occasion for redemption. But this point is moot as well if you read the whole story. Hosea's marriage to Gomer was not for Gomer or Hosea's salvation. It was a pitiful sight for all who saw Hosea: a cuckolded husband and three children who were waifs. Instead, the marriage was for Israel's salvation.

Today, marriage is not the usual metaphor by which people describe their relationship with God. While you hear people frequently speak about God as a guide or friend, few describe God as lover, wife, or husband. The family metaphor is about as close as we come to that.

A long time ago, St. Augustine used the family metaphor to describe our relationship with God when he wrote in the sixth century CE, "He who has God for father, also has Christ for brother and the church as mother." Since all understanding of the divine is dependent on experiences communicated in language used by humanity, relationships with God have been described "as being like..." No one has yet recorded the voice of God on a tape recorder. Nor has anyone ever been able to produce a photograph of God speaking to a human. We, like the Hebrews, are still dependent upon the language of humanity to describe the experience of God.

Since there is no unique verbal language by which God communicates, human language presents a challenge because there are limits to meanings by different generations and in different cultures. For example, marriage is a metaphor that was used widely by the prophets of the scriptures, in the monastic period of the Christian church, and during the Protestant Reformation. But it is fraught with problems today. It's not so much that views of marriage have changed with time, but that sexuality employs a language that engenders a defensive attitude when it is used in a place of worship.

John Burgess addresses this issue in his article "An Interminable Debate? Can't stop talking about sex" [*The Christian Century,* August 4, 1993]. He describes how one Protestant denomination spent almost thirty years talking about sex, beginning with divorce in the 1960s, moving on to pre-marital and extra-marital sex in the 1970s and '80s, and, now, homosexuality in the 1990s. He writes: "Without being aware of it, the sexuality debate has become the vehicle for getting at one of the most basic questions of faith: What does it mean to be human before God?" Burgess draws attention, I think, to another basic question of faith: "What does it mean to know God?"

Hosea fails in his first attempt to get the Israelites' attention to their condition. So Plan B comes into effect: a soap opera right before their eyes. A decent, law-abiding prophet engages in a sordid marriage. He flaunts decent morality right in their faces, day after day—he, and this woman of the night, and their three children (all of whom are given uncomplimentary names that will haunt them their entire lives). And to make matters even more tabloid-worthy, the marriage does not reform Gomer, and on occasion she goes back to the beds of her former lovers or customers.

And this live X-rated advertisement did get the Israelites' attention. All of Israel was talking about this crazy religious man who claimed to announce that Israel must change her ways in order return to God's prosperity. Yet he, God's messenger, was a wimp at home with three pitiful children, cuckolded by a prostitute-turned-wife. What were they to learn from this craziness?

Sex is the most intimate of human physical acts. Marriage is the most basic human agreement or contract. Together, they require the most fundamental of human emotions necessary for a family, society, or nation to survive: mutual trust. Marriage takes Hosea's metaphor one step further. When one partner crawls into another lover's bed for sex, it is a betrayal of trust and the emotional contract. When a partner refuses to share the parenting of children, bread at the table, or the roof over one's head, it's a betrayal of the civil contract. Trust comes before love.

Hosea says that Israel has climbed into another lover's bed: Ba'al. Israel has looked for excitement in other beds instead of working on the relationship in her own bed. Denial of her own untrustworthiness has led her to other gods who promise her self-esteem. Israel is so wrapped up in satisfying her own desires that she has neglected the needs of her husband and children. She has forgotten her own children at home. She has refused to share bread at the table with the poor or to share the roof over her head with the blind, the lame, or the widow—those who have no control over their condition.

But back on the soap opera, Hosea welcomes Gomer back again and again, even though the broken trust has made him the laughingstock of everyone. Soon Gomer learns that there is nothing she can do that will separate her from Hosea's desire to be her husband. She has tested every limit, and still Hosea remains faithful to her. Finally, Gomer comes home for good and is a faithful wife and a nurturing mother.

By this time, the audience gets it, so to speak. Husbands look at their wives; wives look at their husbands. Not so much the joy, but the pains of their broken marriage fidelities—sexual and contractual—become self-evident. Gomer is Israel; Hosea is God; their children are the next generation. If conditions remain the same (as their names foreshadow), "what they sowed" "will not be pitied" and they will "not be a people."

What is the way out of this? What is the prognosis? The prophet returns to his indictment, the knowledge of God. In the scriptures, "to know" has a double meaning. Like in our language, it refers to mental skills, but it also means sexual intercourse. Thus, "to know God," from a biblical perspective, means commitment of mind *and* body to God. Our relationship to God is not expressed in words only, but also the behavior and emotions upon which marriages are built: trust, sex, and love.

While imagining God as lover, spouse, or sexual partner is beyond our parameters of language, it was not in the Hebrew world. Things were more earthy then. But the focus remains clear to all generations: God never gives up on us. We may do everything possible to break the trust that God has placed in us to be joyful and loving people, yet God always welcomes us back to begin a new relationship. Our responsibility is to come back to God. God will do the rest.

Impending Judgment on Israel and Judah

5 ¹⁰ The princes of Judah have become
like those who remove the landmark;
on them I will pour out
my wrath like water.

Respecting landmarks

Sermon by Richard Murdoch | East Lansing, MI | September 5, 1993

"It's time to walk the boundary," my grandfather announced. It was a ritual without meaning for me, but during each summer's visit to the family farm, I dutifully participated because I was the eldest grandson. Each time our destination was a notched tree, a marked fencepost, or a large boulder. These marked the corners of land that had been in possession of our family since 1860. On one such annual occasion, when I was seven (I know it was then because the summer before, I had taken my first solo train ride to visit my other grandparents in Iowa), it was discovered that a new neighboring farmer had erected a replacement fence. A portion of my grandfather's fence—already in disrepair—had been torn out. In deep thought, rubbing his prominent and bony chin, my grandfather's anger erupted after measuring the foot or so difference. "What can you expect from a Lutheran?" (He, of course, being a Baptist.)

In no uncertain terms, my grandfather was intimating that Lutherans were bad people. They were dishonest people who moved fences to their advantage. I remembered the event as one of those childhood "awakening" experiences. My other grandfather in Iowa was a Lutheran, and he was nice—at least I thought so. Did he also secretly move fences in the night, grabbing other people's land? The inner conflict was so great that I asked my father about it. His response made sense to me, as bizarre and offensive as it may sound today: "Your other grandfather is Swedish Lutheran; this new farmer is German Lutheran." It was during the time of the Second World War, and everyone said any German— even German-Americans—did bad things!

In biblical times, moving a boundary stone, a landmark, was an offense punishable by death. It represented a violation of turning a sacred trust into a personal gain. However, the violation was seen not so much as an individual sin against one's neighbor, but as a sin against the whole nation, the People of God. It violated the sacred trust that God had given the Hebrews: "Be fruitful and multiply the earth" (Genesis 1:28). The Genesis covenant went beyond simply the procreation of children. It was the stewardship of the whole earth, including the productivity of the land. Hebrews (unlike a majority of later Christian leaders from the sixth through the twelfth century CE) believed in the capitalistic notion of owning land, but viewed their ownership of land as temporary and corporate, held in trust for the next generation.

Typical of a prophetic warning, Hosea (in the role of the prosecuting attorney) says, "Hear the Word of the Lord, O Israel, for the Lord has a controversy with the inhabitants of the land." What follows is a formal bill of indictment listing the charge being brought by God against the Israelites in the seventh century BCE: "There is no faithfulness or kindness, and no knowledge of God in the land." He follows this with the charges of lying, killing, robbing, adultery, and murder. The consequence of this individual and corporate behavior is a land that is dried up and a people who are dried up, having lost their means and purpose for living.

Finally, in this quasi-legal courtroom drama, the bailiff summons two groups who stand for the accused: priests and tribal princes (or leaders). While each of these two groups has failed at its leadership of Israel, Hosea is harsher on the princes of Judah than on the priests, calling the princes the most despicable and shamed who "act like men who move their neighbor's landmark."

In the unforested and semi-arid land of the Israelites, stones alone acted as landmarks. And these landmarks would often move mysteriously by unscrupulous folks interested only in their own gain if they were not watched diligently. Hosea says that the leaders of Israel seek only their own interest; mutual trust and promises are no longer respected. Even the cornerstone of their economic security—their landmark—is not respected. How can a people survive when they don't respect what has been entrusted to them by God?

There are many different kinds of landmarks that define life's boundaries in addition to property. Every society depends upon boundaries: economic boundaries, political boundaries, emotional boundaries. Basic for any society or nation to survive, there must be mutual trust. I was reminded some years ago just how important trust is and how we take it for granted. It was before the collapse of communism, when I made a trip to the Soviet Union. As travelers often do, I needed to purchase things. I noted that everyone used cash. There were no personal checks or credit cards. If you wished to purchase an item at the Soviet department store, it took waiting in three lines: one line to view the item, a second line to pay for the item and receive a receipt, and finally a third line to claim your purchase. Upon inquiry, I was told that bank drafts could be gotten from a bank, but there was no such thing as a personal checking account. "Why the waiting in lines?" I inquired. I was told the lines existed "because a customer could leave with the item in one hand and the cash in the other hand!"

Hosea says that Israel was transgressing the boundaries established by God between those who lead and those who are led. Both priests and princes not only participate in, but also allow, common landmarks of human respect to be violated. Instead of life being sacred because it is in the image of God, it is cheapened by murder and violence for individual gain. Instead of property being productive, it is taken by others for individual gain. Hosea says there is no "knowledge of God" in the land. If Israel had any understanding of the divine, they would know that any gain at another's expense degrades all of humanity. Violating boundaries or moving landmarks at another's expense leads to the disintegration of a people.

There is not a day that either a newspaper or a TV show does not illustrate the indictment of Hosea. His words are as contemporary today. Boundary after boundary is violated, whether it be theft, rape, or murder. The disintegration of a society is characterized by its disrespect for the landmarks that are set for the common good of all. These landmarks—which can also be called morality—are based upon basic religious precepts: If we are created in the image of God, and if God has given us the earth and all its productivity to be stewards, then we must respect the landmarks between us in order to survive. When those landmarks are moved for personal gain at the expense of another, then we are not treating the other person as one who is made in the image of God. Hosea calls this "the knowledge of God." Without this simple universal trust, then the land and the people shall dry up and wither away just like seventh-century Israel, twentieth-century Bosnia and Somalia, or perhaps twenty-first-century America.

✡ Hosea 6:4-6, 11:3-9 ✡
Impenitence of Israel and Judah

6 ⁴ What shall I do with you, O Ephraim [Israel]?
  What shall I do with you, O Judah?
Your love is like a morning cloud,
  like the dew that goes away early.

⁵ Therefore I have hewn them by the prophets,
  I have killed them by the words of my mouth,
  and my judgment goes forth as the light.

⁶ For I desire steadfast love and not sacrifice,
  the knowledge of God rather than burnt offerings...

11 ³ Yet it was I who taught Ephraim [Israel] to walk,
  I took them up in my arms;
  but they did not know that I healed them.
⁴ I led them with cords of human kindness,
  with bands of love.
I was to them like those
  who lift infants to their cheeks.
  I bent down to them and fed them.

⁵ They shall return to the land of Egypt,
  and Assyria shall be their king,
  because they have refused to return to me.

⁶ The sword rages in their cities,
  it consumes their oracle-priests,
  and devours because of their schemes.

⁷ My people are bent on turning away from me.
  To the Most High they call,
  but he does not raise them up at all.

⁸ How can I give you up, Ephraim?
  How can I hand you over, O Israel? ...

My heart recoils within me;
  my compassion grows warm and tender.
⁹ I will not execute my fierce anger;
  I will not again destroy Ephraim;
for I am God and no mortal,
  the Holy One in your midst,
  and I will not come in wrath.

Love
with abandon

Sermon by Richard Murdoch | East Lansing, MI | September 19, 1993

We have a pair of beautiful cardinals who make their home with us. They nest in our blue spruce, bathe in our birdbath, feed at our bird-feeder, and perch upon our fence. From there, they usually complain loudly about another member of our family, Sam, our cat. One after-noon this past summer, these complaints were extra noisy, causing me to investigate. Mother Cardinal was especially vociferous. Hunting for her whereabouts, I sighted her in the neighbor's old and twisted apple tree, flitting between it and the fence. Seeing Sam napping on a bench below the tree, I scooped him up from his nap and was carrying him inside when I realized that Father Cardinal was giving Baby Cardinal his first flying lesson.

I returned to watch the drama. Father would demonstrate the cor-rect way to fly, then turn around as if to say, "It's easy; follow me!" The loudness of Mother Cardinal fit her role as cheerleader. On occasion, when her fledging offspring seemed to perform well, it received a bite of food as a reward from her. Beginning on the lowest of branches, closest to the fence, the day's lesson progressed ever so slowly, finishing on the highest branch of the apple tree for the grand finale: A solo flight directly home to the blue spruce. It was a flight fifteen to twenty feet in the air with no branches to cushion a fall. And I'm happy to report that Baby Cardinal made it, much to the clucking delight of parents.

The cycle of life is imitated in each of nature's creatures, isn't it? As with birds, so with us. Of the skills parents teach, mobility is the key to survival, freedom, and independence. The minute you teach your daugh-ter or son to walk, you have instilled him or her with the power to be-come an adult.

Do you remember teaching your child to walk? How old were you? How many times did he or she fall? Like Mother and Father Cardinal, did relief and pride overwhelm you when the security of your out-stretched hands was reached? Can you remember the risks that you allowed to get your child to take those first steps—to change from a little primate on all fours to a miniature up-right, two-legged *Homo sapien*? Do you remember the changes that occurred in your household when this newfound mobility expressed its power? Vases not placed out of reach were dashed to the floor. The medicine cabinet yielded more than the usual number of colorful strips of Band Aids to cover the "ouchies," from bumps on the head to split lips. It takes some pretty young and lively parents to keep up with a toddler!

It's this kind of parent that's described in our third and final message from the Hebrew prophet Hosea. But again, it is not the usual image we have of God. Unfortunately, our metaphor for religion is conditioned by our earliest memories and rarely changes. Children often confuse God and Santa Claus. It's probably the white beard and the kindly face of a grandfather that does it, don't you think? After all, who would think of God as young enough to change diapers? Who would think of God as agile enough to run after a toddler? Yet that is the picture that Hosea describes for us: "Yet it was I who taught Ephraim (Israel) to walk, I took them up in my arms."

Hosea's God is no bearded old gentleman. Hosea's God is described as a new father young enough to teach a child to walk and as a young mother lifting an infant in her arms (as in a painting of the Madonna). Hosea's God is willing to take risks in order for a child to survive. Just as Mother and Father Cardinal knew, a bird cannot stay in its nest forever if it is going to live. In spite of the risks of cats and heights, Baby Cardinal must be taught to fly. He must be taught the skill of mobility against great risks. For a child, bumps will be endured, and vases broken.

God did the same for Israel—taught Israel how to walk, put Band Aids on their ouchies, led Israel tenderly on one of those child leashes you might see at the mall, fed them their cereal, and taught them how to chew instead of slurp their food. But then, all of a sudden, God became parent of an adolescent, a young adult. Israel had her own ideas about things. To Israel as a youth, freedom meant irresponsibility. Her room was messy; his chariot got in later and later. Things seem to go from bad to worse.

And finally, God said what every parent eventually says sometime during the worst part of watching children grow up: "Why did I even have children; they don't appreciate all I have gone through for them!"

Or even, in the words of the Tough Love movement: "Out of my house, until you can live with my rules!"

The bonding of childhood turns into the agony of rebellious youth. Israel has forgotten what childhood was like. Now God is the parent of youth, dealing with the struggle of identity and struggle of independence. Israel is both male and female, boy and girl. Israel, as *he* doesn't know appropriate boundaries, stealing land in the middle of the night. Israel as *she* is a wife who sleeps around, being unfaithful to her husband and neglecting her children. Hosea says that God has ample justification to abandon his offspring, Israel. "I'm fed up with you!"

But there are too many parental memories for God to abandon Israel in its rebellious youth. "My heart recoils within me, my compassion grows warm and tender; I will not execute my fierce anger." Parents of adolescents are tempted to act upon their anger, but there are the memories of childhood that draw one back to reality: the first steps walking, the first birthday, the first day of school, the first bike ride. God remembers Israel's triumphant exodus from Egypt, his wandering in Sinai, and her battles at Jericho.

"What shall I do with you? Your love is like a morning cloud; like the dew that goes away early," says God. Israel has so much potential, but she is immature. She tries so hard to make up for the past mistakes. She offers to sacrifice anything to say that she's sorry for the past. She wants to come back home. He wants to bridge the chasm that has developed. But God says sacrifices are not necessary to show remorse. Israel doesn't have to come back with head bowed and shoulders slumped. Hosea says that God isn't the kind of parent who screams and says, "I told you so!" God doesn't delight in humiliation. The solution does not rest in assessing blame. But how easy that is in our frame of reference. "Don't spend time blaming what went wrong; spend your time on the solution. Fix it!"

God "doesn't delight in sacrifice but in steadfast love." How can we get back in God's good graces? Steadfast love is the solution, not blame. So do not forget, it is love with abandon that lights the world.

✡ Isaiah 9:2-7 ✡
The Righteous Reign of the Coming King

9 [2] The people who walked in darkness
   have seen a great light;
those who lived in a land of deep darkness—
   on them light has shined.

[3] You have multiplied the nation,
   you have increased its joy;
they rejoice before you
   as with joy at the harvest,
      as people exult when dividing plunder.

[4] For the yoke of their burden,
   and the bar across their shoulders,
   the rod of their oppressor,
      you have broken as on the day of Midian.

[5] For all the boots of the tramping warriors
   and all the garments rolled in blood
   shall be burned as fuel for the fire.

[6] For a child has been born for us,
   a son given to us;
authority rests upon his shoulders;
   and he is named
Wonderful Counselor, Mighty God,
   Everlasting Father, Prince of Peace.

[7] His authority shall grow continually,
   and there shall be endless peace
for the throne of David and his kingdom.
   He will establish and uphold it
with justice and with righteousness
   from this time onward and forevermore.
The zeal of the Lord of hosts will do this.

Journey to Jerusalem

Sermon by Richard Murdoch | Omaha, NE | December 7, 1980

Isaiah was no fanatical John the Baptist running through the wilderness eating locust and honey; nor was he an Amos or Hosea dressed in rags or dancing the whirling dances of a dervish. No, Isaiah was counsel to the kings. He had access to the temple and the royal palace. He spoke with authority at councils of war and the courtyard meeting of the priests of Aaron. He was commissioned not only by God, but also by Uzziah to be the Royal Prophet. He dressed in fine robes and maintained a certain status in the royal household.

Uzziah, the king of Judah (southern kingdom of Palestine), was remembered second only to Solomon for economic, military, and moral success. He ruled for many years (783-742 BCE) upon the throne of David, as a direct descendant of that royal dynasty. But Uzziah's strength became his weakness. The Book of Chronicles tells us that he grew proud to his destruction and attempted to usurp the power of the priesthood by entering the temple to burn incense on the altar—a privilege reserved for the priests of the house of Aaron.

Azariah, the chief priest, followed by eighty other priests, pleaded with him not to go beyond the bounds of his power. They said, "It is not for you Uzziah, to burn incense unto the Lord, for it is the priests of Aaron, those who are consecrated to do this. Go out of the sanctuary. Let those who are appointed do it; it will bring you no honor." But Uzziah was angered, because he was the king. They were all his servants—including Isaiah. Uzziah was angry, and as he proceeded to burn incense upon the altar, leprosy broke out on his forehead. He was banished from the temple and the palace—living his days separated from his people, his priests, and his son, Jotham, who became regent.

The succeeding Jotham died within five years, placing Ahaz on David's throne. And Ahaz had more than his share of problems with his neighbors and cousins. The Assyrians to the north had just conquered the northern kingdom, Israel, and sent its people into captivity. Assyria had also plundered Samaria and left it in ruins. In the southern regions, the Moabites were being used by Assyrians to taunt Judah, Egypt, and Babylon. King Ahaz consulted Isaiah as to what might be the best way to get out of this political mess—not only to save his own skin, but also the skin of his beloved people. And he did what any sensible politician would have done: He tried to negotiate. He sent emissaries to Assyria and said, "Why don't we be friends? We can let you travel through our land, and supply you with goods—just don't destroy us." So, with gold from the temple and silver from the palace treasury, off goes the king with his tribute to save the country. Isaiah warned Ahaz, however, not to try too hard to be friends with Assyria's King Tiglath-Pileser III. "Just do what you have to and come home."

Isaiah's words were tempered to this effect: "Remember, the Lord God is the ruler of history, not Tiglath-Pileser." To make a long story short, when King Ahaz reached Damascus, his eyes bugged out. He was treated as royalty—as the long lost brother. He was wined and dined. He was entertained. He was educated, and he became enamored with the Assyrians' religion—it was so current, alive, and feeling. He ordered a copy of the great altar of the Damascus temple to be copied and installed in the Jerusalem temple. He changed the garb of the priests—none of that drab blue and white wool anymore! No, rather rich reds, brilliant golds, and deep indigos. It made no difference whether there was any rationale, it just looked elegant. And of course, the Assyrians were greatly impressed with the sincerity of their new friend and convert in Judah.

Well, the stakes were too high. Ahaz came back bragging about how his new friends would take care of them, and save them from their enemies. Isaiah reminded him that God was the lord of history—not the Assyrians. Ahaz preferred to believe, as did many Israelites, in the might of the Assyrians whom they could see, rather than a God whom they could not see. It is always more comforting to see armor and spears than praying hands and an altar, isn't it?

It was not long before the Assyrians were forgetful of their fine friend Ahaz; and Assyrian enemies were constantly running over Judah. Judah was plunged into darkness—militarily, economically, and morally. There was no aid—their gold and silver were long gone. They cried to Egypt to come to their aid. They cried for Ethiopia to come to their aid.

But no one came. And finally they called upon Isaiah, the elder states-man and prophet. Isaiah's words were couched in a vision, which then was followed by the familiar words of today's scripture: God as the lord of history would provide his servant/king in his good time. And when it was appropriate for him, he would indeed send a messiah. He would restore Judah. He would restore Jerusalem. Most importantly, he would restore the throne of David.

The prominence of Jerusalem was overshadowed by Bethlehem, which was called the city of David, although the word literally means "house of bread" because it was in the fertile plains of grain. But the sleepy village of Bethlehem was far from Isaiah's throne of David (in Jerusalem). It was the whole force of the throne of David that gave be-lief to the prophecy—that of his authority there would be no end.

We really can't perceive how important it was to the Israelites to have their monarchy. For us in a modern era, the only monarchy we know is that of Queen Elizabeth in Great Britain. Yet, in many ways, she has only a ceremonial kind of function. The great force of her office has been removed. In fact, it is almost ironic that the president of our coun-try has more power than the monarchy, which the colonists saw as so powerful in their days. But for the Israelites, their monarchy was the assurance that God was in their land. They—and the neighboring peo-ples—believed in the divine right of kings.

Isaiah really felt, knew, and believed that God was the lord of history. Of course, many of the Israelites gave lip service to that in their temple, but in their hearts they would feel more secure with the Assyrians and the Egyptians looking after their interest. That is the human dilemma for many of us today: Shall we trust in the lord of history or the warlords of history? It has always been a tension between those who, on the one hand, feel that God has ordained them to subdue the world, and those who are purely pacifist on the other side. History is full of examples of both extremes. The purists will have nothing to do with the destiny of a land and withdraw. The activists cite their God-ordained goal to enter.

Isaiah can be accused of neither of these positions—he clearly tried to steer a center road between the two. But what he did most signifi-cantly was to set straight the relationship between the two: God is the lord of history. We trust not in our own design for history, but we can be used as a means by which God may bring that history to pass.

The Suffering Servant

52 ¹³ See, my servant shall prosper;
   he shall be exalted and lifted up,
   and shall be very high.

¹⁴ Just as there were many who were astonished at him
   —so marred was his appearance, beyond human semblance,
   and his form beyond that of mortals—

¹⁵ so he shall startle many nations;
   kings shall shut their mouths because of him;
for that which had not been told them they shall see,
   and that which they had not heard they shall contemplate.

Journey to Babylon

Sermon by Richard Murdoch | Omaha, NE | December 14, 1980

Often, we glibly pass over the Babylonian captivity of the Israelites as an event of history—something objective and factual. For us, it is merely a note in a history book, because we have invested no emotional energy in it. But for those whose Jewish traditions are respected, it was an experience like that of Egypt with the Passover, and like that of Nazi Germany with the Holocaust. And it has been put into ritual, always to be learned and experienced through ritual to the next generation.

We, as Americans, have been fortunate in our 200 years of national history. We have never been wrenched from this homeland of ours and taken to a land of foreign tongues, foreign cultures, and foreign servitude. Few of us know what it is like to be dragged from our homes by conquering invaders, parents ripped from children; taking only the clothes on our backs; leaving all our possessions to chance.

In 598 BCE, that is what happened to the educated, merchant, and ruling classes of Judah. Babylonians took the cream of the crop. They completely liquidated the assets of all those who could provide any leadership for the people. They were taken to Babylon to augment the highly technological culture which was developing there. It was, for all intents and purposes, a brain-drain. It left Judah in the hands of shepherds, fishermen, and small farmers. Tradesmen and artisans were all that remained of the once proud Israelites of the Southern kingdom. Eleven years later, Babylon returned again dragging them too, along with as many peasants as they could round up for the fantastic building programs in progress, including irrigation systems, public buildings, and the famous Hanging Gardens of Babylon.

Before the captivity was ended by Cyrus the Great, four generations had been deprived of their native land and their religion in exile. Fathers had been buried in the alien land, children had become great-grandfathers. And during this exile, the words of the prophet Isaiah offered the words of God as had his namesake Isaiah two centuries before. But there was a significance in the theme—instead of the throne of David in all its glory, it was a suffering servant—a servant not unlike what the exiles themselves knew.

His words were to wait and to be patient as the Lord would deliver them. But you can well imagine that four generations is longer than most would want to wait to return to their hometowns, houses, native grounds, and merchant stalls.

Let's consider the theme of patience from Isaiah's words. In English vocabulary, the word "patience" can be used as an adjective to mean a character trait. Then there is the second use of the word as a noun, "patient," which is someone a physician attends. Oftentimes, we wrongly state that the doctor healed the patient. Actually, a patient is one who waits for healing to occur by the bodily process, encouraged by a physician's skill; but it is the body that does the healing, and the person waiting for that healing to occur is rightly called a patient.

If you can transpose this thought, you will be able to catch Isaiah's theme, that of enduring suffering while the healing takes place. We have medications today which may cover the conscious pain while healing is taking place in bodily cells, organs, bones, muscles, and limbs. Discomfort takes place. In fact, we are not at ease, hence the word "dis-ease." In all healing, there is an element of suffering, which if not preceding healing, certainly maintains someplace in the healing process. As Benjamin Franklin printed in the little volume *Poor Richard's Almanac*: "No gain without pain."

Second Isaiah is a story about the necessity for suffering in order to heal the wounds that Israel had inflicted upon herself because of apostasy from Yahweh. The Israelites made bad alliances. They refused to see the moral decay from within. They rested on their laurels of the past. They trusted in their own goodness and righteousness and were caught by surprise—something prophets had repeatedly warned them about. They believed they were God's chosen people, so nothing could go wrong. But something did go wrong, because in their understanding of chosen-ness, they saw it as special privilege—which Yahweh never intended. Yahweh intended chosen-ness to mean special opportunity. Privilege is passive and opportunity is active. Privilege is bestowed, opportunities are grasped, sought out.

Second Isaiah sees the whole Babylon captivity as a growing experience—a growing back towards their God with a sense of opportunity. Their privilege has been removed; they are slaves in a foreign land. While probably not shackled, they are not free persons. They are under obligation to other masters, forced to walk barefooted, without sandals, as a sign of their slavery of spirit.

Isaiah says that waiting is part of the healing and suffering is part of the process of growing. That is often difficult for us to understand, isn't it? We all want microwave theology. Instead of all afternoon to defrost the frozen meat, presto, it's defrosted in seconds. Then, instead of cooking it for hours, we cook it for minutes. But the process of history is not to be microwaved: It thaws in its own time.

God's People Are Comforted

40 ²⁸ Have you not known? Have you not heard?
The LORD is the everlasting God,
 the Creator of the ends of the earth.
He does not faint or grow weary;
 his understanding is unsearchable.
²⁹ He gives power to the faint,
 and strengthens the powerless.

³⁰ Even youths will faint and be weary,
 and the young will fall exhausted;
³¹ but those who wait for the LORD shall renew their strength,
 they shall mount up with wings like eagles,
they shall run and not be weary,
 they shall walk and not faint.

Reflections of a theological tour host

Sermon by Richard Murdoch | East Lansing, MI | July 31, 1994

I want to introduce you to two friends who were significant in my life: Thornton Burgess and Richard Halliburton. And, unfortunately, I have never met them, so they will never know how they molded my life. They are what our school librarian called "book friends." Burgess was the author of a series of children's books which included the *Old Mother West Wind* series, published starting in 1910 (not that I was a child then), and a series in the 1940s, when I *was* a child, titled *Bedtime Story-Books*. My Aunt Connie in Royal Oak, Michigan, made a ritual of giving a book to my brother and me for each holiday or birthday. She believed that books were the "window to the world." My favorite, titled *The Adventures of Grandfather Frog*, has her inscription: "For Richard and Larry, Your mother and I liked these stories very much. Love, Aunt Connie, 1944."

The summer of 1944 was one of several during which my brother and I were sent unaccompanied on the train from Baltimore to Iowa because of the war scare and rationing. We took our books to keep us company on the trains and read them under the watchful eye of the porter our parents had engaged to get us off one train and onto another in Chicago, finally winding up at my grandparents' home in Iowa.

One evening, while the rain was playing its music on the tin roof of the sleeping porch, my grandmother saw me reading that book, and then went to her closet, pulling out more books that my aunt and my mother had read: *Old Mother West Wind*'s "How" and "Why" books.

The nights were long and hot for us kids on the sleeping porch. We could hear every creature, every patter of rain on the tin roof. We entertained ourselves with the how and why of the world of nature of which Mr. Burgess wrote. At our age, it was a time of discovery. My brother, who is the engineer in our family, took dibs on the "How" book at that early age. And I, being the philosopher-type, took the "Why" book— portents of things to come! Stories such as "Why Striped Chipmunk is

Proud of his Stripes" interested me more than "How It Happens Johnny Chuck Sleeps All Winter."

Christmas 1952 brought another book from Aunt Connie: *Richard Halliburton's Complete Book of Marvels*. I spent those winter months reading and rereading about the marvels of the Occident and the Orient, with my book friend, Mr. Halliburton, including the 10 Wonders of the Ancient World.

I'd like to share his tantalizing introduction, which was read by this farm-bound thirteen-year-old boy:

> *When I was a boy in school, my favorite subject was geography and my prized possession was a geography book. It was filled with pictures of the most exciting things. Sometimes I pretended I had a magic carpet and without bothering about tickets or money or farewells, I would skyrocket to New York or to Rome or to Grand Canyon or China across deserts and oceans and mountains and then suddenly to return back home in time for the school bell at recess. I often said to myself, "I wish my father, or somebody, would take me to all these wonderful places. If I ever grow up and have a son, we are going to travel together. I'll take him to Gibraltar and Jerusalem, the Andes and the Alps because I'll want my boy not only to study geography—I'd like him to live it too." Well, I'm grown up now. But as yet I haven't any son or daughter to go traveling with me. And so, in their places may I take you? Your friend, Richard Halliburton.*

Mr. Halliburton's book was timely because my Uncle John, who was a Baptist minister, was hosting a group that very summer to the World Baptist Alliance in Europe, with a side trip to the Holy Land. My family was abuzz with talk because he would be the first ever to take a foreign trip, as it was called in those days. When he returned, it was like having Halliburton's book come alive in our living room through slides, souvenirs, and stories.

While Uncle John's destination was a convention in Switzerland and a tour of traditional sites in the Holy Land, it became apparent that his greatest interest was not just in visiting destinations. It was in experiencing moments of discovery. I learned later that he shocked his

Baptist ministerial colleagues with slides of the Jordan River and artwork from early Christian churches showing that the familiar and traditional form of immersion for baptism was impossible in the Jordan River except at the traditional Mediterranean rainy season. Instead, John the Baptist no doubt took a shell, scooping up the water and pouring it over Jesus's head. Now, for a Southern Baptist preacher, this discovery was heresy. Everybody knew the "truth": Jesus was dunked by John the Baptist, and so was everybody else!

Those who travel to destinations or places are usually interested in the *where*. But *Old Mother West Wind*'s Thornton Burgess, Mr. Halliburton, and my uncle John instilled within me an inquiry—an obsession with the *why* of life. Some of you have traveled with me to Oberammergau, Germany, to the eclectic culture of Spain, and through the steps of St. Paul. You know how the ancient cultures of Phoenicia, Greece, and Rome fascinate me; how I've said that every opera and TV soap opera plot is a replay of before; and how, with exception of two gospels, Matthew and Mark, all other books of the New Testament, were written outside the Holy Land—that's twenty-five out of twenty-seven. To understand Christianity is to understand the Hellenistic world. And to travel is to live it.

I cannot ever forget the experience of being in Corinth, Greece, and looking up at that great mountain against which it is framed, understanding for the first time 1 Corinthians 13. "If I have faith enough to move a mountain—that mountain there—and don't have love, I am a sounding gong and a clanging cymbal. Faith is of little use." Or standing in the amphitheater at Ephesus, overlooking that vast shopping mall where St. Paul's preaching threatened the profits of the shopkeepers and hence he was rushed out of town by his friends, to keep him from reprisals by the local Chamber of Commerce. Travel, for me—as for Mr. Halliburton, Mr. Burgess, and my Uncle John—has been more than a destination. For me, it is discovering the very essence of the scripture, the *why* of humanity. Because what you've heard is not always the whole story!

As I have reflected upon my nine years with you here at this church, my role has not been unlike that of a tour host—and note that I say "host" not "guide." A guide leads you and tells you the significance of the place that you might visit. On the other hand, a host provides the framework in which you might find the significance for yourself.

Like a good host, I have not been so concerned about providing answers, but instead, I've focused on providing connections or situations in which you can find your own answers to your own questions. Of course, it's a lot easier to get a guide to lead you, but it doesn't last as long as the experience of discovering your own road signs and benchmarks. This September 18 will mark my thirtieth year of ordination to the professional ministry—a benchmark that comes all too soon.

But as I look back upon these nine years at this church and the twenty-one years divided between three other churches, I am no closer to answering the riddle of why God permits evil and suffering than I was before. But I do know that each time I try to explain, it gets more difficult, because it becomes more personal. As a theological tour host, I have not answered every question of life to everybody's satisfaction. I have instead—as your host—invited you to discover for yourself the wonders of both the tragedies and comedies of this journey called life.

Isaiah says that we should not grow weary. We should mount up with wings like eagles. We shall run and not be weary. I challenge you to continue to explore this world, always seeking the very essence—the why of humanity.

✡ Jeremiah 23:1-8 ✡
Restoration after Exile / The Righteous Branch of David

23 [1] Woe to the shepherds who destroy and scatter the sheep of my pasture! says the LORD. [2] Therefore thus says the LORD, the God of Israel, concerning the shepherds who shepherd my people: It is you who have scattered my flock, and have driven them away, and you have not attended to them. So I will attend to you for your evil doings, says the LORD. [3] Then I myself will gather the remnant of my flock out of all the lands where I have driven them, and I will bring them back to their fold, and they shall be fruitful and multiply. [4] I will raise up shepherds over them who will shepherd them, and they shall not fear any longer, or be dismayed, nor shall any be missing, says the LORD.

[5] The days are surely coming, says the LORD, when I will raise up for David a righteous Branch, and he shall reign as king and deal wisely, and shall execute justice and righteousness in the land. [6] In his days Judah will be saved and Israel will live in safety. And this is the name by which he will be called: "The LORD is our righteousness."

[7] Therefore, the days are surely coming, says the LORD, when it shall no longer be said, "As the LORD lives who brought the people of Israel up out of the land of Egypt," [8] but "As the LORD lives who brought out and led the offspring of the house of Israel out of the land of the north and out of all the lands where he had driven them." Then they shall live in their own land.

Between already and not yet

Sermon by Richard Murdoch | East Lansing, MI | November 13, 1988

Two weeks ago Tuesday, on November 1, to be exact, I walked through the door of my friendly neighborhood store to drop off some film. I was stunned when I was greeted with a full array of Christmas decorations, because in my hand were undeveloped pictures of the bright sunshine and flowers of early fall in Louisiana. How could it be?

I was being told by my eyes, "Christmas is already here!" but my confused head said, "But it's not yet Thanksgiving." I would assume that I was not the only customer who had that experience, because the local papers carried several letters soon after to the editor on the same subject. Moreover, in idle conversation, several people mentioned having had the same reaction as mine. And it may be that you, too, have responded with the same bewilderment that November 1 is just too early for tinsel and bells.

Not too long ago, Christmas shopping began with the Thanksgiving Day parade that ended in presenting Santa Claus. We came to expect a certain orderly flow of the holiday season. Now Thanksgiving gets lost in the shuffle, and our friendly letter carriers bring us Christmas catalogs even in the midst of the August heat. The orderly progression of the calendar means nothing to retailers for whom Christmas gifting is the difference between profit and loss, between staying in business and going out of business. How we wish that life might return to its orderly progression, instead of jolting out of one season into another before we have been able to finish the first properly.

We could do that, of course. We could throw the catalog back into the face of the one who delivered it with, "Here take it back. It's too early. When it's the proper time, bring it back!" We could boycott and picket the store with signs saying, "Unfair to Thanksgiving." We could cancel our magazine and paper subscriptions with a note of protest stating, "When you start to advertise Christmas at the right time, I'll resume reading your publication." There are definitely some actions that we could take to reorder our lives in the way which we remember. But I think few of us will.

Why won't we? Because deep down in our hearts, the order which we desire is a fantasy that we enjoy only in our minds. Our life experiences, for the most part, are exactly opposite. One event bumps into another throughout the seasons of life. There is no clear beginning and no clear ending. Diapers give way to training pants, but it's hard to say when. Somehow, nursery school turns into kindergarten and middle school evolves into high school—but don't ask a parent to name the date. Romance turns into passion and passion into love, but don't ask a couple when, because they won't agree upon a date.

In real life, seasons bump into each other.

No matter how flexible one plans, it is impossible to include every eventuality. Elie Wiesel, the celebrated Jewish author, tells of a faithful rabbi in Jerusalem who tried to do just that. When his daughter was to be married, the nuptial agreement was brought to him for his approval and signature. He stunned his daughter by taking a pen and adding these words before his signature. "This agreement is null and void should the Messiah come before the wedding." The daughter left, feeling relieved but anxious. The rabbi, retiring to his bed for the night, left instructions with his servant to awake him if the trumpet sounded, just as he had instructed for a score of years. In the early morning haze, a trumpet sounded from the Mount of Olives, blown by a prankster. The servant immediately woke the rabbi, who, wiping the sleep out of his eyes peered out the window to see a driver beating his donkey. He went back to bed, muttering to himself, "I don't have to see anything else. So long as people still beat their donkeys, the world is not redeemed, the Messiah has not yet come."

Jeremiah the Prophet says a shocking thing in Chapter 23, verses 7 and 8:

> *7 Therefore, the days are surely coming, says the LORD, when it shall no longer be said, "As the LORD lives who brought the people of Israel up out of the land of Egypt," 8 but "As the LORD lives who brought out and led the offspring of the house of Israel out of the land of the north and out of all the lands where he had driven them." Then they shall live in their own land.*

As you can recognize, the place changes in this verse. Egypt is changed to "the north." In all of the worship and theology of Israel, God's action in leading the people out of Egypt (called the Exodus Event) was the proof of power and blessing. The Exodus was commemorated in the most important worship service called Passover. The Exodus led to the giving of the Ten Commandments and the Torah, the written basis for Judaism. The ordering of Judaism for a thousand years was founded and passed with the affirmation that it was the God who brought them out of Egypt that made all things happen.

But Jeremiah upset that. He said, "The day is coming when that will be no longer true. The people will swear by the God who brings Israel up out of the North Country!" "Heresy! A thousand years we have been wrong?" they would have cried. They would have been as confused as Roman Catholics were in our day when they were suddenly told that eating fish on Friday no longer has merit and that St. Christopher was no longer a saint who could protect travelers when his statue is perched upon a dashboard!

The world is rushing ahead of itself, and we're caught in between. Or, as philosopher Ernst Bloch states in *The Future of Hope*:

> *The world is regulated by forces of opposition from yesterday and the day before yesterday. To make matters worse, the old does not want to pass away, the new does not wish to come into being.*

We are not the only ones who are between *already* and *not yet*. The bumping of life's seasons into each other—the confusing of the old order and the new—is an experience very common to humanity. More of our days are spent living between the beginning and the ending of events. Our time spent in initiating and closure is far less than our days in the middle, yet we are ill prepared for it.

Many people give up on religion. "What good has it done?" they ask. Take, for example, the Middle East. Jewish fighting against Jewish, Christian fighting against Christian, Muslim fighting against Muslim, Christian fighting against Muslim against Jewish.

Another example reminds us of religion's ineffectiveness: "My only child was taken by a strange and unexplained illness. Not a prayer to spare him was answered!" Someone else might tell you, "If all the real estate and holding of churches were sold—with true people meeting in homes like the Amish—there would be enough money to house and feed every homeless and hungry person in this country and Canada." Finally, we are reminded by some people that they "don't go to church because people who do are hypocrites. They don't practice on Monday what they read about on Sunday!"

And of course, the answer can be *yes* to all of the above. It's all true. But it's true because we live between the times. The season of love runs into the season of hate. The season of healing runs into the season of death. The season of charity runs into the season of greed. The season of grace runs into the season of sin. While peace is encouraged between the super powers with arms limitation pacts, war is waged in the Middle East with weapons bought from the same!

We sometimes have a reason to be discouraged and a reason to feel hopeless. We even have reasons to feel cynical towards faith, if we expect the world to be orderly and if we look for completed events that will last forever. Did you see the television interview this past Veterans Day with three World War I veterans? When asked the difference between World War I and other wars, a ninety-one-year-old gentleman answered: "The difference of our war is that we fought for a cause, not against a people. We believed we were fighting a war to end all wars. We were on a mission for all times; that's why my entire engineering class left Princeton to fight. But just because it didn't end war, doesn't mean we died for naught."

Each two steps ahead and one step backward comprises the opportunity for hope between two points in time. Just because not everything is completed nor all promises come true, is no justification to deny that it will happen in the future. We live between the times, and we are comfortable with that because we have faith, not because God brought Israel up and out of Egypt, and not because God brought Israel up and out of the North Country, but because God continually brings us up and out into life today.

Hananiah Opposes Jeremiah and Dies

28 ^{1} In that same year, at the beginning of the reign of King Zedekiah of Judah,

in the fifth month of the fourth year, the prophet Hananiah son of Azzur, from Gibeon, spoke to me in the house of the LORD, in the presence of the priests and all the people, saying, ^{2} "Thus says the LORD of hosts, the God of Israel: I have broken the yoke of the king of Babylon. ^{3} Within two years I will bring back to this place all the vessels of the LORD's house, which King Nebuchadnezzar

of Babylon took away from this place and carried to Babylon. ^{4} I will also bring back to this place King Jeconiah son of Jehoiakim of Judah, and all the exiles

from Judah who went to Babylon, says the LORD, for I will break the yoke of the king of Babylon."

^{5} Then the prophet Jeremiah spoke to the prophet Hananiah in the presence of the priests and all the people who were standing in the house of the LORD;

^{6} and the prophet Jeremiah said, "Amen! May the LORD do so; may the LORD fulfill the words that you have prophesied, and bring back to this place from Babylon the vessels of the house of the LORD, and all the exiles. ^{7} But listen now to this word that I speak in your hearing and in the hearing of all the people.

^{8} The prophets who preceded you and me from ancient times prophesied war, famine, and pestilence against many countries and great kingdoms. ^{9} As for the prophet who prophesies peace, when the word of that prophet comes true, then it will be known that the LORD has truly sent the prophet."

Which prophet is right?

Sermon by Richard Murdoch | East Lansing, MI | August 24, 1986

I have a friend of mine whose vocation is career guidance. As an opening to his interviews with people making mid-life career adjustments, he states with amazing accuracy that there are only two jobs that consistently pay well for consistently unreliable information: weather forecasters and economists! Most all other jobs only last as long as the employee can produce positive and reliable results or products.

You can easily tell if a product is reliable. My mother has been buying Morton salt for 60 years. It's been right for her because "when it rains it pours." She's tried other brands. Some work, some don't. But going down the grocery aisles, her hand has always reached for the blue round box with the yellow umbrella and the girl. No name was needed to identify it. We knew which product was "right."

It's not quite as easy to tell whether a result is reliable. Consider the practice of teaching grammar. My youngest brother and I are eleven years apart. We both went to the same high school. I diagrammed sentences and learned parts of speech until I was blue in the face. He, on the other hand, learned grammar contextually, by reading literature. The teacher would draw the students' attention to correct and incorrect paragraphs. Students would then imitate the correct style by composing their own paragraphs. One of us learned by analyzing and the other learned by synthesizing. I am not sure whether you would be able to tell from our letters or from our verbal communication which method was more effective. In a sense, both methods were right because we can both read and write English. But through my daughters' education, I sense that the debate is still being pursued in pedagogical circles today.

In the more weighty issues of life, persons charged with the government of a country, the management of a national corporation, the direction of a religious denomination, or the fostering of foreign trade are often selected on their rightness in analyzing or forecasting what ought to be done. They may be appointed, elected, or ascend into their positions. But with responsibility goes the sense of being right in the face of challengers representing another sense of rightness that is different from the persons in power.

For example, who is really right in South Africa? The state department follows its administration's leadership in a program of constructive non-engagement, which is a form of moral encouragement to slowly dismantle apartheid. The Congress wants to move in a more active form of moral encouragement by certain economic sanctions. The business community sells assets to subsidiaries held on paper by South African nationals and the economy backfires on the very people that need to be helped. Social historians, diplomatic historians, economists, political leaders, philosophers, ethicists, religious bodies, banks, and even travel agencies have entered the foray of whose way is right to discipline this unruly child of Colonialism, whose ways conjure up the 100-year past of two world super-powers: America's slavery era and Russia's czarist era.

Any claim to rightness is best supported by some authority. It may be the authority of elected office: "See how many people voted for me, I represent the majority. The majority is right!" Or it may be the claim of analyzing the data: "These conditions prevailed in 1861 in America and in 1867 in Russia, therefore we can expect that given the same circumstances, the same result will occur in 1986 in South Africa."

Or it may be the claim of divine knowledge, by appealing to either the scriptures or specific divine revelation: "Slavery is mentioned in the Bible; therefore it is a fact of creation." Or a Moses-like prophet might claim, "The word of the Lord came to me in a dream that a great war will arise among the white masters of South Africa, unless they let my people go!" Or one might claim economic and political disaster (based upon expert studies of a blue-ribbon committee that a neutral body might volunteer) such as, "In the name of world order, the whole precious metal market will be ruined and all currencies with it, unless we proceed slowly!"

So, who is the right prophet about South Africa? Who is the right prophet in Judah? Is the only difference in the question the year: fourth century BCE or twentieth century CE?

Most people thought Hananiah was the right prophet, and no doubt so would you. He spoke words of encouragement and hope in an election year, so the prophet spoke hope for those left in Jerusalem. Relying upon a divine revelation from God himself, he prophesied the Babylonian masters would be defeated! The Israelites will come home from their exile! Yahweh is a strong god! He is a powerful god! God is in his temple! His sacred gold and silver objects taken to Babylon in captivity will be brought back to adorn his house again!

Hananiah stated all would be done with the help of the Egyptians, neighbors with whom the Judeans would court and favor through Zedekiah, king in Jerusalem. Hananiah (court prophet and prophet to the administration of Zedekiah) had a responsibility—discharge his commission with great aplomb. The temple crowd at worship outside was awed and encouraged by this foreign policy announcement. The Jerusalem stock and bond market was poised for a bull run *until* pesky little Jeremiah (from that dump of a town Anathoth) stood up declaring he had the right word from God on this Egyptian alliance against Babylon!

Jeremiah was not with the in-crowd. He was an outsider when it came to the courtly ways of Zedekiah's group of prophets, but he was not unknown. His prophetic utterances were always crowd-getters due to his visual aids. And this time was no exception. He wore a wooden yoke around his neck—as if he were an ox—to make his point. His message was from the very same God who had spoken to Hananiah. But it was different this time: "Don't join the Egyptians in this alliance against Babylon. If you do, the cure is worse than the disease. Instead of being free of bondage, you'll be in deeper bondage. Bide your time. Babylon is a place of penance for your sins. Build homes; take marriage partners; have children; establish cities. When your penance is over, God himself will deliver you without the aid of anyone else!"

Hananiah was not pleased. He stormed out of his special place of announcement—maybe even a pulpit—and proceeded to break the wooden yoke from Jeremiah. Hananiah announced that God had broken the yoke of Babylon just as he had Jeremiah's. But once the scuffle was over and Jeremiah had recovered what dignity he could muster, Jeremiah flatly denied the yoke was broken. He took an iron one to make his point!

Now, if you were in that temple crowd, worshipping and hearing this press conference on foreign policy (our modern idea of separation between faith and politics was not known in that age!), bewilderment would certainly set in. Which prophet brings the right word from God—

the official administration or the challenger from the country? Or is it the prophet who speaks hope for the future, the one who lifts the flagged spirits? Or is it the prophet who speaks of endurance and suffering; pain and trial; slowdown and thriftiness? Is it the one who speaks for the majority of people? Or the one who speaks from the committed minority?

Doesn't the dilemma sound familiar? Doesn't it sound modern? Doesn't it sound personal?

You have probably already guessed who had the right word from God. Jeremiah. In effect, he said it was better to be Babylonian than dead. Those who made the alliance with Egypt—those who said better be dead than Babylonian—*were* dead, including both Zedekiah and Hananiah. Jerusalem was completely leveled by Nebuchadnezzar. There was not a stone left standing, nor food stored in a single larder when he finished. There was not even a temple to bring the sacred relics back to when God himself was ready to deliver them (as Jeremiah had prophesied). Jeremiah survived. Hananiah did not.

So we have the first test of a "right" word from God. You don't know who speaks the right word until time has passed to prove the word. Again, take the weather forecaster and the economist. You'll know if the weather prediction is correct only after it has happened. You will know if the economist is right only after the year's annual growth and inflation indicators are available.

The second test of a right word from God lies in the integrity of the one who speaks. Where is the self-interest and motivation? Hananiah had a position to maintain, so people might have been a bit suspicious about his integrity from looking at his actions. About as suspicious as you would be of the weather forecaster who predicts a sunny day, but is seen sticking an umbrella under his coat. Or the economist who predicts a bull market for the next several months, but is seen trading his stock in for gold bullion. Jeremiah had nothing to lose in exile—Hananiah would lose everything.

The third and last test of a right word from God lies in its context. How does it fit in with the values we associate with God's kingdom: love, justice, mercy, and peace? Can deeds and words of hate bring love? Can deeds and words of vengeance bring mercy? Can a process of prejudice and discrimination bring justice? Can peace be brought by violent methods? Is a peace wrought by the sword really peace? Is love involuntarily forced by the threat of punishment really love? Is mercy extracted by emotional blackmail really mercy? Is justice held in place by pitting special interest groups against each other with unequal favors really justice? The context of Jeremiah was that of penance. Israel needed time for reflection and penance in Babylon for her unfaithfulness to God. (Hananiah said Israel was saved; it was the heathen Babylon that needed chastisement by God, not Israel!)

Which is the right prophet who speaks the right word of God from the fourth century BCE to the twentieth century CE? The one whose word stands the test of time, whose actions speak of integrity, and whose word is within the context of the eternal values of God's kingdom.

Context:
More History

Ezra – Nehemiah – Esther

During the years of exile in Babylonia (597-538 BCE), the history of the nation of Israel became detached from the geographical land, and the formal religion of Judaism began. At this time, people were remaining loyal to their God, but the type of worship and culture had begun to change, or adapt. It now needed to be mobile.

On came a resurgence in looking at the traditions of the faith. The Torah was edited and polished into a central text for the people, to bring them—and keep them—together.

Then, in 539 BCE, Cyrus of Persia overthrew the Babylonians, and the post-exilic era began. In the Bible, this period is presented in the Books of Ezra and Nehemiah.

Ezra/Nehemiah

(In the early scriptures, these two books actually form a single book. In later Christian Bibles, they were split and named after the main character in each book.)

In stark contrast to the Assyrian and Babylonian kings, Cyrus advocated a policy of religious and cultural independence. So, eventually the exiled were allowed to return home to Jerusalem.

Jerusalem was now part of the Persian province of Yehud (Aramaic for Judah). In these books, we follow the Jewish leaders Zerubbabel, Joshua, Ezra, and Nehemiah as they attempted to reconstruct what had been lost, while maintaining harmony with Persian policies.

This period is known as the Restoration, or Second Temple Period, because of the reconstruction of the temple and Jerusalem. Many challenges arose, including hostile surrounding communities, the results of intermarriage, and different views of what constituted "Jewish identity."

Reforms were also instituted to rebuild the people's faith. To rally the people, there was a celebration and public reading of the Torah (to renew the Mosaic covenant).

Esther

During this same time period, the Book of Esther presents the story of Jewish people remaining in Persian Babylon. Read the sermon for the full story.

Meanwhile...

In Asia, new traditions erupted onto the scene. The *Tao Te Ching* was penned by Lao Tzu (a wise old scholar and keeper of the Chinese imperial archives according to one tradition). It features thoughts on the natural way of the universe, urging its readers to follow the *Tao* ("way" or "path") rather than the will of a specific creator deity.

In China, Confucius began teaching an ideology based on the importance of five main virtues: humaneness, righteousness, ritual propriety, knowledge, and integrity. His followers collected the teachings in a book known as the *Analects*, which would influence Chinese politics, education, and culture for more than two thousand years.

And then Siddhartha Gautama appeared on the scene in India, shedding his royal upbringing for the path of Nirvana, and brought Buddhism to his students. Learning the Four Noble Truths and the Noble Eightfold Path, the students strove to find the middle way and ultimately liberation from attachment to both matter and thoughts. The Dhammapada distills the essence of his teachings in a written form.

Across the world, Mayan cities started to appear in Mexico. Influenced by the Olmecs, these city people worshiped a pantheon of gods, each of which had a benevolent side and a contrasting malevolent side. For the Maya, science, life, and religion were interdependent, leading to impressive systems of astronomy and math.

Persia invaded Greece, kicking off the Greco-Persian Wars. Lasting over fifty years, the brutal battles have provided sensational content for bestselling books and hit movies, as well as the inspiration for the marathon run. In the end, the Greeks were able to hold off the Persians at the battle of Thermopylae and force them out. Persia would go its own way, as Greece entered its Golden Age.

Not too far away, the Roman Republic was established and set in motion its expansion over the Mediterranean world.

Haman's Downfall / Mordecai's Advancement

7 [1] So the king [Ahasuerus of Persia] and Haman [a high-ranking advisor under the king] went in to feast with Queen Esther [the Jewish queen of Ahasuerus]. [2] On the second day, as they were drinking wine, the king again said to Esther, "What is your petition, Queen Esther? It shall be granted you. And what is your request? Even to the half of my kingdom, it shall be fulfilled."

[3] Then Queen Esther answered, "If I have won your favor, O king, and if it pleases the king, let my life be given me—that is my petition—and the lives of my people—that is my request. [4] For we have been sold, I and my people, to be destroyed, to be killed, and to be annihilated. If we had been sold merely as slaves, men and women, I would have held my peace; but no enemy can compensate for this damage to the king."

[5] Then King Ahasuerus said to Queen Esther, "Who is he, and where is he, who has presumed to do this?" [6] Esther said, "A foe and enemy, this wicked Haman!" Then Haman was terrified before the king and the queen.

[7] The king rose from the feast in wrath and went into the palace garden, but Haman stayed to beg his life from Queen Esther, for he saw that the king had determined to destroy him.

[8] When the king returned from the palace garden to the banquet hall, Haman had thrown himself on the couch where Esther was reclining; and the king said, "Will he even assault the queen in my presence, in my own house?" As the words left the mouth of the king, they covered Haman's face.

[9] Then Harbona, one of the eunuchs in attendance on the king, said, "Look, the very gallows that Haman has prepared for Mordecai [Esther's uncle], whose word saved the king, stands at Haman's house, fifty cubits high." And the king said, "Hang him on that."

[10] So they hanged Haman on the gallows that he had prepared for Mordecai. Then the anger of the king abated.

Esther's special place

Sermon by Richard Murdoch | Rye, NY | September 28, 1997

As many of you know, I served as a ship's chaplain on a Greek ship a year ago during the month of September. Not only was it an exhilarating experience visiting the ancient wonders of the Aegean Sea with its classical and Christian sites scattered throughout its islands and coastal cities, but it was also a humbling one. Humbling, because most any traveler to that part of the world quickly realizes that America is but a fleeting speck of 200 years in the history of the world; that our technology and art is reflected in what ancients discovered. Personally, I also quickly came to realize that Presbyterians (being on the other side of the world's religious fence) are a minority.

I will hasten to add that I am sure that none of those with whom I ministered probably ever detected this last self-revelation. In fact, several times over, those with whom I ministered in worship and pastoral visitation were more than solicitous to offer my name to their bishops and rabbis to fill vacancies in their parishes and synagogues!

As you may not know, a ship's master oversees the religious responsibility of his passengers at sea. There are no bishops, no presbyteries, no dioceses, no synods, and no religious executives over the seas. A ship's captain, and especially a Greek one, takes this very seriously.

At daily morning Eucharist, Friday evening Shabbat, and Sunday afternoon ecumenical services for four weeks, I met no more than half a dozen Presbyterians (or those married to such) throughout the entire month that included four week-long cruises of six hundred passengers each. To put this into context, my leaving for Greece coincided with the denominational media's accompanying furor of the General Assembly's Amendment "B," which dealt with the place of homosexual members in the Presbyterian denomination. Colleagues wrote and spoke often with dire predictions about the Presbyterian Church splitting in half. The discussion included serious questioning, depending on the outcome. Would there even be a Presbyterian denomination in 2020? Maybe after four hundred years, we would be obsolete and irrelevant if not actually self-destructing.

It struck me at the time that should the Presbyterian denomination indeed self-destruct over this issue, it probably would receive little less than a passing notice in the contemporary newspapers of the world and would earn hardly more than a footnote in church history. After all, what are a mere two and half million Presbyterians compared to hundreds of millions of Roman Catholics, Eastern Orthodox, and assorted Protestants? We're just a couple of small stars in the Milky Way of the religious galaxy. What influence do we have in the world as a minority compared to the vast majority of the others? What influence do we have bringing the kingdom of heaven upon earth? Why not just retire to the corner into our own little world?

No doubt, the Jewish people in Persia during the time of Esther were tempted to do the same. Theirs was a small group who remained after the great exodus of people in Persia who returned to Palestine under Ezra and Nehemiah. Set free to leave Persia four generations after the great Babylonian captivity, a few remained in Persia instead of joining the crowds returning to their own sacred Promised Land. We learn in the book of Esther that one of those remaining in Persia was a man named Mordecai, under whose charge was his niece, Esther.

Esther has a special place in Judaism. It is because of her and her uncle that those of Jewish faith celebrate Purim, a festival in late February or early March. The book named after her also has a special place. It is the only book of the Bible that makes no explicit mention of God's existence, action, or intervention. It lacks even the name of God. In other words, there is nothing godly about it.

You will forgive the irreverence of a somewhat contemporary translation, but I assure you that what I share with you from pages 44 and 45 from a book entitled *Uppity Women of Ancient Times* by Vicki Leon accurately gives the explicit story line from the complete book of Esther in the context in which it was written. But what it does not do is delve into the implicit theological implication of the story.

About 460 B.C., in a worldwide star search for a virgin with cover-girl looks for King Artaxerxes of Persia, Esther's name (which means "star") came up. Was this fate? No, Hollywood: Her real name was Myrtle. Myrtle lived with her uncle Morty in Susa; both were part of the Jewish population who remained in Persia after the exile. The star-makers spent months lubing Esther with myrrh and other oils, the standard purification ritual, while Morty advised: "Smile, and for God's sake, don't tell him you're Jewish."

At last, Esther auditioned for the king, who liked what he saw, and, bingo, she was in... eventually (the Bible says she didn't get the ring for seven years). Despite new family ties, Morty got into a beef with the king's right-hand man, Haman, who decided to get rid of this upstart and his tribe as well. Using the king's seal, Haman issued a bogus order to destroy all Jews on a certain date. A panicky Morty leaned on Esther to lobby her man; she waffled until he said, "Star or not, you won't escape just because you're in the fancy house, Myrtle."

And the rest we know from today's reading. Esther earned her special place in Judaism and the scriptures. While it is true that the festival of Purim remembers Esther for saving her people from destruction, these Hebrews are not—in usual biblical style—led back to the Promised Land, or to freedom and prosperity as was Abraham, Moses, Ezra, or Nehemiah. Instead, they stay put where they are. They remain in Persia, a foreign and "pagan (aka not Jewish)" land. The actions of Esther and Mordecai force the Persians to create a space on the other side of the fence, where they live as a minority.

As I have shared before, my mother's family was Swedish. When they immigrated to this country, they settled around a small town in northwestern Iowa, which later was assigned a rather un-Swedish name of Burnside by the railway company. It was all Swede—one church, one school, one store, one station, and one post office. A town close to it was all Norwegian, another Danish, and another Finnish.

When my Aunt moved from Burnside to a larger town, she moved from a homogeneous culture to a diverse one. Dayton had "diversity" (as my aunt remarked one time). They were mostly Scandinavian, and the Swedes were in the majority. But when my aunt moved in later life to the county seat, Ft. Dodge, she moved from being part of the majority to becoming part of the minority. To her, Ft. Dodge was not only diverse (meaning Scandinavian), but it was "multi-cultural" (meaning Roman Catholic, German, African-American, Mediterranean, Pentecostal, and Baptist). Her Swedish Lutheran culture was no longer a majority influence as it had been in her younger years (when the pastor of their Lutheran church was always an honorary member of the village board). She never felt at home in Ft. Dodge; she didn't know what to make of living as a minority.

Minority is defined by its context. The question is always, "which minority in relationship to what larger space?" In relationship to the world's population, most of us in this room, being Caucasian, are definitely in the minority of the world's population. Yet if you narrow that space to the boundaries of the North American continent, Caucasians are in the majority. In the religious space of the world, we Protestants are a definite minority. Yet if one narrows the space to within North America, Protestants still have a majority.[1]

But there is not even one of us in this congregation who has not had the experience of being a minority. It doesn't have to be physical space, it can be mental space. How many times have you voiced a minority opinion or held a minority viewpoint, only to find that it put you on the other side of the fence? Most of us are uncomfortable thinking about being in the minority. There is a certain feeling of powerlessness that causes us to slide into the corner on the one hand or feel victimized on the other.

Last week, at the annual meeting of the American Association of Family and Marriage Therapists, Rev. Jesse Jackson addressed the group on the theme of racism and healing families. Receiving an applause that echoed the halls afterwards, he told of talking with a young man about his inability to stay out of truancy. I will paraphrase as best I can his example: When Rev. Jackson asked him about his lack of interest in school, the man responded, "You know Reverend, I do drugs because I have to have something to make me feel good because nothing has ever gone right for me. My dad ran off when I was a little boy, my mother did not have time to pay attention to me while working. There wasn't any money for the things other kids had, so I didn't really fit in at school. There was no space for me. So I left home. I joined a gang because they made a place for me." Rev. Jackson responded, "You know son, lots of people, even me, had exactly the same experience.

But you can't blame your life on other people all your life; you'll have to grow up sometime. Why not start now before it's too late?"

Neither did Mordecai and Esther shrink nor retreat nor submit to "victim-thinking." Instead, they sought each opportunity to make space for their place as a minority. When Mordecai discovered a plot against King Xerxes,[2] for the good of the majority, he shared the information, which preserved the rule of the king. When Xerxes was looking for another wife, Mordecai was not embarrassed to groom his own niece for the position, regardless of her dubious chances as an outsider. Changes in society are never made by a majority. Changes come from the other side of the fence, the minority.

It was a minority of vassals who raised the question of capitalism against the landed aristocracy. It was a minority of democratic thinkers that questioned the divine right of monarchies. It was a minority of colonial business entrepreneurs who raised the question of taxation against King George. It was a minority of abolitionists who raised the question against slavery. It was a minority of civil rights leaders who raised the question of equality of public accommodations. It was a minority of college students who raised questions about the morality and legality of the Viet Nam war. Without minorities, majorities destroy themselves with power and repression as in the great Inquisitions that almost destroyed all of Europe.

We need to become comfortable and make effective use of our role as minorities to enhance the world in which we live. Mordecai and Esther did; so can we!

[1] Written in 1997. According to the Pew Forum on Religion & Public Life's *U.S. Religious Landscape Survey* (conducted in 2014):
- 70.6% of Americans are Christian. Protestants comprise the largest portion of that percentage (46.5%) followed by Catholics (20.8%), Mormon (1.6%), Jehovah's Witness (0.8%), Orthodox (0.5%) and Other Christian (0.4%)
- 22.8% of Americans identify as "unaffiliated," up 6.7% from the last survey in 2007
- 5.9% of Americans identify as a non-Christian religion including Jewish (1.9%), Muslim (0.9%), Buddhist (0.7%), Hindu (0.7%)

[2] King Ahasuerus (as referred to in the Bible) is usually identified as Xerxes of Persia

Context:
Poetry & Wisdom Writings

Job – Psalms – Proverbs – Ecclesiastes – Song of Solomon

Even if you've never picked up a Bible, odds are you are familiar with many verses in these books. They permeate our culture from song lyrics, to sayings in fortune cookies and stickers on car bumpers.

The writings are from various times, and are independent of each other—they do not form a cohesive collection. They vary from the other books so far, since they don't deal specifically with the nation of Israel.

Job, Proverbs, and Ecclesiastes are often categorized as wisdom books. They do not claim any divine revelation or historical timeline, but rather deal with the trials and tribulations of the human condition. Psalms and Song of Solomon provide the poetry.

Job

Job is the primary character, a righteous man who challenges the belief that there is a moral world order. He feels he is afflicted by God, and is being treated unfairly. He questions why God allows injustice and evil. The format is three speeches on suffering, where we see him truly hit bottom.

Psalms

The name Psalms comes from a Greek book *Psalmoi,* meaning songs played on a stringed instrument. In Hebrew, the book is referred to as *Tehillim* (praises). Early Jewish and Christian traditions attributed the psalms to David. However, modern scholars believe it is more of an anthology, comprised of many songs that were written by various people at different times and places over a thousand years.

There are many types of psalms included. Praises (or hymns) are upbeat and contain praise for God. Laments (or petitions) are more moody. They generally begin with a cry to God followed by a complaint by an individual or a community. You'll also find psalms of confession, and psalms for festival or royal use.

Proverbs

The Book of Proverbs contains observations, or statements of wisdom, based on all kinds of things. They aren't specific to any particular culture, but are more like practical wisdom you would receive in a family, handed down by generations. Often comparing a familiar aspect of life to a moral or spiritual truth, they provide directions for a happy life. The most common format is a two-line sentence where the parts have some sort of parallel to each other. For example, "As iron sharpens iron, so one person sharpens another." (Proverbs 27:17)

Ecclesiastes

Often translated as "preacher" or "teacher," from the Hebrew *qoheleth* and Greek *ecclesiastes*, this book was one of the most controversial, and debated fiercely as to whether it should be contained in various canons. It has a pessimistic tone, but, ultimately, that provides the basis for the overarching idea that humans live in a world in which they have no control. From this book comes the famous lyric: "To everything there is a season." ("Turn, turn, turn" was added later!)

Song of Solomon

Hands down, the sauciest of the Bible's books, Song of Solomon is also its only love poem. The author is unknown, but it is traditionally attributed to Solomon. Some Jewish readers see it as an allegorical account of love between God and Israel. Conversely, some Christians use it as a representation of the love between Christ and the church. Some readers (and scholars) state that it is simply what it appears to be—a love poem.

✡ Job 38-40 selections ✡
The Lord Answers Job

38 [1] Then the LORD answered Job out of the whirlwind:

[2] "Who is this that darkens counsel by words without knowledge?
[3] Gird up your loins like a man,
  I will question you, and you shall declare to me.

[4] "Where were you when I laid the foundation of the earth?
  Tell me, if you have understanding.
[5] Who determined its measurements—surely you know!
  Or who stretched the line upon it?
[6] On what were its bases sunk,
  or who laid its cornerstone
[7] when the morning stars sang together
  and all the heavenly beings shouted for joy?

[8] "Or who shut in the sea with doors
  when it burst out from the womb?—
[9] when I made the clouds its garment,
  and thick darkness its swaddling band,
[10] and prescribed bounds for it,
  and set bars and doors,
[11] and said, 'Thus far shall you come, and no farther,
  and here shall your proud waves be stopped'?

[12] "Have you commanded the morning since your days began,
  and caused the dawn to know its place,
[13] so that it might take hold of the skirts of the earth,
  and the wicked be shaken out of it?
[14] It is changed like clay under the seal,
  and it is dyed like a garment.
[15] Light is withheld from the wicked,
  and their uplifted arm is broken."

...

39 [26] "Is it by your wisdom that the hawk soars,
  and spreads its wings toward the south?
[27] Is it at your command that the eagle mounts up
  and makes its nest on high?
[28] It lives on the rock and makes its home

in the fastness of the rocky crag.
²⁹ From there it spies the prey;
　　its eyes see it from far away.
³⁰ Its young ones suck up blood;
　　and where the slain are, there it is."

40 ¹And the LORD said to Job:

² "Shall a faultfinder contend with the Almighty?
　　Anyone who argues with God must respond."

³ Then Job answered the LORD:

⁴ "See, I am of small account; what shall I answer you?
　　I lay my hand on my mouth.
⁵ I have spoken once, and I will not answer;
　　twice, but will proceed no further."

⁶ Then the LORD answered Job out of the whirlwind:

⁷ "Gird up your loins like a man;
　　I will question you, and you declare to me.
⁸ Will you even put me in the wrong?
　　Will you condemn me that you may be justified?
⁹ Have you an arm like God,
　　and can you thunder with a voice like his?

¹⁰ "Deck yourself with majesty and dignity;
　　clothe yourself with glory and splendor.
¹¹ Pour out the overflowings of your anger,
　　and look on all who are proud, and abase them.
¹² Look on all who are proud, and bring them low;
　　tread down the wicked where they stand.
¹³ Hide them all in the dust together;
　　bind their faces in the world below.
¹⁴ Then I will also acknowledge to you
　　that your own right hand can give you victory."

Who needs God?

Sermon by Richard Murdoch | East Lansing, MI | February 25, 1990

To say that we need to eat is quite different than we want to eat. The former indicates recognition of a physical condition to be satisfied for survival; the latter indicates a desire or a wish to fulfill an expectation. To say that we need God is to admit a deficiency.

Rabbi Harold Kushner, the spiritual leader of a synagogue in the Boston area, discusses this topic in another of his books making the *New York Times* bestseller list. His first venture in publishing five years ago explored the age-old question posed by Job: "Why do the righteous suffer?" The good rabbi stated it just a bit differently: *When Bad Things Happen to Good People.* His book was listed for over twelve weeks.

But his second book did not stay on the *Times'* list more than a week. Those who read the *New York Times* advertisements for $10,000 broaches by Tiffany may have found that the book hit a bit too close to home. The rabbi addressed rampant materialism in his second book, *When All You've Ever Wanted Isn't Good Enough.*

But now he's produced another bestseller, *Who Needs God?* You can find somewhat the same wisdom in the Books of Psalms and Job (from which Rabbi Kushner quotes liberally). However, he organizes the information a bit more handily, and that is worth our consideration.

The book's theological bias is implicit in the title. Humans need God for seven reasons, each of which is conveniently discussed in seven chapters, preceded by an introductory chapter, and followed by a summary chapter.

1. We need God to make sense of creation.
2. We need God because we need a soul as well as a body.
3. We need God because we need morality.
4. We need God because we need companionship.
5. We need God because we need to be relieved of guilt.

6. We need God because we need to communicate beyond ourselves.
7. We need God because we need security in death.

According to Rabbi Kushner in *Who Needs God?*:

There is a kind of nourishment our souls crave, even as our bodies need the right foods, sunshine, and exercise. Without that spiritual nourishment, our souls remain stunted and undeveloped. In the physical realm, we understand that our ancestors' hard physical work built muscles and burned off calories, but we today are the victims of a modern lifestyle, so we need to diet, to jog, to work out at the gym. So, too, the king of spiritual communion our forebears knew is less accessible to us—because the world is so noisy and full of distractions, because we are so dazzled by our power and success, because religion in the late twentieth century is often badly packaged or presented by people we cannot trust or admire.

In one way, the rabbi's thesis is quaintly old-fashioned in our modern world. The modern era followed the Victorian era in cultural tradition. Just as Kaiser Wilhelm and Queen Victoria—descendants of the House of Hanover, but rulers of two different countries, Germany and Great Britain—dominated the end of the nineteenth century and ushered in the twentieth, so did America's technological prowess guide the modern twentieth century. The modern world that we ushered in was an age of applied science. The Marxist-Leninist bias against organized religion "as the opiate of the people" carried over into scientific debate. That viewpoint attempted to eliminate superstition and ignorance with the accumulated wisdom of the ages—measured by scientific method. It sincerely believed that humanity could be brought closer to the truth about solving the world's ills in scientific inquiry than by believing "myths of outdated religious ritual," as Pavel Gurevich notes in *Religions and the Battle of Ideas*.

So, to be modern was to streamline theological knowledge to fit scientific knowledge. Few of us, I believe, have realized how much the Marxist-Leninist religious critique affected the way we did theology. Miracles were stripped of the miraculous; parables were made plain;

worship had to have a rationale; church education had to have observable goals; and every biblical verse had to be explained. There was nothing left to chance. Religions and their theologians felt they had to have an answer to every question.

But we are past the modern age. Cultural historians tell us that we are in a postmodern age. This postmodern age will take us into the twenty-first century. There are new metaphors and similes to be used. New paradigms are developing from artificial knowledge. Baby-boomers, who know nothing of "years between the wars," look at things differently. They embrace questions without answers. They consider the mystical as a possibility not opposed to the scientific method, but included within it. Space exploration has shown how many scientific assumptions did not hit the mark. But most of all, a whole culture based upon the scientific dialectic of Marx as implemented by Lenin has been acknowledged as impotent.

From the silent world of repressed spiritual aspirations has come a foundation upon which completely new cultures awaken to new vitality in living. To be constitutionally promised an economic system that takes care of the minimum needs of food, shelter, and clothing for eighty years proved to be more than a disappointment. It was a ruse. Why had the needs of the physical been able to suppress the needs of the spirit? Why were food, clothing, and shelter the ends that supported life? Unknown to the Marxist-Leninist perception of reality, there existed—in the quiet recesses of an older generation—remembrance of a spiritual tradition that was shared with their unwilling children. Even Gorbachev has admitted that he was baptized as an infant. That unwilling generation has become a generation willing to question why the miraculous cannot be in a miracle; why all questions must have answers; why humanity must be so proud as to say we need nothing.

I remember a management course I took in which the instructor paraphrased the Bible this way: She said, "The first great commandment of administration is 'I made a mistake.' And the second is 'I need help.' Upon these two, the health of any organization shall rest." And not only organizations, but also families, churches, communities, and individuals. While the scriptures state that we are made in the image of God, we are not made as gods. The definition of God is simply *needing nothing to exist*. When Moses asked God what name he should call upon on the mount, the response was simply, "I Am Who I Am." God is the great "I AM." No other adjective, role, or further description needed.

There is no shame in admitting a need. It is a part of our humanness. But we have no need to call the kettle black, so to speak. Like the Marxist-Leninists, we declare ourselves as self-sufficient, needing nothing from anyone. We call it a strength. Yet, in many ways, it is a weakness beyond all weaknesses.

In today's scripture lesson from the Book of Job, we encounter a very self-sufficient figure who challenges God's direction. Job not only challenges God's place in the events of his life, but challenges God's involvement in creation as a whole. Job's story tells of our need for God. Our need is not a deficit, but an asset. To acknowledge God's presence is a source of strength into which we might tap to be truly free.

But a very important corrective must be cited. Needing God is not the same thing as needing religion or needing the church. Needing God satisfies a part of the soul that all share. Not all need religion and not all need the church. The Marxist-Leninist confused all three as one and equal in themselves. The theologians of the Middle Ages, did the same. One of their maxims was: "He who has God for a father, must have Jesus as his brother and the church for his mother." Religion is an intellectual construct of words that we employ when speaking about our knowledge of God. The church is a social system that has been drawn together by those words as they are lived out in a community.

But neither religion nor church is a necessity to satisfy the human need to experience God. God is a need; religion and church become expectations that we might want in order to nurture ourselves. Job is declared as a believer in God, but no place is he mentioned as being attached to a community of faith.

Both the Book of Job and Rabbi's Kushner's book have universal appeal in any culture because they recognize that humanity is a unique inhabitant of this cosmos, and needs not only food, shelter, and clothing, but a spiritual dimension that extends beyond purely physical and survival needs. While the need for organized religion and community may not be chosen by all, the need for God is a universal need that has become authentic for our postmodern culture.

God's Eternity and Human Frailty

90 [1] Lord, you have been our dwelling place
    in all generations.
[2] Before the mountains were brought forth,
    or ever you had formed the earth and the world,
    from everlasting to everlasting you are God.

[3] You turn us back to dust,
    and say, "Turn back, you mortals."
[4] For a thousand years in your sight
    are like yesterday when it is past,
    or like a watch in the night.

[5] You sweep them away; they are like a dream,
    like grass that is renewed in the morning;
[6] in the morning it flourishes and is renewed;
    in the evening it fades and withers.

...

[13] Turn, O LORD! How long?
    Have compassion on your servants!
[14] Satisfy us in the morning with your steadfast love,
    so that we may rejoice and be glad all our days.
[15] Make us glad as many days as you have afflicted us,
    and as many years as we have seen evil.
[16] Let your work be manifest to your servants,
    and your glorious power to their children.
[17] Let the favor of the Lord our God be upon us,
    and prosper for us the work of our hands—
    O prosper the work of our hands!

Does parenthood come with a warranty?

Sermon by Richard Murdoch | East Lansing, MI | June 19, 1994

Warranties and guarantees are the cutting edge of marketing revenue in our consumer-fueled society. It is not that these instruments are new. For years, we have sent in manufacturers' postcards for new things we have purchased to ensure that we are registered as the owner of a watch, a Crock-Pot, a hair dryer, a television, or some other item. More recently, items requiring larger investments (such as automobiles and homes) are marketed in the same manner.

Some observers suggest that consumer demand for warranties and guarantees is a direct reaction to the public's impatience with shoddy manufacturing or planned obsolescence. Others suggest that the demand comes from a movement away from old-fashioned personal retailing, in which the customer directly knew the owner of the store, who stood behind whatever product was sold personally. Now we have no such personal bond or pledge by a storeowner. Instead, many stores represent large warehouses of goods marketed by some distant management who is more interested in bottom lines than in customer satisfaction.

But business analysts suggest that the need for warranties and guarantees is precipitated by a distrust between citizens and structures of society, resulting in the need for "consumer rights." And those observers who are more philosophically oriented point out that we are no longer a culture of hope and risk-taking, no more the vast frontier of a new world. We are no longer seeking to make life better for the next generation. Our vision is today; our goal is security and satisfaction. And if our goal is not met, we look around for sources of accountability in order to influence the reaching of that goal.

But warranties and guarantees are set to take new directions. As colleges and universities find their pool of potential customers declining, as graduates find the job market sparse, and as employers find the cost of benefits and training increasing, a new product warranty is emerging. Eleven years ago, a little-known college in Nebraska embarked on an educational experiment to counter its declining enrollment. Doane College is just a few miles from Lincoln, Nebraska, in a little prairie town named Crete. It's a small college with just sixteen hundred students that found it difficult to make ends meet. The college began to offer employers a guarantee of its graduates as well as a guarantee of placement to their graduates in education.

The latest issue of *UCC News* [June 1994] reported that a dozen small colleges offering the same option have seen their enrollments increase and their finances stabilize. Doane College offers a warranty to school districts that hire its graduating seniors. If the school district finds the beginning teacher unable to perform at its expected standards, the teacher can return to summer or evening courses for re-education at no expense to the school district. And if a graduating senior fails to be placed within six months, he or she can return to the college, tuition free, for another year to study a different teaching area or even change careers. Has this innovative marketing paid off? Professor Dick Dudley is reported as saying that there have been 400 graduates in eleven years, and the return rate has been less than five percent. He said that warranties have worked extremely well at minimizing the risk for employers and students in our unsettled times, as well as enhancing the college's reputation as an institution of excellence.

As our society becomes more complicated and uncertain of its values, the desire to seek warranties and guarantees is extending far beyond manufactured goods to services, and even into life itself. On a professional basis, the medical world finds itself on the firing line—as do the fields of psychology and education. But most remarkable is the incursion of this issue into families. I am sure that you have seen reports of two recent court cases in which adult children are suing their parents due to "inadequate parenting" that allegedly impaired them, and made them unable to develop to their full potential as self-supporting individuals. These emotionally explosive cases involve a completely new field of litigation and social service laws. The extenuating circumstances are too involved to go into here, but the philosophical assumption is an indication of expanding cultural expectations that life should have certain warranties and guarantees.

Religion has never been exempt from this expectation. There is a reasonable assumption that if you believe in God with all your mind, heart, and soul, there should be something in return for your belief. Regardless of the specific religion, there is the expectation that a divine being should protect those who believe in her, him, it, or them (in the case of polytheism). In the Judeo-Christian tradition, much of the biblical writings concern events that seemingly didn't go according to plan. Yahweh did not give victory and success to the Hebrews as a people when they needed it the most. After Jesus's death, the Twelve Apostles did not understand why God allowed their master to die the death of a common criminal when they believed he had not committed a crime.

Yet in the history of religion, the opposite has often happened, leading to the development of a system of guarantees—though not in this life. Through pietistic living or through large donations of resources, one was guaranteed. El Greco's famous painting in Toledo, Spain, *The Burial of the Count of Orgaz*, was considered the proof of such guarantee to succeeding generations. In the painting, St. Peter is depicted as personally coming to the burial of Don Gonzalo Ruiz in order to escort him to paradise because at his death Ruiz had willed his fortune to provide for the city's poor. Since Ruiz felt that his faith had not been honored by God while he was alive in the world, he developed strategies to garner God's honor in the world to come.

But the Reformation changed the face of religion for some Christians. The reformers—influenced by the rational thinkers of a new world rising—could offer no such proof positive for faith. Faith brought no guarantees, only opportunities. Humanity created its own crises. It was up to humanity to be accountable and redirect its energies—from offering a guarantee in the future world, to creating opportunities in this world to expand and enhance God's creativeness. The reformers felt that accountability rested not with God, but with humanity. And if God's blessing was absent, then it was up to the individual who found him or herself with a lemon to make lemonade! Don't blame it on God!

In May, we celebrated Mother's Day, a tradition just barely a hundred years old in our culture, but one that has roots in the human family that are centuries old. Today, our calendar is marked with Father's Day, a tradition that dates from 1910 in America, and without any roots in the human family. Both observances indicate the need in our culture to lift up the importance of the role of parents in families, the smallest and most basic of social systems. Parenting is the most basic and important human service to a society, but it comes with no guarantee. There are no warranties either for parents or for children. Just risks and opportunities.

The influence of the feminist movement in this country for the past twenty-five years has influenced forever the expectations of the American family. It is only within the last ten years that another movement has arisen, called the men's movement, which has forced a younger generation to re-examine male cultural expectations in light of the changing cultural expectations of women. The result of all this introspection into gender roles will yield no guarantees of a society or culture that will be at ease with itself; nor will the clarification result automatically in more competent parenting.

Women and men historically have blurred gender lines because of the tasks that have been put before them for the survival of a society. The task before us is not negotiation between two warring camps of expectations, but a simple decency and tolerance which sees life as a moving sea, the boats of which rise and fall with the tide of mutual hopes—and desires for a world whose children will love as they have been loved. But what we shall need for this is not a warranty nor more knowledge, but wisdom.

Ode to a Capable Wife

31 ¹⁰ A capable wife who can find?
   She is far more precious than jewels.

¹¹ The heart of her husband trusts in her,
   and he will have no lack of gain.
¹² She does him good, and not harm,
   all the days of her life.

¹³ She seeks wool and flax,
   and works with willing hands.
¹⁴ She is like the ships of the merchant,
   she brings her food from far away.
¹⁵ She rises while it is still night
   and provides food for her household
   and tasks for her servant-girls.

¹⁶ She considers a field and buys it;
   with the fruit of her hands she plants a vineyard.
¹⁷ She girds herself with strength,
   and makes her arms strong.
¹⁸ She perceives that her merchandise is profitable.
   Her lamp does not go out at night.
¹⁹ She puts her hands to the distaff,
   and her hands hold the spindle.

²⁰ She opens her hand to the poor,
   and reaches out her hands to the needy.
²¹ She is not afraid for her household when it snows,
   for all her household are clothed in crimson.

²² She makes herself coverings;
   her clothing is fine linen and purple.
²³ Her husband is known in the city gates,
   taking his seat among the elders of the land.

²⁴ She makes linen garments and sells them;
   she supplies the merchant with sashes.
²⁵ Strength and dignity are her clothing,
   and she laughs at the time to come.

²⁶ She opens her mouth with wisdom,
and the teaching of kindness is on her tongue.
²⁷ She looks well to the ways of her household,
and does not eat the bread of idleness.

²⁸ Her children rise up and call her happy;
her husband too, and he praises her:
²⁹ "Many women have done excellently,
but you surpass them all."

³⁰ Charm is deceitful, and beauty is vain,
but a woman who fears the LORD is to be praised.
³¹ Give her a share in the fruit of her hands,
and let her works praise her in the city gates.

Does God have a wife?

Sermon by Richard Murdoch | East Lansing, MI | May 9, 1993

Teaching Sunday church school is no picnic these days. Kids are not afraid to speak up and speak out. Actually, that's always been the case, hasn't it?

A young girl asked her teacher, "Does God have a wife?" The teacher answered directly, "No, God doesn't have a wife." But as kids will do, the girl continued to probe. "Why not?" The teacher reflected a moment and replied, "Because God doesn't need a wife. God can do everything for himself." Still the little girl continued, "Well, my mommy says everybody needs a wife!"

Little did the teacher know that this girl was reflecting the milieu around her. Had the teacher read the newspapers, she would have discovered an advertisement in the New York City area for a fast-growing service franchise called "Your Wife." For a weekly fee, the service will pick up and deliver your dry cleaning, take your car to be serviced, do grocery or incidental shopping, arrange a catered dinner for guests (including sending invitations), and be present for house repair and maintenance appointments. In fact, the service will do anything excluding house cleaning, childcare, and food preparation. The advertisement goes on to pose the question: "Who uses the service most? Not single men, but couples and single women." The text stated that everybody needs a wife.

The advertisement also says that good wives are hard to find today. And that's just what the mother of King Lemuel said in the Bible more than two and a half thousand years ago. And who should know better than a mother? Just who is this Lemuel, the royal son whom the queen mother instructs? There is no historical king recorded as Lemuel, although the name is literally translated "devoted to God." The literary form of this scripture passage is not the unusual, dry biblical history. It is an acrostic. All twenty-verses begin with a different letter of the Hebrew alphabet, progressing in order from A-Z, so to speak. It seems that the author, whoever she or he is, wants to cover the entire subject on womanhood. After you have read this poem, it is obvious that this is no average housewife. This is a super-mom.

Part of the impact of the Book of Proverbs' treatment of womanhood is cultural and part is status. In the early days of the Bible, when the Hebrews were a nomadic people and polygamy was the norm, a wife's status was much higher than in Jesus's day when the Hebrews were a settled agricultural and business culture. The role of the wife described in Proverbs is much more like an executive officer in the military. A major or captain may command the company, but it is the exec who makes it happen. A wife in the days of Lemuel managed servants who, in turn, managed the household. A husband might have the authority to command, but he was absent much of the time, so it was the wife to whom the day-to-day happenings were entrusted. It was an arrangement of responsibility. Not one person could do everything for himself or herself. Wives—especially a head wife—were entrusted with enormous responsibility for business and family.

But wifedom falls to a lower state later on in the Christian New Testament. The Hellenistic culture didn't look kindly upon the role of women. No longer was a wife an executive officer of a family corporation. In both the Letter to the Colossians and the Letter to the Ephesians, wives are told to submit and obey. Likewise, in the Letter to the Corinthians, she is told to keep her mouth closed, her head covered, and keep to herself in the company of other women. Instead of being entrusted with responsibility, she is stripped of it.

In the ancient world, before the Greek Olympus gods defeated the Titans, the gods were maternal gods. Mother gods such as Astarte, Ceres, or Demeter were first responsible for creation and its population. But when the Olympian gods defeated the Titans, it was the father god who was responsible for creative force in the world. Zeus, the king of the Olympian gods, was the first to have a wife, Hera. Gradually, the influence of masculine gods replaced the feminine gods responsible for mother earth. Maternal religions gave way to fraternal religions in the Western world, which became Christianized.

But even in Christianity, the need for a nurturing, feminine side of God was evident in the referring to the church as "mother" and other churches as "sister" churches, and most obviously in the special place afforded the mother of Jesus, the Virgin Mary. In a very complicated theological formula formulated by Origen, a famous Christian scholar, which was voted by the Synod of Ephesus in 431 CE and Chalcedony in 451, Mary was declared to be *Theotókos*, or bearer of God, which became a standard of conservative Christian doctrine. Not even the Protestant reformers would renounce these two synods' declaration of Mary as the mother of God, so ingrained was the need for gender roles.

It is a unique modern phenomenon that perceives a need to divide God into user-friendly gender roles of language. Some people feel so strongly about this that worship services using only female language for God have been instituted. Others make a definite point to create a new language that is neither male nor female with which to speak to God. And this isn't new! I remember attending a state denominational meeting almost twenty years ago that met at Eisenhower College in New York State. We spent almost an hour on parliamentary procedure after a motion was introduced to address our prayers to S/HIM. I remember all that seriousness with amusement because, at the time, my children named our new female cat Shim since the cat replaced a male cat named Him.

All references to God are limited by human language. Since the divine by definition is not human, there is simply no language to describe God in God terms. So we have to fall back on human metaphors and experiences in order to understand or make sense of how the divine relates to humans. In some languages, it is easier than others. English tends to be especially difficult, because it is polyglot language.

God, by definition, hardly needs a wife. By simple definition, God is all sufficient and dependent on no human. If God were dependent upon creation and its creatures, then God is no God at all—just an extension of the human psyche. But the little girl's question had a second implication: Does God have relationships? The relationship she knew most clearly was the relationship between her parents, a woman and man who—because they married—were wife and husband. And because they had conceived and birthed her, they were mother and father. Whenever she was confronted with information about relationships, her only way of understanding was to be found in her experience. She was dependent upon metaphors she could experience to understand the working of God.

The teacher would have been wise to explain that God is both like a father *and* like a mother (Jeremiah 31:9 and Matthew 23:37) and then proceed to inquire what she knew about mothers and fathers. She might even have asked what the little girl knew about wives and husbands, because God is sometimes like a husband *and* a wife (Isaiah 54:5 and Revelation 21:9). And—if the little girl were a bit older—the teacher could have mentioned that God is sometimes even like a man *and* a woman (Genesis 1:26 and Isaiah 49:15).

The gender of the divine is irrelevant, and its advocates search in vain. The burning question of theology is: Does God relate to creation and its creatures, or does God simply preside over the creation? While the Hellenistic (or Greek) gods would be content with the latter, Jewish, Christian, and Muslim peoples would claim the former. God does have relationships with creation and its creatures: God is loving; God is merciful; God is just; God can be trusted; God can be loved. These are all words couched in human relationships.

But relationships between men and women, wives and husbands, and fathers and mothers are not automatic. They are very special, but they require energy and skill, love and devotion, mutual respect and forgiveness. There is pain and sorrow, joy and laughter. All of these are found in the words of Lemuel's mother. Since Lemuel means "devoted to God," some scholars have advanced the thought that—similar to the Song of Solomon in which the bridegroom could be God and God's followers could be the bride—this passage is an allegory about our relationship with God. God is Lemuel and we are the collective wife—an unusual gender twist, but certainly possible.

The words to Lemuel—spoken by a woman about women—become more than a "guide to a happy royal household." They are words about relationships between women and men—the roles they share and the joy they share. But even beyond that, they become words about relationships between God and those of faith—a faith whose credibility is not based not on gender likeness, but on the willingness to let faith be understood by using our human experience of relationships, as fragile and as vulnerable as they might be.

✡ Ecclesiastes 3:1-15 ✡
Everything Has Its Time

3 [1] For everything there is a season, and a time for every matter under heaven:

[2] a time to be born, and a time to die;
a time to plant, and a time to pluck up what is planted;

[3] a time to kill, and a time to heal;
a time to break down, and a time to build up;

[4] a time to weep, and a time to laugh;
a time to mourn, and a time to dance;

[5] a time to throw away stones, and a time to gather stones together;
a time to embrace, and a time to refrain from embracing;

[6] a time to seek, and a time to lose;
a time to keep, and a time to throw away;

[7] a time to tear, and a time to sew;
a time to keep silence, and a time to speak;

[8] a time to love, and a time to hate;
a time for war, and a time for peace.

[9] What gain have the workers from their toil? [10] I have seen the business that God has given to everyone to be busy with. [11] He has made everything suitable for its time; moreover he has put a sense of past and future into their minds, yet they cannot find out what God has done from the beginning to the end. [12] I know that there is nothing better for them than to be happy and enjoy themselves as long as they live; [13] moreover, it is God's gift that all should eat and drink and take pleasure in all their toil. [14] I know that whatever God does endures forever; nothing can be added to it, nor anything taken from it; God has done this, so that all should stand in awe before him. [15] That which is, already has been; that which is to be, already is; and God seeks out what has gone by.

Making each minute count

Sermon by Richard Murdoch | Omaha, NE | January 1, 1984

The potential of each minute is almost unlimited. There are 365 days stretched out before us in each New Year. And each day contains 1,440 minutes. You might have reflected sometime in this past week about New Year's resolutions, with a glimmer of remorse in your mind as you remembered that some things you wanted to get done didn't get done simply because there wasn't enough time. Then we usually resolve to organize ourselves in the New Year so that won't happen again!

Let me stretch your imagination with what can happen in a minute. But first, why is a minute a minute? It's indeed a curious division of time, set forth originally by monks with their water-clock invention. Using it, they divided an hour into sixty pieces by allowing sixty drops of water to fall from the same height, which then moved the hands of the "clock" by one notch of a wheel.

If statistics hold, you can expect that each minute in this New Year will bring the following results[1]:

6 babies will be born
2 teenagers will run away from home
44 car accidents will happen
4 couples will get married and 1.5 will get divorced
3,472 cups of coffee will be drunk
$38 will be spent to fight dandruff
7 people will take their first airplane ride
7,590 cows will be milked
62,500 stamps will be sold by the Postal Service
4 people will reach their 65th birthday
122,785 eggs will be made
and 3.8 hot dogs will be sold at Chicago's O'Hare Airport.

There's a lot that happens in a minute isn't there? There's so much potential in our minutes, and we never seem to have enough! In fact, it is in the very measure of time that we often experience anxiety about life. For in our culture of "more is better," we have developed impossible contradictions. For example, the employee who spends more time at his or her job is cited as being extra productive and extra loyal. The parent who spends more time at home is noted as being a better parent. The student who spends more time studying is a better student. The pianist who practices long hours is a better pianist. It is assumed that more time used in an activity will result in better performance, so, simply put, more is better.

Time is a commodity we use to purchase what we want: fame, respect, loyalty, love, and esteem. We believe success is directly related to the ticking of the clock each minute of the day. Ben Franklin's old saying in *Poor Richard's Almanac* professes: "Watch the pennies and the dollars will take care of themselves." A newer version of this adage is found in the popular book *The One Minute Manager,* in which we are advised to watch our minutes and let the hours take care of themselves.

If you read the entire Book of Ecclesiastes, you'll find that the *qoheleth* (a Hebrew name that translates to *ayatollah* in Arabic or *preacher* in English) would disagree with our perception of time and what it brings. These eight verses from the Book of Ecclesiastes are perhaps the most quoted biblical verses in song, literature, and philosophy the world over, with the exception of the Christmas passages from Isaiah and Psalm 23. The preacher's message is quite simple and to the point. He had tried the time-honored formula (as we know it) from the wisdom literature of the Proverbs, the Prophets, and the Psalms: Follow the Torah rules; go to the temple; be kind and generous; share with the poor; make each minute count. The result was a blessed and prosperous life full of joy and happiness.

The preacher had done that; but the result was just an empty shell. It didn't happen the way it was supposed to. He found that the righteous *did* suffer; that crooked people *did* win rewards; that hate got more attention than love; that intimidation secured more than sharing; that cheating was sometimes rewarded, and honesty neglected.

In qoheleth's verses, the list of opposites—negatives against the positive ideal—is obvious to every reader. There is little redemption of time in the mind of preacher, beyond the fact that this is the way it is, there are good times and bad, so get used to them because you can't change them. Many people have neglected this book's wisdom and yet this concept appears again in the Gospel of John as well as in the Letter to James.

There is a clue in the preacher's opening words for this chapter: For everything, there is a season and a time. There is a distinction here that helps us understand. Critics fail to recognize that in the verse there is a distinction made between season and time. This means a distinction in keeping time. One reference is to the trees, the other to the forest. Simply put, different perceptions are seen by different people. Some people see the individual trees and other people note the complete picture (or forest). Time (in the sense of Ecclesiastes) is the chronological time that you and I live in: minutes and hours and days. Time is chopped up, used up, consumed, exchanged, wagered, bought, and sold.

In the Book of Ecclesiastes, the season is the forest, the bigger picture. It is not the minutes, hours, and days. Season refers to *kairos,* a Greek word for "time above time," that sense which can't be measured. Maybe you don't know the word, but you know the feeling. Sometimes an experience can seem hours long, but when you look at your watch, it took only a minute or two. Maybe you've seen a car wreck? Time holds in slow motion. You want to turn it back, but you can't, and it seems to take hours for it to happen. You feel suspended in time.

Kairos is a measurement of time that has no divisions or chronicling. A season simply is an experience that fulfills people's being. Within the forest, within the seasons of life, there are trees—the time for love, the time for hate, the time for life, and the time to die. God doesn't hold every minute of the *chronos* in his hand, but he holds the season in his hand. God's purpose is often unclear in individual minutes, but in the sense of the whole season, there is sense to be made of it. Of course, that is not always revealed to us when we want it.

I heard on TV about a preacher who told people that, based on his study of the Book of Revelation, there was no doubt that Christ's second coming would be before the year 2000 arrived. He doesn't seem to realize that chronological time has little bearing on kairos time. When it comes, it comes. You're not going to hurry it. You're not going to lengthen it.

Reflect back, not on your minutes, but on your seasons. Was there joy in your heart this past year? Did it come from a child's birth, a marriage, an emotional renewal? Was there a sense of newness in your life? Was meaning renewed? Was there a sense of hope in God's purpose for you? Did you experience a sense of grace, a sense of mercy, a sense of sharing? It's the seasons that count, not the minutes.

Marguerite Higgins, a war correspondent, received the much-coveted Pulitzer Prize for international reporting based on her coverage of the Korean War. In her articles, she referred to many interesting and deep-seated experiences. One article described the Fifth Company of Marines (which originally numbered eighteen thousand) in combat with more than one hundred thousand Chinese Communists. It was particularly cold—forty-two degrees below zero—on the morning of the battle, and reporters were standing around. The weary soldiers, half frozen, stood by their dirty trucks, eating from tin cans. A huge Marine was eating cold beans with his trench knife. His clothes were as stiff as a board. His face, covered with heavy beard, was crusted with mud. The correspondent asked him, "If I were God and could grant you anything you wished, what would you most like?" The man stood motionless for a moment, then he raised his head and replied, "Give me tomorrow."

---

[1] I attempted to find out where these statistics came from to provide correct attribution and credit, but was unable to determine the source.

Between Malachi & Matthew

Welcome to one of the most hotly debated topics about the canons of scripture in Judeo-Christian history.

Between Malachi and Matthew, the books that appear in any Bible will depend on the version you are viewing, and what specific religious denomination it stems from. As a child, my King James Version simply concluded the "Old Testament" with the Book of Malachi and then began the "New Testament" with the Gospel of Matthew, which left about four hundred years unaccounted for (approximately 445 BCE to 6 BCE). It wasn't until I started writing this book and began flipping through my stack of borrowed Bibles that I asked myself, "What's up with this Apocrypha?"

To answer that question, we need to step back a bit and talk about how the Bible evolved. The Bible is a collection of writings that were originally written on scrolls made of animal skins, with most of the scrolls measuring from twenty to thirty feet long. (Although paper was invented in China in 100 BCE, it hadn't arrived yet in the land from which the Bible came.)

These Hebrew scrolls were kept at the temple, and read through during worship services. The idea of a Bible kept in a person's home did not exist yet. (I wonder how these folks would have reacted to hearing these results of a 2013 study by the Barna Group: Eighty-eight percent of adult households in the United States have a Bible, and, on average, each house has four different versions!)

Each scroll was hand copied and dispersed to individual synagogues. The collections in the synagogues varied widely, so there was no single "Bible" maintained consistently. As the scrolls were copied, they were often edited, so archaeologists have found many different versions of the same writings, and we can learn a lot from the differences that appear.

Which brings us to the Septuagint, the first canon translated into Greek. Why Greek? By the third century BCE, Alexander the Great had conquered Persia, creating an extensive empire that stretched from

Greece to Egypt as well as India. As this empire grew, Greek became the common language binding people together.

So the Septuagint included a number of writings that had been in circulation since 445 BCE, and these were used by the Jewish people who were living in foreign countries since the Exiles, and thus spoke Greek. The Septuagint was authorized by the Sanhedrin (the Jewish high council) and used up until about 60 CE.

So what happened? Why did some books go missing? One theory is that as the Jesus movement began, and used the Septuagint, Judaism sought to return to its roots and removed everything that had not originally been written in Hebrew or Aramaic (thus removing the Greek-only writings). There's no consensus by scholars as to what date the Jewish canon was set, but the final version is attributed to the Council of Jamnia in the late first century CE. After much debate, some books were left out and eventually became the Apocrypha (from the Greek word for "hidden").

Today, rabbinic Judaism includes only twenty-four books in the authoritative canon of the Hebrew scriptures, or Tanakh. However, many modern Jewish people accept some of the books of the Apocrypha as providing valuable historical information about that time period (as well as the original accounts of the temple purification in 164 BCE and the resulting festival of Hanukkah).

So, what about Christian Bibles?

That controversy continues to the fourth century CE when Pope Damascus asked the scholar Jerome to create a translation of the Bible into Latin (hence the Latin Vulgate). No surprise here, since Rome was shaking off its Greek heritage. Emperor Constantine became the first Roman emperor to convert to Christianity.

Jerome called attention to the status of the apocryphal texts in cautionary prefaces to the books. Then somewhere down the line, these prefaces were removed by a copier, and the books became part of the canon approved by the Roman Catholic Church. Today, you will find these books, with some variations—in most Roman Catholic, Greek Orthodox, and Russian Orthodox versions.

Later, the people who created the English translation and the Protestant reformers in the 1500s and 1600s removed these books completely or set them aside in a separate Apocryphal section. Hence why my King James Version did not include these books, and why I don't have any sermons from them. Yet it's turned out to be one of the most interesting parts of my learning, because it is important to understand the climate and culture in which Christianity began.

So let's dig in for a brief overview of this time period "between the testaments" before we move on to the Christian writings.

As you may recall, Jerusalem and the temple were destroyed by the Babylonians (under Nebuchadnezzar) in 586 BCE. During this time, many Judeans were exiled to Babylon, beginning what we often refer to as the Jewish Diaspora (from the Greek word for "scatter or disperse"). About 50 years later, Persia's King Cyrus allowed the exiled to return. Many returned, but many did not, continuing to live in diaspora, creating Jewish communities in Babylon and other countries.

The Persians ruled the Near East (including Judah) for two centuries. It was the largest empire the world had seen, well surpassing that of the Assyrians before them. The empire now extended to the edges of India. The Persian prophet Zoroaster (Zarathushtra) had developed a monotheistic religion, writing the Gathas to define its precepts. Based on belief in one universal, transcendent, Supreme Being—Ahura Mazda—it was the world's most powerful religion.

During this time in Jerusalem, the temple was rebuilt and rededicated. The Torah and other writings were edited and refined. And the daily drama of ancient life went on.

The Greco (Greek)-Persian wars began around 499 BCE. For fifty years, the two sides battled, leaving a rich history that has since inspired myriad exciting books and blockbuster movies. Eventually, Alexander the Great conquered Persia and ushered in the next great empire. He would name seventy cities after himself, and even one after his favorite horse, Bucephala. (The word "ego" comes to mind here.) Egypt and Judah were now under Greek rule.

The immense size of Alexander's empire meant that a single culture could be spread throughout the region as trade and commerce expanded within it. Much like English is today's common language for business, Greek became the common language, and with it came Hellenism (from *Hellas,* the Greek word for Greece). Hellenism affected the arts, literature, architecture, and philosophy across different countries as it intermingled with local cultures. It also affected religion, as devotees had to determine how new ideas conflicted or merged with their own religious ideals.

After Alexander died in 323 BCE with no clear heir, his kingdom was divided among his generals. Judea (the Greco-Roman name for Judah) became a hotbed of conflict during this time, changing hands between the Seleucid (Near Eastern) Empire and Ptolemaic Egypt. By 301 BCE, things had settled down a bit and the winning Ptolemies ruled Judea in relative political peace for eighty years. However, Hellenization was driving a wedge in Judaism, as the upper class in Jerusalem adopted more and more Greek ways, while the lower classes clung to their ancestral Hebrew roots.

In 169 BCE, the Seculid ruler (aka the Greek king) Antiochus IV invaded Egypt to fight the Ptolemies in hopes of reclaiming land, including Judea. On his return from Egypt, he sacked Jerusalem. (There are many theories why, from anger about his defeat, to financially raiding the temple, to believing Judea was in revolt.)

Revolt did ensue, leading to Antiochus outlawing the Jewish religion (including the teaching of the Torah). Then he ordered the worship of Zeus in the temple. This final act brought the Jewish revolt into full swing, under the leadership of the Hasmonean family, led by the priest Mattathias and his five sons. One of Mattathias's sons was nicknamed Maccabeus ("the hammer"), so the revolt became known as the Maccabean revolt.

After seven years of guerrilla warfare, the revolt ended in victory led by Judah Maccabee. The temple was cleansed and brother Jonathan installed as high priest. Thus, after four hundred years of foreign rule, Judah was now finally again independent. The "Maccabees" would rule for the next eighty years (aka the Hasmonean dynasty). However, constant struggles for power would create a crack and let Rome in.

Now, stick with me, as this gets a bit complex...

The Seculid (Greek) Empire was under constant attack by the rising powers of the Roman Republic and Parthian Empire, both of which had come to power after the destruction of the Persian Empire by Alexander. During this time, as the Seculids were losing power, the Roman Senate recognized the Jewish state of Judah (139 BCE). But not far off, the Hasmonean high priests, Hyrcanus II and Aristobulus II, would find themselves involved in a power struggle that would ultimately bring the entire area under Roman occupation.

Let's dig into that soap opera.

Hyrcanus II and Aristobulus II were brothers. Upon their father's death, their mother named the eldest son, Hyrcanus II, successor to the throne—so we clearly know where this is headed. Not surprisingly, Aristobulus II rose in rebellion, attacked, and was victorious. But the victory was short-lived. Hyracanus II's chief advisor, Antipater (Herod the Great's father), convinced him to fight back. An ancient Arab group called the Nabataeans backed Hyrcanus II, and civil war broke out.

Not too far away, Pompey the Great had finally defeated the Seleucids, and moved into the area, attempting to bring law and order to the region. Hearing of the civil war, he sent his lieutenant to sort it out. The brothers both pleaded their cases. Before Pompey made his decision, Aristobulus jumped the gun, heading for Jerusalem and angering Pompey in the process. Pompey then chose to back Hyrancus, and the result was the three-month Siege of Jerusalem in 63 BCE. An estimated twelve thousand people died.

When the dust settled, Hyrancus II was reinstated as high priest, but stripped of much of his power. Judea was autonomous, but now paying tribute to Rome and under its thumb.

During this fiasco, Judaism was splitting. Many reasons fueled the schism: anger at the Hasmonean military monarchy, reactions to how much Hellenization should be adopted, and concerns about greed in the temple affairs. The result was Judaism was no longer a united religion. The sects of the Hasideans, Pharisees, Sadducees, Essenes, and Zealots were now on the scene.

Meanwhile, two deaths in the 40s BCE would lead to instability in the Mediterranean—first Pompey, then Julius Caesar. Aristobulus's son attacked Judea and captured Jerusalem, proclaiming himself the king. But Rome stepped in and instead appointed Herod the Great to rule as "King of the Jews."

Many Jewish people, however, disagreed with Herod's lineage. And they disagreed with his philosophy that playing nice with Rome was the best way to secure the welfare of the nation. Although Herod started reconstruction of the temple, worked towards unifying his people, and strengthened Judea's economy, unrest continued. The ends just did not justify the means. People were suspicious of his intentions and violent actions. They wanted to be free.

It's interesting to note that in the Roman Empire there was not a national religion based on a creed or sacred writings. Polytheism abounded, but not everyone worshipped the same gods. Some gods were localized to certain places. When people were conquered, they often inherited the gods of their conquerors. And there were greater gods that stood above these. In the Greco-Roman world, there was a pyramid of power in the divine realm, with a few great gods at the top, and many less powerful gods at the bottom. Some people even believed only in one god at the top—the Greek Zeus or Roman Jupiter.

Plurality was commonplace, and no one would argue that if you worshipped a certain god you couldn't worship another one as well. The exclusivity we see in many of today's religions simply wasn't present. There was a lack of doctrine in these practices—gods were worshipped through prayer and sacrifice with a focus on living in the here and now, not towards some future salvation, redemption, or reward. And for the most part, all gods were seen as "valid."

So, in the beginning, the Jewish people were given a lot of religious freedom to worship their own god. It wasn't inconsistent from a Greco-Roman point of view. But where the trouble happened (as it frequently does) is in the meeting of politics and religion. Being dominated by a foreign power was unacceptable (as it would be for most people). Social, political, and religious uprisings continued, not only between the Jewish and Roman, but internally as well, as the divide between the rich and the poor was widening.

It was into this unrest that a boy named Jesus was born.

Meanwhile...

The Silk Road came into massive use, connecting people, increasing trade, and spreading cultures. Many people in the Mediterranean got a face-to-face introduction to Far Eastern culture, seeing silk and the precursor to modern paper for the first time.

The increasing urbanization of India had brought a wide diversity of beliefs. Within this environment, the *Bhagavad Gita* was written. Over time it would become a handbook for ancient Hindus and modern yoga students alike. Mahatma Gandhi would later refer to it as his "spiritual dictionary."

Mighty building projects were happening all over the globe. The Great Wall of China was built to protect China from its northern invaders. Across the globe, the Maya constructed a large-scale temple, as well as forty urban cities where they established sophisticated mathematics, astronomical study, and a complex 365-day calendar.

Scientific exploration abounded. In Alexandria, taboos no longer restricted medical dissections of human bodies, making new findings in anatomy possible. Eratosthenes of Cyrene tabulated the first circumference of the Earth. The Chinese wrote the earliest known book of medicine, the Nei Ching. Nearby, Lui Xin documented over 1080 different stars. The Romans developed concrete, as well as the first germ theory. The seeds of the science vs. religion debate had begun.

Then Queen Cleopatra, the last active Pharaoh of Egypt, died. According to tradition, she committed suicide by the bite of an asp. Her son ascended to the throne briefly but was killed by Octavian. Egypt finally became a province of the Roman Empire. Rome seemed unstoppable.

The "J" Word

"Let the one who seeks not stop seeking until he finds.
When he finds, he shall be troubled.
When he becomes troubled, he will be amazed,
and shall come to transcend all things."
—The Gospel of Thomas

Sometime around age thirteen, I stopped saying the word Jesus.

Oh, I'd go ahead and read the prayers aloud at church with everyone else, but when the word "Jesus" appeared, I'd be silent. This wasn't out of reverence, such as when people of the Jewish faith stay silent while reading the word for God in the Torah. I admit it was the opposite. Somewhere along the line, I had gone from a little girl in ponytails singing, "Yes, Jesus loves me!" to a teenager who got a knot in her stomach when she saw or heard Jesus's name.

I don't know specifically how, when, or why it happened. But now, as an adult, I have a name for it: doubt. The influential theologian Paul Tillich said, "Doubt is not the *opposite* of faith, it is an *element* of faith" (emphasis added). So does that mean I was normal?

My father thought so, when I spoke with him on the subject. "Dad, I can't say 'Jesus' in prayers anymore," I told him. "Well, that's certainly an interesting development," he replied. So I continued, "I don't believe in Jesus." Never one to let me off the hook easily, my father asked, "What don't you believe about Jesus?"

I don't recall the rest of the conversation exactly. I probably mumbled something and tried to leave the room. I simply didn't have the language to be able to describe my thoughts. I do remember him telling me it was okay to question, and to talk with him anytime about it. But I was too embarrassed. I felt as if I were a doctor's daughter saying, "Dad, I don't believe in medicine." How could I talk about this thing that he had committed his life to in that way? Better to avoid it. Go focus on school and boys.

Today, I'm still not sure if I can articulate how I feel about Jesus. But while writing this book, I've had the pleasure of speaking to a bunch of people—of various religious traditions—on the subject. And what I heard surprised me. People I considered fine, upstanding Christian folks admitted to me, "I'm not really sure if Jesus lived." Or: "I think he was the son of God like I'm the son of God—just a better person." Or: "I put him in the category of great teachers like the Buddha, Gandhi, and Martin Luther King, Jr." Some pointed to the similarities between Jesus and other ancient stories that sounded similar, such as Horas or Mithras. One asked me if I had heard that Jesus spent the so-called missing 18 years from the Bible studying in India. And there were others who said, "He saved my life" or "He is the divine Son of God." The answers were all over the place.

So, I set off to find out who Jesus really was. I quickly learned that many of the things I thought I knew about Jesus were likely misconceptions. He wasn't an only child. (He had brothers and sisters.) Christmas isn't his birthday. (December 25th was decided upon in the fourth century CE. And interestingly, in 2008, some astrologers pointed to June 17th as a more likely date.) He wasn't born in a wooden barn that looks like my nativity set. (More likely a cave, or a lower floor of a home.)

As I dug deeper to try to find out just who exactly Jesus was—at least, according to the scholars—I also found myriad descriptions. And I learned that even while Jesus lived there was debate about who he was—in fact, that is a common theme in the gospel stories about him: "Who do you say I am?" (Mark 8:29)

Also, contrary to popular belief (and what some churches may want us to believe), there were enormously diverse viewpoints about who Jesus was in the early "Jesus movements" after his death. People varied widely on who he was, what he was, what his death meant, whether he was resurrected, and so on. But you have to dig past the Christian Bible to see this—much of the variety was stripped out as the movement became an organized religion.

Well, that was news to me! Somewhere inside me, my thirteen-year-old self was telling my forty-something-year-old inner self that there was only "one truth" about Jesus, and you either believed it or not. Luckily, my wiser forty-something-year-old won out, and I realized that not being sure who Jesus was is similar to not being sure exactly what God is.

Ultimately, it's just not that important to me that I can't find the perfect Wikipedia entry to solve my question. As Vietnamese monk

Thich Nhat Hanh says in *Living Buddha, Living Christ,* "It is our duty to transcend words and concepts to be able to encounter reality."

So I began to approach Jesus's teachings and the stories about him with a big grain of salt and my beginner's mind. I set aside what I thought I knew and looked at it as another "language" to learn—that of a Jewish reformer and the early Christians.

Sermons from
the Christian scriptures

Context: The Gospels (Life of Jesus)

What child is this?	*Luke 2:1-11*
A rumor of angles to shepherds	*Luke 2:8-20*
What do the stars hold?	*Matthew 2:1-12*
The human experience of trust	*John 1:21-34*
Disappearance of sin	*Mark 1:14-20*
God is the answer?	*John 3:1-13*
In pursuit of perfection or excellence?	*Matthew 5:45-48*
Concerning prayer	*Matthew 6:9-15*
The sighted blind	*John 9:1-11*
When is enough, enough?	*Luke 10:25-37*
The celestial garage sale	*Mark 10:17-31*
Trading stamps as a way of life	*Mark 10:35-45*
Prayer changes things	*Matthew 21:18-22*
Humility	*Matthew 23:27-28*
Greatness reversed	*Luke 22:14-30*
I thirst	*John 19:16-29*
It is finished	*John 19:30*
Resurrection: reaction and response	*John 20:1-16*
Void if detached	*Luke 24:36-53*

Context: History of the Faith & Church

What dreams!? What visions?	*Acts 2:1-18*
When Christians murmur	*Acts 6:1-7*
To pray...	*Acts 12:1-2, 4-17*
Faith, hope, and... love	*1 Corinthians 13:1-13*
Flags, flags, and more flags	*Romans 13:1-7*
How are your callouses?	*Ephesians 4:17-24*
Are we worth more dead than alive?	*Philippians 1:22-27*
When you rekindle the fire	*2 Timothy 1:3-14*

Context: Revelation

Will my dog go to heaven?	*Revelation 21:1-4*

Context:
The Gospels (Life of Jesus)

Matthew – Mark – Luke – John

So here's the thing: Jesus didn't leave us any direct writings. No diaries. There's no video of his actual Sermon on the Mount posted on YouTube. Instead, the stories were originally passed around orally, because texts were not in wide circulation—and if they had been, they would not have been very useful, since most people could not read.

Then, starting around 70 CE, after being passed around for forty years, texts about Jesus's life and teachings—called gospels—were written down and shared. And although many are attributed to certain disciples (such as Matthew, Mark, Luke, and John), scholars are not confident who actually wrote the books. Or how often they were edited over the years before we got to the versions we have now.

Likewise, scholars have yet to have solid agreement on what exactly the historical Jesus said. Which is often frustrating—I want to be able to go straight to the source—to read Jesus's own words. I live in the world after the invention of Guttenberg's printing press. I trust what I see in print. (Or at least I did pre-Internet.)

So I searched a little further for more sources, and I found other gospels that are not in my Bible. In 1945, near Nag Hammadi, Egypt, forty-five additional books from the second and third centuries were found. The find included gospels from the Egyptians, Thomas, and Philip. There's a Gospel of Mary Magdalene dating back to the fourth century CE, and even a Gospel of Judas that has been carbon-dated to 280 CE.

I found at least three dozen gospels (or accounts of Jesus's life) that aren't in my Christian Bible, but which were used by many early Christian groups, not to mention a plethora of non-gospel texts about Jesus and early Christianity. The Bible is only the tip of the iceberg in the available writings to explore. Yet, we can't be sure these contain Jesus's exact words either. They are simply additional perspectives.

But since my father's sermons focus on the four canonical gospels found in the Christian Bible, I have to narrow our focus there.

Of the four canonical gospels, three are very similar, so they are called the "synoptic" gospels (Greek for "together" and "seeing"). The Gospel of John has a very different literary style, and so it stands off on its own. But even among the three synoptics, there are a lot of discrepancies that are very hard to reconcile. They simply don't agree on a lot of things. Some are timing details: For instance, was Jesus crucified on Wednesday, Thursday, or Friday, and was his ministry one or three years in length? Some are related to places: Was Joseph and Mary's hometown Nazareth or Bethlehem, and where exactly did the risen Christ appear to his disciples? Still others are variations in the stories Jesus shared.

There are also discrepancies within the books themselves. And this isn't surprising, because—similar to the Hebrew scriptures—multiple writings often were edited together to make one book. Ancient editors just didn't seem to be bothered so much when their numbers didn't add up, or stories didn't agree.

So, I think a good approach is to look at each of the four gospels as a human perspective, or one person's take on something that was very powerful. Each author focused on a slightly different part of that story based on what was important to him, her, or them as there is some evidence that each gospel represented a different early path of the faith.

Mark

"Wait," you think, "you're supposed to start with Matthew!" True, in most Bibles, Matthew is the first gospel to appear. But scholars believe that the Gospel According to Mark was actually written first, around 66 to 70 CE, about thirty-five years after the death of Jesus. It's the earliest surviving gospel available. So let's start there.

Although this book was originally authored anonymously, it was traditionally attributed to John Mark, who had authored it based on the Apostle Peter's preaching. However, there is little evidence to support this tradition. Plus, the issue is further complicated since during this time, most people did not have last names (this is why you find descriptions such as "Mary, mother of," "Jesus, son of," or "James, brother of.") But regardless of who wrote this gospel, common usage still refers to it as the Gospel According to Mark, or just Mark for short. So, to keep it simple, I'll do the same.

This gospel doesn't say anything about the birth or childhood of Jesus, but instead starts with the adult baptism of Jesus by a minister named John the Baptist. From there, the gospel focuses primarily on Jesus's ministry in Galilee, his ministry in Judea, and his final ministry in Jerusalem. Included in the ministry are various parables, stories of miracles, and accounts of issues between Jesus and one group of the Jewish faith—the Pharisees.

Then, it provides details about the last week of Jesus's life (often called the Passion Narrative, as the word *passion* is Greek for "suffering"). This includes how Jesus is arrested and tried before the Roman prefect Pontius Pilate of Judea, where he remains silent. Found guilty, he is crucified. The only words he utters are: "My God, my God, why have you forsaken me?"

In the various ancient versions of the Gospel According to Mark that have been recovered, scholars have found three different endings. In all of the versions, Jesus is buried. In the first version, after the burial, three women (Mary Magdalene, Mary the mother of James, and Salome) appear at the tomb to anoint the body, a common practice of that time.

However, Jesus is not there. Instead, they find a young man (or possibly an angel), who tells them that Jesus is risen, and will meet them in Galilee. The book then ends abruptly: "So they went out and fled from the tomb, for terror and amazement had seized them; and they said nothing to anyone, for they were afraid."

The second—or "short"—ending concludes with the women passing on the news: "And all that had been commanded them they told briefly to those around Peter. And afterward Jesus himself sent out through them, from east to west, the sacred and imperishable proclamation of eternal salvation."

The third—or "long"—ending includes Jesus appearing to Mary Magdalene, followed by two other disciples on the road. Jesus then appears to the eleven remaining disciples (Judas is not present) at a meal before being "taken up into heaven."

An interesting feature of this gospel is that most people around Jesus consistently don't understand what Jesus is teaching, and are full of misunderstandings. The author of Mark portrays Jesus as a special "Son of God," and "the Messiah." You may recall that *messiah* is the Hebrew word for "anointed one." In the Jewish messianic view, it was believed the messiah would overthrow the enemies of the Jewish people, bringing victory and a new world order. The Greek translation for messiah is *Christos*, and is where the word "Christ" comes from. In the Book of Mark, Christ's role as messiah is new—to suffer and die at the hands of those aligned against God and God's people.

Yet, when people do recognize Jesus as a messiah, he tries to hush them, to keep his identity secret. Meanwhile, even though Jesus is faithful to the (Jewish) law, and is not portrayed to stand in opposition with Judaism, Jewish leaders want to kill him, his neighbors take offense with his actions, and his family thinks he is crazy.

Matthew

The Gospel According to Matthew appears to have used the Gospel of Mark as a source. And like Mark, it was written anonymously, and then later attributed to Matthew, the tax collector. Scholars aren't sure who wrote this gospel either. But they think it was written about ten years after Mark, around 80 CE.

Matthew adds many events not present in Mark. For example, it starts with the genealogy of Jesus, to show the lineage back to King David. And it covers the story of Jesus's birth (including the Wise Men). After that, it includes some basic details of Jesus's childhood—such as a flight into Egypt for safety, and then a return to Nazareth.

Moving on to Jesus's ministry, the Gospel of Matthew includes teachings of Jesus that are not present in the Gospel of Mark, primarily the Sermon on the Mount, which includes the Lord's Prayer, the Beatitudes, and the Golden Rule. The author also includes a passion narrative, but it varies a little from Mark. Here, Jesus does speak, albeit briefly, to answer "You sayest" when asked if he is the King of the Jews. During the crucifixion, as in Mark, he says, "My God, my God, why have you forsaken me?"

After the burial, in Matthew, a guard is sent to the tomb by Pilate to make sure Jesus's body stays put. When the women appear at the tomb, there is a great earthquake, followed by an angel rolling the stone door back from the tomb. The angel tells those present that Jesus is risen, and to go spread the word. Afterwards, Jesus appears to the women as they are traveling. Finally, he appears to the eleven disciples (again, Judas is not present) on a mountaintop, where he encourages them to go out to baptize and teach the world. Then he "was received up to heaven and sat on the right hand of God."

What's interesting is that, of the four canonical gospels, this one has the highest percentage of words devoted to Jesus's teachings—estimated at forty-three percent of the book. It is also the gospel that relies most heavily on the Hebrew scriptures for its basis. (Did you know that many of Jesus's parables were not original to him, but were pulled from older Jewish stories?) The problem for Jesus here is not the Jewish law, practices, or teachings—which he supports—but instead, is the Jewish authorities and Jesus's views on their actions. Likewise, there's a strong emphasis on Jesus being the fulfillment of Jewish messianic prophecy, aka a new Moses.

Luke

The Gospel According to Luke is traditionally attributed to Luke, a physician who traveled with the Apostle Paul. Scholars, however, question this authorship as well, since it was originally anonymous. It is generally dated to about 85 CE.

As you might expect, Luke includes many of the events of both Mark and Matthew. However, there is a strong emphasis on compassion and social issues, shown by more stories about Jesus reaching out to the poor, sick, and oppressed. This gospel begins before the infancy of Jesus, with alternating stories of foretelling of the birth of both Jesus and John the Baptist to their mothers. The birth of Jesus follows, yet this time the shepherds visit (rather than the Wise Men). In fact, there are a lot of differences between the birth stories in Matthew and Luke. (And each Christmas, many of us seem to celebrate an amalgam of the two.)

A childhood story, original to Luke, about Jesus's visit to the temple as a twelve-year-old boy, provides the solitary glimpse into Jesus's teen years in the canonical gospels. After that, Jesus is baptized by John the Baptist, and the familiar stories of the ministries in Galilee and Judea appear. (Interestingly though, the Sermon on the Mount from Matthew is replaced by the Sermon on the Plain in Luke. So the jury is still out on whether it was the same speech, just noted in two different places, or a repeat speech, or a "created" speech containing a synopsis of Jesus's teachings.) Luke is where we find the parables of the Good Samaritan and Prodigal Son.

There are some significant other differences. The Gospel of Luke provides much more detail on the journey to Jerusalem than the other gospels do. Also, in this passion narrative, Jesus is tried before *both* Pilate and Herod (local ruler of Galilee). Pilate is said to be willing to release Jesus, but the people ask for him to be crucified. So in this gospel, the blame is shifted.

Luke paints a very different picture of Jesus on the cross. Here, Jesus is not dismayed. Instead, he shows a concern for others. This is where the famous, "Father, forgive them, for they know not what they are doing" (Luke 23:34) appears. This verse does not appear in the other gospels. In Luke, Jesus is simply playing out his part in a divine plan.

In this gospel, after Jesus's burial, the women see two men at the empty tomb, who explain Jesus is risen. They pass the word on to the Apostles—who don't believe them. Then Peter runs to the tomb and verifies the women's stories. Jesus appears afterward to two disciples, and then to eleven Apostles (but in a different place than in Matthew and Mark). Finally, he is carried "up to heaven," and the disciples head back to Jerusalem.

What is interesting in Luke is that Jewishness is not emphasized the same way as in Matthew and Mark. Although Jesus is seen as a prophet or spokesperson for God, the author is clearly coming from a "gentile" (non-Jewish) perspective. The Gospel of Luke presents Jesus as God's son, the universal savior of humanity—for Jewish and non-Jewish alike. In Luke, the point is not simply Jesus's death and resurrection. It is that Jesus's death prompts people to see their part and repent, and that is ultimately what "saves" them.

John

The most distinctive of the canonical gospels is, hands-down, the Gospel According to John. Here, Jesus is portrayed differently than in the synoptic gospels. How? He's divine. And he talks a lot about his identity. John is the only gospel that explicitly says Jesus is divine—the three synoptic gospels refer to him as "Son of God" in a non-exclusive way. (For those in the first century CE, the terms are often the inverse of what we expect: "Son of Man" refers to someone divine, and "Son of God" refers to someone human—many people were referred to as Sons of God.)

Another distinction is the opening, or Johannine Prologue, which gives this book a very different start than the other gospels. There's a mystical description of the "Word" of God becoming human in Jesus Christ. So, naturally, there is no other birth story in John. And neither is there the story of the baptism by John the Baptist. But, there is more information on the beginning of Jesus's ministry that is not found in the other gospels—however the teaching parables familiar from the other gospels (such as the Sermon on the Mount/Plain) are absent. Instead, we find the unique words from the Feast of Tabernacles, including, "I am the light of the world," "The truth will make you free," and other words about Jesus's identity—no secret or hush-hush in this gospel!

Jesus's ministry, which seems to be longer in duration then the other gospels (it includes three Passovers rather than one), focuses heavily on miracles—turning water into wine, healing people, feeding five thousand people on a tiny amount of food, walking on water, raising the dead, and so on.

Some other differences? The passion narrative is similar to the synoptics, but it is preceded by a long speech—often called the Farwell Discourse—to Jesus's disciples. During the trial with Pilate, Jesus is much more talkative than in the synoptic gospels (and he does not appear before Herod). And upon the cross, his words are different. He utters both, "I thirst" and "It is finished" rather than the words stated in the other gospels.

After burial, Mary Magdelene appears alone at the tomb, and when she sees the tomb is open, runs to tell a couple of the disciples, who come back to investigate. When the disciples leave, Mary remains, distraught, and has a conversation with an angel. Jesus then appears to her. As in the other gospels, he also then appears to the disciples. In John, this happens in four different configurations of disciple groups; then the book ends without noting an ascension.

One troubling thing about the Gospel of John is how it has historically been used very negatively towards those of the Jewish faith.

Scholars believe that the author's community had been excluded from the local synagogue (because of their belief in Jesus as a messiah), and that's why the gospel seems to express antagonism towards the Jewish religion and people. So it's important to read these portions understanding that the author may have had an axe to grind.

✞ ✞ ✞

So what really happened? Which of these events are undeniably "true?" It's hard to know.

Indeed, many of the stories in these gospels seem truly fantastic to our modern ears—especially in the Gospel of John. But it's important to remember the context of the ancient world. Jesus was not the only miracle-working "Son of God" of that time. The term was used widely in Greek mythology (think: Apollo and Dionysus). The Hebrew scriptures named Adam, descendants of Seth, and the kings of Israel to be Sons of God. Even Alexander the Great and Julius Caesar used the term about themselves. So ancient listeners likely would have been familiar with the concept. Furthermore, the concept of "real" in the ancient world was defined differently than those of us living after the Age of Reason, obsessed with scientific inquiry to prove our truth.

As for healing miracles, you can either believe they were divinely inspired, or look to many of the modern descriptions of the ancient events. Your choice. I'll try to stay out of that debate, but I have read recently some compelling scientific studies that prove that how we think about our body significantly effects how we heal. (For example: You know about the placebo effect? There's actually a related effect as well. People who don't have faith in their medicine have less chance of it working.) The role of conscious thought in pain perception and healing is an area of extensive research these days as Western medicine meets Eastern. Someday, we may better understand the link.

Wherever you net out—the stories are true, not true, or don't really know what you think—as with the Hebrew scriptures, I think there is much to be explored and pondered.

Meanwhile…

Sadly, after having played a notable role in Ancient Greek mythology, lions became extinct in the region. Conversely, human populations were booming all over the globe. Major urban areas were centered around rivers—the Ganges, Tigris, Yangtze, Nile, and Po.

According to the Han dynasty's census in 2 BCE, China boasted an impressive fifty-seven million inhabitants and occupied a tremendous amount of land, including Vietnam. Over in the pre-Columbian Americas, Teotihuacan claimed the prize for largest city, with an estimated one hundred thousand inhabitants, becoming the area's most important religious center.

Rome was the largest city in the world, with an estimated population around one million residents. The Roman Empire was in its Golden Age, steadily increasing domination over Europe, the Near East, and Africa. Even so, Greek culture was still prominent in art and architecture (hence the term Greco-Roman). And the language that united the Empire was still Greek.

Suddenly the *codex*—an early form of the modern book—appeared in Rome, and began to replace the use of scrolls throughout the area. Due to its portability, the codex would make it increasingly difficult for Rome to stop the spread of ideas—including those that came from the influential Jesus and his persuasive followers.

The Birth of Jesus

2 ¹ In those days a decree went out from Emperor Augustus that all the world should be registered. ² This was the first registration and was taken while Quirinius was governor of Syria. ³ All went to their own towns to be registered. ⁴ Joseph also went from the town of Nazareth in Galilee to Judea, to the city of David called Bethlehem, because he was descended from the house and family of David. ⁵ He went to be registered with Mary, to whom he was engaged and who was expecting a child. ⁶ While they were there, the time came for her to deliver her child. ⁷ And she gave birth to her firstborn son and wrapped him in bands of cloth, and laid him in a manger, because there was no place for them in the inn.

⁸ In that region there were shepherds living in the fields, keeping watch over their flock by night. ⁹ Then an angel of the Lord stood before them, and the glory of the Lord shone around them, and they were terrified.

¹⁰ But the angel said to them, "Do not be afraid; for see—I am bringing you good news of great joy for all the people: ¹¹ to you is born this day in the city of David a Savior, who is the Messiah, the Lord."

What child is this?

Sermon by Richard Murdoch | East Lansing, MI | December 23, 1990

In last Sunday's *Detroit News*, this headline appeared: "Analysts: Chrysler Shouldn't Hold Breath Awaiting a Savior." Within this week, countless articles have analyzed the impact upon the automotive industry, the Michigan economy, the unions, the stockholders, and the State of Michigan Pension Fund by the sale of twenty-two million shares to Los Angeles financier Kirk Kerkorian. The analysts are divided on the impact, but they are united on one issue; Chrysler is headed for trouble one way or the other. And the company is looking for a savior.

Unlike titles such as priest and prophet, which have come to us from primarily religious usage, the term "savior" has come from secular usage. The root of the Hebrew word means "to develop without hindrance." Originally, savior was a title applied to successful military generals or warring kings (as mentioned in II Kings 13:5 or Judges 3:9). David was declared a savior because as a chieftain he had conquered the neighboring Philistines, making it safe for Israelites to travel and work without hindrance.

The term savior, then, is a title reserved for situations in which individuals, nations, or even companies like Chrysler are threatened by hostile takeovers. The one who turns things around—making it safe and secure to live—is called a savior. The headline I cited is unusual, because today we think of a savior primarily in religious contexts. We have reserved this title for Jesus as *the* savior, *our* savior, or *my* savior. However, this is actually a post-biblical development of the title (even though we assume it is part of Jesus's original understanding).

Dr. Robert Coles, the Harvard psychiatrist who gained a national reputation with his study, "Children of Crisis," has continued over the past twenty years to monitor the status of children in the world. His most recent study, which he admits was the most difficult to secure funding, is titled "Children and Spirituality: Religious Values in Children." Dr. Coles and his staff have interviewed hundreds of children in this country and abroad, seeking to determine what part religious values play in healthy child development.

His interview style is organized on themes. He asks one question at a time about the significant figure within one's religious tradition. Dr. Coles reports that he is almost embarrassed to admit that children are able to articulate words about faith better than he. He recounts an interview with two girls aged seven and eight. He asked the girls the question, "Who is Jesus?" Summarizing the interview, the first girl volunteered, "He's the one who takes care of things when things go wrong." The second girl piped in, "Sometimes he doesn't help, but my mother does; but that's all right, he is still my savior."

Our belief that a personal savior assists in an individual's situations reflects considerable movement from the belief in the Hebrew scriptures that a savior is one who rescues an entire nation or a whole people. The title "my savior" postdates the gospels, and most use appears in the late first and early second century CE. It appears in only one of the gospels, Luke, where it is mentioned in the Christmas story.

By this time, the Roman Empire had been using the title "savior" for the Caesars, due to their splendid military and political rescues from chaos to order. "Caesar is my savior" was a common oath required of citizens. Over the gates of many cities was inscribed "Caesar-Savior" to inform all who entered that the power of Rome protected the area. The cult of Caesars was an anathema to Christians. They replied collectively and individually, "Not Caesar, but Jesus is my savior." Because of this refrain, Christians were accused of treason, beginning the extensive waves of persecutions in the second and third centuries CE, culminating with Diocletian. Over twenty thousand Christians are believed to have been killed in his reign alone.

While the first-century creeds described Jesus as "lord," the second and third centuries added "savior," resulting in a dual affirmation, "Jesus is Lord and Savior," by the fourth century. (It was not until the Protestant revivalism of nineteenth-century America that the individual possessive pronouns "my" and "our" come into religious affirmations.)

As a title, savior has received more attention in times of turmoil, when things are out of control. After the Roman Emperor Constantine converted to Christianity in the fourth century, most martyrdom in the Roman Empire ceased, and "lord" became more prominently used.

Then during the so-called Dark Ages of the church, "savior" was more important. And then in the Renaissance, there was a return to "lord." Through the ages, in times of peace and prosperity, we see "lord," but in times of war or depression, we see "savior."

Today, many of the unchurched, as well as those in the mainline denominational churches, are unconvinced they need a savior. "Saviors are for people out of control," they state. And very few of us are going to admit publicly that we are out of control, that we can't handle everything. Isn't that what we learned from our first steps? "I can do it myself!"

Likewise, I remember an advertisement on television during the time that ATMs were first being introduced. The script went something like this: "Don't you want to take charge of your money? Then why do you let your bank tell you when you can get your money? We'll let you take charge twenty-four/seven, fifty-two weeks of the year with our new ATM. Take charge!"

We are taught to be take-charge people. We have the power to make things happen. Our bookstands are filled with self-help authors telling us how to be in control—right now! Very few of us feel the need—when we are in control—for a savior. The only time we admit that we need a savior is when the situation is out of control: a tragic accident, death, illness, divorce, unemployment, business failure, financial failure, or personal failure. Whether we admit it or not, we secretly await a savior to restore us to a place where "there is no hindrance."

Those of us who have gone through a crisis will hardly deny the sense of alienation we feel from God and from the rest of humanity when our lives are out of control. We lose self-esteem. We operate with reduced energy and resources. Then we count ourselves fortunate if a physician, teacher, business associate, banker, lawyer, friend, parent, or spouse responds in a way that lifts our heavy anxiety and helps end our paralysis. We can see the light of day again. We are grateful that he or she has saved us.

While many of us might feel uncomfortable giving direct credit to Jesus for saving us in such situations, there are Christian traditions that make public testimony of such belief. In their worship services, they acknowledge how Jesus has taken charge to turn things around. Remember the eight-year-old girl's comment? "My mother helps, but he is still my savior." In that little girl's tradition, the mother is in cooperation with Jesus. We may be much more likely to believe that Jesus works through other people. In this way, we don't have to acknowledge directly and publically that we are out of control.

There is a refreshing pause for us in the Christmas story from Luke, because we have to recite each year these words about a savior. By this very recitation, we acknowledge that in some ways we are out of control. We await a savior, perhaps not as Chrysler does, but certainly like Dr. Cole's young interviewees. We are forced to acknowledge at least the possibility that at times our lives are out of control. We do not only need a lord to whom we can appear in our self-respecting pride to show our good works and deeds. We also need a savior who does not need to humiliate us in our failures, but lifts us up "without hindrance."

The Shepherds and the Angels

2 **8** In that region there were shepherds living in the fields, keeping watch over their flock by night. **9** Then an angel of the Lord stood before them, and the glory of the Lord shone around them, and they were terrified. **10** But the angel said to them, "Do not be afraid; for see—I am bringing you good news of great joy for all the people: **11** to you is born this day in the city of David a Savior, who is the Messiah, the Lord. **12** This will be a sign for you: you will find a child wrapped in bands of cloth and lying in a manger." **13** And suddenly there was with the angel a multitude of the heavenly host, praising God and saying,

14 "Glory to God in the highest heaven,
  and on earth peace among those whom he favors!"

15 When the angels had left them and gone into heaven, the shepherds said to one another, "Let us go now to Bethlehem and see this thing that has taken place, which the Lord has made known to us." **16** So they went with haste and found Mary and Joseph, and the child lying in the manger.

17 When they saw this, they made known what had been told them about this child; **18** and all who heard it were amazed at what the shepherds told them. **19** But Mary treasured all these words and pondered them in her heart. **20** The shepherds returned, glorifying and praising God for all they had heard and seen, as it had been told them.

A rumor of angels
to shepherds

Sermon by Richard Murdoch | East Lansing, MI | December 19, 1993

What do you know of shepherds and their sheep? When I delve back into my memory bank, a collage of images comes to my mind. The earliest I recall are from when I was elementary school age. I was taken to visit a very old home called the Eakin Place. As part of the buildup, my father pointed out that not only was it the home of my great-great-grandparents, but for a hundred years, it had been known for its sheep.

Initially, we kids were disappointed because the house did not live up to our expectations. Maybe in the past it had been a famous place, but now it was a primitive and ill-kempt place. But for us children, it soon acquired a magical quality. Over several visits, stories abounded about Revolutionary and Civil War times, punctuated by a cousin's pointing to a special piece of furniture or a visit one foggy night to the family graveyard—complete with a stone wall and squeaky gate.

The most curious and fascinating object to us was a piece of equipment that had an extended arm with a pair of shears at the end. At its base was a treadle that was similar to a sewing machine's. This contraption was Cousin James's mechanical sheep-shearing machine. If I remember the story correctly, at the State Fair in 1908, he had the quickest shearing time with this new-fangled machine (which the neighbors had ridiculed). "Would you like to see the barn where he kept the sheep at night?" another wizened cousin asked. "Of course!" And off we trudged, having never seen a sheepfold at our tender age.

I remember my father telling me that Cousin James had died more than ten years earlier. And the sheep had been sold. "So don't expect to see the sheep," we were warned as we entered the barn. But we didn't need to know the sheep had been sold; as far as we knew from the stench, the sheep were still there. No one had cleaned the fold; they simply closed the door for all those years. My childhood message about sheep was clear. Sheep were smelly and dirty! From that time on, the sheep in the Christmas crèche took on a different dimension for me.

Of course, as you can infer from this experience, I never met Cousin James (who was indeed a shepherd). But based on family stories, he was a laidback loner, and not so different from shepherds I saw when I later visited Greece. Spending long periods alone in the hillsides, day or night, shepherds often rely on to their daydreams to make the time shorter. They depend upon their *gaida* (bagpipe) and wine flagon for companionship, along with their faithful sheepdog.

Sheepherding is a necessary profession in the semi-arid regions of the Mediterranean, but not necessarily a status profession. While individual, working shepherds are not held in high esteem in their cultures, the owner of the flocks or chief shepherd (who remains home) can be quite wealthy and influential. But it was not to the chief shepherd that the angel came that Christmas night so long ago. Instead, it was to the minimum-wage sub-shepherds.

The real surprise in this angel story is not the angel's appearance, but the shepherds' response. They left their flocks on the hillside, unprotected and vulnerable to night winds and foraging wolves in order to run off to town to chase a dream. Dreaming and fantasy, of course, is expected of shepherds who are alone so much of the time. But it is unexpected for them to put their sheep in jeopardy to follow their dream. "Ah!" you say, "But they took their sheep with them." Well, that's not a possibility. If you have ever seen a shepherd herding sheep across a road (while you watch from a tour bus) you'll know that the speed at which a flock moves is not unlike that of a snail! Nor is it a possibility to rouse a flock of sheep at midnight and drive them braying through the streets of a village in the darkness of the night without sending the whole town into chaos.

The shepherds gave no thought to their charge. They responded on impulse, without thinking. They were awed. They were struck with wonder. They had no time to consider the consequences of their action. "They went with haste," says verse 16. But a more accurate translation would be: "They left immediately, as fast as they could run."

What led them to do such an irresponsible thing as leaving their sheep and running—something that was completely out of character? It was not the angel's announcement that sent them running in awe and wonder. It was what happened after the announcement—the appearance of the "heavenly host."

In first-century apocalyptic Judaism, there had developed a belief in several levels of divine beings who were present with God and did God's work in heaven and on earth. Since the powers of the world at that time (the Roman occupation government) could not be trusted to bring order to chaos, Yahweh's government could and would. God, like a king, was supposed to sit upon a heavenly throne, surrounded by a host of divine beings who provided light, wisdom, and celestial music. This host numbered anywhere from forty-nine million angels to twelve legions of a thousand angels each. They believed that around the throne direction was given by four archangels, two of which appear in the Christmas narratives—Gabriel and Michael—plus two others, Raphael and Uriel. Beneath these four, who were God's primary messengers to the world, were other different levels of angels who served a variety of tasks for God as directed by the archangels: Seraphim, Cherubim, Thrones, Dominions, Powers, and so on.

The idea that each believer has a guardian angel developed in the Middle Ages as early as the ninth century CE. By the Renaissance era (fifteenth century CE), the various levels of angels showed up frequently in religious paintings commissioned by the Christian church. The enduring artistic and literary allusions for an order of angels expressed the need of the human spirit to rise above the everyday events of survival. But little was made of the importance of angels during the Protestant Reformation. The two luminaries of which we hear the most were divided on the subject.

Reformer Martin Luther accepted the work of angels as intermediaries for the divine in this world. He continued to embrace the Renaissance notion of the guardian angel for each redeemed Christian, perched invisibly upon the right shoulder. The left shoulder was reserved, of course, for the tempting messengers of Satan. It was believed that angels were the incarnation of God. (But as the gulf between heaven and earth grew in church theology, Mary became the intercessor before God. And as time wore on, even Mary became remote, and guardian angels were considered the closest presence of God to humanity.)

But John Calvin—the other notable Protestant reformer—rejected all notions of angels, saying that they detracted from the redeeming work of Jesus. Angels weren't needed, and neither were priests. Believers could access God for themselves directly through prayer, Bible, and discipleship. In fact, one reason for the elimination of Christmas celebrations in Calvin's reformed church was his quandary of what to do with all the angels.

Many of us have inherited the Calvinist quandary with angels. We are reasonable and rational human beings who would be hard-pressed to defend a visit from an angel to our friends or work colleagues. Yet, at least one time of the year—during the Christmas season—many of us are comfortable singing carols and listening to scripture lessons about angels as if they were everyday occurrences. Some, such as Peter Berger, author of *A Rumor of Angels: Modern Society and the Rediscovery of the Supernatural,* have suggested that our wonderment today is not vast, that we have no need of angelic beings to remind us that there is a tremendous world out there yet to be known. Ancients marveled that angels could fly. They were jealous of beings that could travel so fast and so effortlessly. Yet if flight is considered as criteria for judging angels, there are millions and millions of angels today—every passenger on any airplane flight.

There is a recent surge of interest in angels. For example, Sophy Burnham's book, *A Book of Angels: Reflections on Angels, Past and Present, and True Stories of How They Touch Our Lives,* is now a *New York Times* bestseller that has sold over a million copies. In it she suggests that our sense of wonder today extends no less beyond the technological than our ancestors. The difference today is that it is not about survival (such as food, shelter, and transportation), but it is now about promoting health and longevity in order to enjoy technology. We seek the newest advance in research on cancer or AIDS, which is rushed upon as a wonder drug. Likewise, any procedure to restore health or prolong life is considered a wonder. People sit in wonder as their lives are spared on a commuter train, when those right next to them are killed by random shots from an unknown assailant. Nations are awed by a seventy-year alliance of Soviet republics disintegrating before them, making competing arsenals obsolete.

Regardless of whether or not we need angels to represent the wonder beyond which we have control, our need for wonder today is no less like that of the shepherds. We hurry to see whatever will help us make sense of the world in which we live. For the shepherds, it was the news of a second chance for their beloved Israel to be freed from the clutches of Roman occupation; for us, it is a second chance from the clutches of our uncertain personal worlds.

We listen without wonderment, that's the story. Where has the wonder gone? It's time to embrace the wonderment of the world.

The Visit of the Wise Men

2 ¹ In the time of King Herod, after Jesus was born in Bethlehem of Judea, wise men from the East came to Jerusalem, ² asking, "Where is the child who has been born king of the Jews? For we observed his star at its rising, and have come to pay him homage."

³ When King Herod heard this, he was frightened, and all Jerusalem with him; ⁴ and calling together all the chief priests and scribes of the people, he inquired of them where the Messiah was to be born. ⁵ They told him, "In Bethlehem of Judea; for so it has been written by the prophet:

⁶ 'And you, Bethlehem, in the land of Judah,
   are by no means least among the rulers of Judah;
for from you shall come a ruler
   who is to shepherd my people Israel.'"

⁷ Then Herod secretly called for the wise men and learned from them the exact time when the star had appeared. ⁸ Then he sent them to Bethlehem, saying, "Go and search diligently for the child; and when you have found him, bring me word so that I may also go and pay him homage."

⁹ When they had heard the king, they set out; and there, ahead of them, went the star that they had seen at its rising, until it stopped over the place where the child was. ¹⁰ When they saw that the star had stopped, they were overwhelmed with joy. ¹¹ On entering the house, they saw the child with Mary his mother; and they knelt down and paid him homage. Then, opening their treasure chests, they offered him gifts of gold, frankincense, and myrrh. ¹² And having been warned in a dream not to return to Herod, they left for their own country by another road.

What do the stars hold?

Sermon by Richard Murdoch | Rye, NY | October 26, 1997

Two millennia ago, an entourage of some very influential figures from a world-class power visited Palestine, which was classified as part of the Third World. However, there are no corroborating sources for this visit in the other gospels or in any secular sources. Thus, whatever is to be known about it must be gleaned not only from reading the Gospel of Matthew, but also from reading between the lines.

At the very beginning of Christianity, we are introduced to astrology and astronomy—neither of which has been much welcomed by the church since. Astrology, which believes that human destiny is controlled by the stars, has never been widely accepted by Christianity. It is often considered part of the "unscientific occult," accented by tarot cards and fortune tellers. Astronomy, representing the scientific study of the stars, has not fared much better.

Consider Galileo, for example. In 1633 CE, Galileo was excommunicated from the Roman Catholic Church because of his scientific claim that the earth revolved around the sun. Not until 1992—three hundred and fifty-nine long years later—did the Vatican finally revoke his excommunication.

In the very beginning, astrology and astronomy were a significant part of the Christian story. What did the stars hold for the writer of Matthew that the church later found difficult to reconcile with its belief? And what do the stars hold today?

Astrologers promise to divine the secrets of the stars under which one is born. Being born under the sign of Capricorn, for example, can have different results than being born under another sign of the zodiac. To most early Christians, the names of these constellations invoke incantations of a primitive religion that was centered in creation, not the Creator. And for many years, astronomy—because it often used the same names—was considered one short step from astrology, leading to cries of idolatry and demands for punishment at a burning stake. For daring to explain the difference between how the two explained what the stars held, Galileo was excommunicated.

Stars were serious business not only in primitive religions that worshipped nature, but also in the religions of more so-called advanced civilizations such as the Greeks and the Egyptians, as well as in Judaism. By looking to the sky, sailors found navigational direction, fishermen predicted their catch, farmers measured the season to plant or harvest, and millers ground their meal. If an error was made, their very survival was at stake.

But there was more at stake than their livelihood: They believed that their very lives were at risk if the stars were not read correctly. They saw a purpose and plan in the stars. The stars were fixed in place, and no matter how people devised ways to manipulate them, the stars were beyond their control. Surely, they were creations or agents of the divine.

Now before one dismisses this as uncritical thinking, how many times have you heard people say that God has a plan in this or that situation because an unplanned event has turned out to make sense when viewed from hindsight? The biblical psalms reflect many times that God has set the stars in the heavens to give boundaries to the world. Since the arrangements of stars in the constellations were observed to be unchanged from generation to generation, it indicated to people a power greater than themselves. They believed the earth below was a reflection of the heavens above. By observing what happened above, they could predict what might happen below.

It is clear that, according to the Gospel of Matthew, neither Mary nor Joseph regarded their visitors' message of a "natal" or birth star as out of the ordinary or contradicting their faith. Nor does the book have any negative teaching about it. It is reported that Jesus was born under a special star that had the power not only to direct these diplomatic visitors to find him but also to predict his future.

While the name of the constellation or the zodiac rendering is missing, the intent is still clear. This star held a unique opportunity; a unique potential for the infant Jesus. And the visitors demonstrated their commitment with three very expensive and significant gifts.[1] This was not some publicity stunt—these men stood behind their years of research. Now that they had reached their destination and their wisdom was revealed, it was expected that Mary and Joseph would guide their son in fulfilling his potential as predicted by his birth star. And it is evident that the Roman occupational government of the time (headed by Herod) took the prediction of the star just as seriously—though in a negative and defensive way. An order for the slaughter of all males under two years old was issued in Palestine soon after the departure of the visitors (one aspect of the story that can be substantiated from secular sources).

While we may use different terminology in our contemporary world, the desire to predict a successful outcome in our lives still occupies the energies of many people. Whether it is in the commercial world of financial, commodity, real estate, or manufacturing markets—or in parenting to predict the educational opportunities our youngsters need to succeed—accurate predictions are definitely a plus. And getting those predictions to come true takes a great deal of our time and energy.

To say that a star holds our destiny is another way of saying that potential has boundaries. Reaching beyond our grasp is what propels us forward in our lives. The runner—not content to simply match a record—reaches just a bit further to feel the thrill of victory. The inventor—who dares to push beyond established convention—can further the progress of humanity. But reaching for potential is directly related to what resources are possible. The physical condition of that runner will set his boundaries. The capital available to an inventor will set hers. In a sophisticated twenty-first century, and in a technological and democratic society, this is a difficult belief to hold because we have grown up believing that our boundaries are endless.

Geneticists are discovering more and more about our potential and our boundaries. Balancing supporters and opponents of each theory, the truth is probably somewhere in between—and as incredible as suggesting that our destiny is controlled by stars. Since the 1953 discovery by James Watson and Francis Crick, we have known about the double-helix model of DNA and that the genes contained in six feet of DNA set individual boundaries within which each of us can develop and interact. Bio-medical researchers at Swiss Federal Institute of Technology in Zurich have now discovered a step beyond—this six feet of genes are woven around each other in three-dimensional spirals that unwoven equal one hundred and thirteen billion miles or the equivalent of fifteen round trips from the sun to the farthest planet Pluto![2] Suggesting that our destiny is held under the old-fashioned influence of a star might be simpler to comprehend than this new discovery!

The dawning of the twenty-first century is bringing a renewed energy of people striving to put meaning into their lives. This weekend's edition of *Parade* magazine reports that a new career service had joined dozens already opened this year in the Denver area. It is designed to assist people in securing secular jobs that match not only their skill and financial potential, but also their spirituality potential. The article goes on to report that while traditional means of assessing and predicting both skill and financial potential were readily available, the real challenge for the career service's owners was finding a way to do the same for spirituality. They had found that their initial clients could articulate their perception of potential, but perceiving their boundaries was uncharted territory.

Our potential is perceived to be the sky, but the concept that there are boundaries is unfamiliar. Boundaries can change the very fulfillment of our perceived potential. What the stars held for the infant Jesus—the visitors believed—was a kingdom of peace and love as an earthly ruler. Yet the boundaries of that potential were turned in a different direction and ultimately made clear in the final week of Jesus's life. The sin and cruelty of the world has no power over God. Jesus's destiny of his untimely death was to bequeath of all humanity the truth that God is God—in life and in death.

What the stars hold for us individually is a lifetime journey, one that we can feel in our heart when we serve God and our fellow humanity.

[1] Interesting note: Scholars are not sure how many wise men there were. The tradition of three wise men is based on the three gifts that were mentioned (assuming one man carried each gift). However, there could have been many more wise men, or two carrying three gifts, and so on.

[2] When my father wrote this sermon, Pluto was still a planet. However, in 2006, scientists at the meeting of the International Astronomical Union voted to remove Pluto's status as a "real" planet. It was reclassified as a dwarf planet. (Did you know Pluto has a twin named Eris? But I digress.) In 2014, some scientists started murmuring Pluto should be reinstated to full planet status. Nostalgically, I agree.

The Testimony of John the Baptist / The Lamb of God

1 ^{21} And they [Pharisees visiting from Jerusalem] asked him [John the Baptist], "What then? Are you Elijah?" He said, "I am not." "Are you the prophet?" He answered, "No." ^{22} Then they said to him, "Who are you? Let us have an answer for those who sent us. What do you say about yourself?" ^{23} He said,

"I am the voice of one crying out in the wilderness,
'Make straight the way of the Lord,'
as the prophet Isaiah said."

^{24} Now they had been sent from the Pharisees. ^{25} They asked him, "Why then are you baptizing if you are neither the Messiah, nor Elijah, nor the prophet?" ^{26} John answered them, "I baptize with water. Among you stands one whom you do not know, ^{27} the one who is coming after me; I am not worthy to untie the thong of his sandal." ^{28} This took place in Bethany across the Jordan where John was baptizing...

^{29} The next day he saw Jesus coming toward him and declared, "Here is the Lamb of God who takes away the sin of the world! ^{30} This is he of whom I said, 'After me comes a man who ranks ahead of me because he was before me.' ^{31} I myself did not know him; but I came baptizing with water for this reason, that he might be revealed to Israel."

^{32} And John testified, "I saw the Spirit descending from heaven like a dove, and it remained on him. ^{33} I myself did not know him, but the one who sent me to baptize with water said to me, 'He on whom you see the Spirit descend and remain is the one who baptizes with the Holy Spirit.' ^{34} And I myself have seen and have testified that this is the Son of God."

The human experience of trust

Sermon by Richard Murdoch | Omaha, NE | December 16, 1979

Water is a commodity that none of us can do without. The ancient Greek philosophers supposed that all life—human, animal, and plant—was composed of four elements, one of which was water. All religious groups since the history of civilization have in some way or another made use of water in its rituals. Water symbolizes life; it symbolizes cleansing; it symbolizes blessing. Water is wet, cool, quiet, and soft.

The ancient Egyptians had a religious myth that combined all three uses in their religion of Isis and Osiris. Each spring, the Nile River would flood, bringing several new inches of fertile earth for the year's crop. It would wash away the debris and cleanse the land of its impurities—and finally bring the blessing of a rich harvest. If this annual cycle was missed, then the whole land was subject to famine. Each season, the Egyptians would trust their gods to send water for new life, cleansing, and blessing.

In fact, water played a big part in Hebrew rituals as well, especially through ritual washing for purification. No doubt when Jacob and his brothers were in Egypt, they had witnessed the Egyptian rituals.

Christian tradition—steeped in the life of the Hebrew prophets and scriptures—also adopted this symbol of new life, cleansing, and blessing. It took the water of baptism as an outward sign of an inward grace. It was a visible sign that either something had taken place or would be taking place. While baptism has been administered in different ways over the centuries, the theological significance has been the same—initiation into the faith.

The human experience of baptism—apart from the theological symbolism—has always centered on trust. Consider the infant baptism story of Queen Elizabeth I of England. In those days (as it still is in many Orthodox Christian groups), the custom was to completely immerse infants in the baptismal font. Often, this was a large marble pillar filled with water. The infant was plunged into the water by the priest, and emerged crying quite loudly. The biography of Queen Elizabeth states that the infant princess cried profusely, as if being birthed from the womb. The royal family was of the utmost trusting nature to allow its heir to be baptized. It was not unknown for renegade priests to drown an heir apparent and change the direction of a monarchy. Entrusting an infant into the hands of another demonstrated an active nature. There was nothing passive or nonchalant about witnessing a baptism in those days. Anything might happen.

Trust has to be an experience of handing over, of letting go, of transferring to another. When we talk about trusting a teenage driver with the family car, we hand over the car keys. When we speak about trusting children to go to a movie by themselves, we are handing over their welfare to them. When we talk about trusting a person with a credit card, we are handing over the decision to make wise purchases. When we speak about trusting a bank with our money, we hand over protection to another.

The scripture reading this morning speaks of the same experience of handing over. John the Baptist is confronted by a group from Jerusalem on the question of baptism. They inquire of John the significance of the baptism. Because John claims to be neither a prophet nor the Messiah, their accusation is similar to false advertising. John answers the question from the viewpoint of trust. He states that he is only the forerunner of the Messiah. There is one in their midst someplace who will be greater than he—and when that person appears, his baptism of water will be handed over, and John will let go. He will transfer the reins to the Messiah. The next day, John the Baptist sees his cousin, Jesus, coming, and in a prophetic state he announces that Jesus is the one. John knows he must trust; he knows he must let go; he knows he must hand over.

Trust is based on a combination of both facts and feelings—probably more feelings than facts. Faith is closely tied to trust, but has more of a rationale or reasonableness to it than does trust. Oftentimes, trust can be a gut-level feeling based on a bare minimum of facts. It is usually based on some previous experiences that have been trustful.

We talk about trusting a friend. If you really trust a friend, you can bare your innermost secret to him or her without fear that it will be broadcast. Once a friend has broken a confidence, your level of trust will diminish considerably. You'll be very cautious about entrusting again—regardless of how good the person may reason that it was in your best interest to tell your secret.

A child who is learning to swim needs to trust the parent or instructor. If that parent or instructor leads the child into deeper water too soon—or takes a hand away from the floating body and lets it sink—the child will be extremely careful not to seek the experience of swimming again soon.

Trust also requires some updating and reinforcement. It is not something that grows by itself. It must be worked at, for it is active. It requires energy on the part of those developing a trusting relationship.

Amy, our five-year-old, looked at her bank book the other day and asked how much money she had. When I told her the amount, she said, "I want to *see* it." I explained to her that it was at the bank. She then said, "Let's go to the bank. I want to see my money." She didn't want to spend it, she wanted to see it. She wanted to be reinforced.

I can imagine the confused face of the bank teller when Amy asks to see her money—which she thinks is kept in a special place in the bank just for her. She will have to develop trust to realize that her money, in effect, is everybody else's money also—it is just transferred around from person to person. But she wants to be reinforced that the bank's word can be kept.

We all must trust. There is no way to live in a world of human beings without in some way trusting people. The greatest barrier to trust is, of course, our fear that it will be broken. Our greatest fear is that when trust is broken that either we won't be able to forgive or that we won't feel that we have been forgiven. Trust is always a risk—because we are putting ourselves on the line. Trust is not for the security seeker. Trust is for the pilgrim who knows that life is never secure in and of itself.

The human experience of trust must be coupled with a supreme trust in God at the very same time we are trusting at a human level. Each time we trust our gut-level feelings about a situation, we must also trust that God has seen fit to put our heart and soul in tune to the right thing.

Each time we reinforce or update our trust, we need to trust God for courage and wisdom to carry it through. Nothing tears down a marriage, nothing tears down a business, nothing tears down a friendship, nothing tears down a partnership, nothing tears down a family like tat-tling, backbiting, and talking behind people's backs.

When we are able to hand over—and let go to God—then both the re-inforcement and the growing comes naturally, as long as we can use forgiveness wisely and knowingly.

Trust, like water, always involves a risk: Too much water can drown us; too little water can dehydrate us. Trust can be both a blessing and a curse—too much of the wrong kind of trust will destroy us; too little trust will cause us to shrivel and lose our humanity.

The Beginning of the Galilean Ministry / Jesus Calls the First Disciples

1 ¹⁴ Now after John [the Baptist] was arrested, Jesus came into Galilee, preaching the gospel of God, ¹⁵ and saying, "The time is fulfilled, and the kingdom of God is at hand; repent, and believe in the gospel."

¹⁶ And passing along by the Sea of Galilee, he saw Simon and Andrew the brother of Simon casting a net in the sea; for they were fishermen. ¹⁷ And Jesus said to them, "Follow me and I will make you become fishers of men." ¹⁸ And immediately they left their nets and followed him. ¹⁹ And going on a little farther, he saw James the son of Zeb'edee and John his brother, who were in their boat mending the nets. ²⁰ And immediately he called them; and they left their father Zeb'edee in the boat with the hired servants, and followed him.

Bible Version: Revised Standard Version (RSV)

Disappearance of sin

Sermon by Richard Murdoch | Omaha, NE | January 2, 1980

The story is told of a young child who was accompanying his parents to worship one Sunday. The preacher asked a rhetorical question, "And do you know what sin is?" And before he could answer his question, a child's voice rang out loud and clear, "It's anything you do that is fun!"

That child's perception of sin is not far from the popular notion of what sin is. Borrowed from the Puritan era, this definition prohibits "pleasure"—especially any departure from accepted cultural norms and values. In the early days of upland Colonial Virginia, where the Scots Irish settled, it was not uncommon to pay the pastor with x number of gallons of whiskey as his salary, since this was a medium of exchange (and an important commodity). The Anglican parishes of the tidewater country paid their rectors in so many hogsheads[1] of tobacco. To the Colonials, paying in alcohol or tobacco was no sin.

Leap forward to Prohibition days. You can imagine it was a sin to pay in whiskey. Leap forward in time again and a hogshead of tobacco might pose a problem as to whether the sin lay in selling it or in consuming it.

To put it in child's language, sin is any no-no.

However, the Puritans (and many of us today) would flunk a Bible quiz on what is sin. The biblical idea of sin is far from a special action. Instead, it has a focus in several definitions.

The classic definition for centuries in Hebrew and Christian theology was that sin is self-pride—pride in believing that all the answers of existence (life *and* death) could be answered by looking inward without any need of a divine or higher being. In the oldest definition of sin, it is pride. St. Augustine declared in his fifth-century writings: "But my sin was this, that I looked for pleasure, beauty, and truth not in him but in myself and his other creatures, and the search led me instead to pain, confusion, and error."

This definition falls short, though. An unhealthy reliance on this definition could mean that people would rely completely on God, without any personal responsibility or ambition. People would not look for better ways to feed themselves. They would rely upon God's miracles to feed them. They would not explore the nature of the body and its illnesses. They would expect God to heal by miracles alone. There would be no need to govern nations—they would rely upon the religious leaders to preach love and everybody would naturally follow their words. In other words, they would do nothing for themselves. They would leave it up to God to have pity upon their condition and create miracles after miracles, as long as they humbled themselves and did not take pride in their own accomplishments.

So a second definition appears (based on the Greek text), from which the Puritans and the Victorians derived their approach. Here, sin means "missing the mark." It is the picture of an archer pulling back a bow, ready to set an arrow flying. His intentions are to hit the bullseye. But because his finger slips, or the string is not waxed, or the shaft is crooked, the arrow misses the mark—not intentioned, but by something that needs improvement. In this view, the bullseye is the moral life and the arrows are behaviors that need to be improved.

A couple of hundred years after St. Augustine, Gregory the Great came up with a list of the Seven Deadly Sins—and ever since, people have had their own lists. Let me list his and then suggest some other ones that have come and gone.

Gregory's list was:

1. *Pride*: Showing that he had at least read his Bible and also read St. Augustine!
2. *Lust*: Meaning any sexual desire except for the procreation of children
3. *Gluttony*: Too much to eat and drink so that one either became obese or drunk
4. *Anger*: The result of which was that all preachers would be peacemakers at all cost
5. *Sloth (laziness)*: From which the Puritans coined the phrase "idle hands are the devil's workshop"

6. *Envy:* Wanting something that someone else has so badly you could taste it
7. *Greed:* Having possessions for the sake of possessing things (rather than for their ability to be useful)

From this last one we get the Shaker ideal of simple homes, straight chairs, and two changes of black clothing. Each culture, each century has added or changed the list to fit. In the 1800s, it became a sin to hold slaves. In the 1920s, it was a sin to drink. At one point in Germany, it was a sin not to have parentage of Aryan descent. In the America of the 1950s, it was a sin to be a socialist.

The list became endless depending on who you were and where you were until finally persons realized that sin was rather relative and relational. There seemed to be no authority to gauge which was which—even the Bible had its contradictions. Why was it not a sin for Abraham, Isaac, Solomon, and the other patriarchs to have several wives, but it was a sin in the New Testament? Why was it not a sin for a couple contemplating marriage in Scotland in the 1700s to have a "trial marriage," but it was in America's New England?

The crowning blow to the list of sins was the decree by the Vatican that after 400 years of not eating meat on Fridays (because it was a sin), it was now okay (if a penance was done instead, or some other food abstained from). What about all those who had eaten meat? Were they now absolved of the sin? The Protestants had been through this when reformer Martin Luther declared that clergy could marry without it being a sin (when some thought St. Paul had plainly and emphatically said in the First Letter to the Corinthians that it was).

This historical prologue is just a brief explanation as to why sin has disappeared from our language as a vibrant expression. It has been replaced with a bland, weak, and simple view of sin being subjective (or disappearing all together). An illustration of this is quite revealing. In 1952, the U.S. Congress voted to require the president to offer a national day of prayer. In 1953, President Eisenhower used the prologue of Lincoln when he declared such a day, saying the following:

It is the duty of nations as well as of men, to own their dependence upon the overruling power of God, to confess their sins and trans-

gressions, in humble sorrow, yet with assured hope that genuine repentance will lead to mercy and pardon.

In the next year, speech writers informed Mr. Eisenhower that the wording was offensive and too negative, that the idea of sin should be soft-pedaled because most Americans did not consider themselves sinful—a little prone to mistakes, but certainly not sinful!

The disappearance of sin, of course, has been assisted by psychologists, educators, and theologians—all of which focus more on the power of positive thinking rather than negative sin. Sin has almost disappeared. But in the recent bestseller *Whatever Became of Sin?* Dr. Karl Menninger calls for a cultural, educational, medical, religious, and psychiatric rereading on the concept of sin and how it can aid in a healthy understanding of ourselves and our society. He writes:

> *Like sheep, all of us have gone astray or followed false shepherds after pausing to kill our emergent prophets. Political leaders we have in abundance, as well as military leaders, social leaders, intellectual leaders. But moral leadership languishes.*

That brings to mind the scripture passage today. Jesus, a new preacher on the scene, speaks to his listeners—former members of John the Baptist's flock of believers. The words are deceiving simple, "Repent, for the kingdom of God has come near." It is here and now, and the time is short to accomplish what must be.

Is the time indeed short to set things right in the world? While we might view this differently, depending on our age, time is quickly ticking away at any age if you consider a few observations.

In two weeks, worldwide:

> *2,122,400 people will die;[2]*
> *294,000 of those people will die of starvation;[3]*
> *5,040,000 babies will be added to the world population.[4]*

Or, in two weeks, in a family, a five-year old can:

> *Be bruised several times on the playground and heal entirely;*
> *Eat 42 meals and 142 snacks;*

Wear out a pair of jeans;
Add 150 words to his/her vocabulary.

Or, in two weeks in the Bible:

Much of what we read in the Books of Matthew, Mark, Luke, and
John took place in Jesus's life.

Time passes quickly, and much must be done within it. Jesus's follow-ers knew that time did not stand still. They had to act and accomplish.

So, what sin was Jesus talking about?

His point was simple and direct: Make amends for your trespasses, whatever they may be. Then hear the good news that God is in the world at work.

[1] A hogshead was a large wooden barrel about 48" long and 30" in diameter. When full of tobacco, it weighed about 1,000 lbs.!

[2] Source: *Population Reference Bureau & The World Factbook* from the Central Intelligence Agency (updated from original sermon)
[3] Source: Poverty.com 6/17/2015 (updated from original sermon)
[4] Source: *Population Reference Bureau & The World Factbook* from the Central Intelligence Agency (updated from original sermon)

Nicodemus Visits Jesus

3 [1] Now there was a Pharisee named Nicodemus, a leader of the Jews. [2] He came to Jesus by night and said to him, "Rabbi, we know that you are a teacher who has come from God; for no one can do these signs that you do apart from the presence of God."

[3] Jesus answered him, "Very truly, I tell you, no one can see the kingdom of God without being born from above." [4] Nicodemus said to him, "How can anyone be born after having grown old? Can one enter a second time into the mother's womb and be born?" [5] Jesus answered, "Very truly, I tell you, no one can enter the kingdom of God without being born of water and Spirit. [6] What is born of the flesh is flesh, and what is born of the Spirit is spirit. [7] Do not be astonished that I said to you, 'You must be born from above.' [8] The wind blows where it chooses, and you hear the sound of it, but you do not know where it comes from or where it goes. So it is with everyone who is born of the Spirit."

[9] Nicodemus said to him, "How can these things be?" [10] Jesus answered him, "Are you a teacher of Israel, and yet you do not understand these things?"

[11] "Very truly, I tell you, we speak of what we know and testify to what we have seen; yet you do not receive our testimony. [12] If I have told you about earthly things and you do not believe, how can you believe if I tell you about heavenly things? [13] No one has ascended into heaven except the one who descended from heaven, the Son of Man."

God is
the answer?

Sermon by Richard Murdoch | Corfu, NY | September 15, 1968

While traveling in New England this summer, I saw the side of a barn painted with these words: "God is the Answer." I would disagree with that sign, for I have found that God most oftentimes is considered the problem rather than the answer.

The other day I was talking with a young man who told me that God was a big teddy bear that people clutched and were soothed by when they were in desperate times, or sick, or needed something beyond their own ability to grasp. And when the need to clutch passed, it was put in the corner until it was needed again.

That person has a real grasp of the problem of God. To him, it doesn't feel like a teddy-bear God is the kind of God worth having or even daring to call God.

Or consider the "foxhole God"—a God that people use only when they are in chaos and need to get out of a crisis.

Nicodemus was concerned about a similar problem. This new teacher on the scene, Jesus, seemed to have something to give. It was a matter of conscience, a matter of human nature. In fact, it was so human that Nicodemus got hung up on the point. He came under the cover of darkness so as not to arouse suspicion, so as not to admit his yearning for something beyond the accepted. And the point of his question is the answer which Jesus had been giving—you must be born anew so that you may see God at work in the world (or the traditional language: "the kingdom of God").

Nicodemus was not referred to as a sage or a brilliant man. He is described as being a respected man, a leader. But his intellect was somewhat embarrassed by the fact that Jesus expected one to be born again—into his cradle of nature. To be ejected again into the same world didn't make much sense to Nicodemus, but he was willing to listen. However, what he heard he could not accept. He heard about a man with human concern, with human sensitivity, who would risk abuse by the law to help a man on the Sabbath, a man who would also risk his reputation and public image by living with the poor, a man who knew something about life as well as the sacred books and laws.

But what he heard was the same sentiment all over again: "You must be born again of the spirit." At this, Nicodemus's mind shut off—it was the same old language about God and such heavenly things. He was sorely disappointed because what he heard was different than what he expected. He came to hear about life today, and instead he heard about life tomorrow. He came to hear about man's hope for himself, and instead he heard the same God language all over again.

God becomes a problem for people when they demand to hear what they want to hear from God, when they seek evidence of his presence in a particular place, when they are no longer are satisfied with the words "the spirit blows wherever it wishes as the wind."

Children and parents have a particular way of arriving at a bargain which is quite similar to our actions with God. A parent will set up a condition to get something done and will offer to reward it by satisfying a desire that is already present. For example, Johnny wants to go to the movie with some friends on Saturday afternoon. As a parent, you're not too enthusiastic about his going. Johnny's room is already messy, and he didn't make the bed or pick up his clothes today. You say, "Well, if you don't clean up your room, you can't go." Actually, Johnny has one up on you because sooner or later the room has to be cleaned anyway, and this way he is killing two birds with one stone. He's happy. You pat yourself on the back for driving a good bargain—so both you and Johnny have set your conditions, and both of you have met them. Both of you have produced evidence.

The God game works much in the same way, although the visible evidence on your part is less demanding than his. There is a need that must be met: "God, if only you let... " and on goes your desire. Then the last part of the vow comes: "...I will do this and this." When the time comes, the need is met, and that is the "evidence" of God—because you have set your own conditions to the situation. So, naturally, you remember the situation as God being there for you when you needed him. Then God is returned to the corner until the next crisis. Is it any wonder that people therefore see God as an answer to a host of little crises, but also as a problem when it comes to life as a whole?

Have you ever stopped to consider the reverse of this situation—that God needs you? This is what Jesus was trying to impress on Nicodemus.

It happens to us too, doesn't it? You go to find an answer to your problem and you don't know yourself that you hold the answer. A new outlook is needed. In this case, see that God needs *you*.

One of the basic needs of life is to have needs: the need to be needed by someone else and the need to need someone else. It's not a morbid need, nor a clutching need. It's not a crutch, nor a defect. It's just a healthy feeling that others can contribute to our lives and that we can contribute to others' lives.

No doubt you have known people who need people around them like a buffer. They go to parties so that they can brag about their popularity. They take trips so that they can let people know how much they are needed at home. They constantly tell you how much they are needed, and how the process would break down without them.

But do you also know people who are needed by others? What a contrast! One uses people, the other is used by and for them. One is vain, the other sensible. One is frantically trying to find a reason for his existence, the other calmly and knowingly is living a good, full life. One struggles to keep the day together, the other knows what can be done for good in a day.

The need to have a God can be almost neurotic. God is not much of an answer to anybody who constantly searches for evidence, who sets up his own situations and then says, "God, now prove it to me."

The reverse is true: God needs you. That does make a difference. When you realize God needs you, it is your life that touches others; it is your money that feeds the hungry; it is your concern for law and order that restores faith in goodness and justice.

God needs you to break apart the callousness of humility, the hopelessness of some people's lives. It is you that becomes a candle to light a house without hope; it is you that does not hide under a bushel when light is needed; it is you that becomes the salt to flavor life with some goodness, some laughter, and some genuine concern for the world.

This is evidence for God's presence in the world. It comes in ways that you cannot condition by your own standards. Sometimes the spirit blows where it wishes, and you don't know where God's presence will shine next. Indeed, you may not even recognize it until after it happens.

But the effect will be the same: Lives are changed, people have hope, two are reconciled, someone is fed, someone is loved.

Nicodemus came looking for an answer. However, the words he heard were so old and so commonplace that he missed the point Jesus was making. He thought he heard Jesus say, "You need God," when in fact Jesus said, "Gods needs you." That is where the problem and the answer lie. If you say "I need God," then you are on the wrong road. If you say "God needs me," then you are in for quite a journey.

Love for Enemies

5 ⁴⁵ In so that you may be children of your Father in heaven; for he makes his sun rise on the evil and on the good, and sends rain on the righteous and on the unrighteous.

⁴⁶ For if you love those who love you, what reward do you have? Do not even the tax collectors do the same? ⁴⁷ And if you greet only your brothers and sisters, what more are you doing than others? Do not even the Gentiles do the same? ⁴⁸ Be perfect, therefore, as your heavenly Father is perfect.

In pursuit of perfection or excellence?

Sermon by Richard Murdoch | East Lansing, MI | May 10, 1992

Last month, Nancy Austin, author of *A Passion for Excellence: The Leadership Difference,* locally presented the thesis of her book, which reworks the old saying, "People will beat down your door if you have a better mousetrap." She notes that in this day of highly competitive markets, companies have to change the way they do business—from production to sales. She emphasized (as does her book) that customers expect—and indeed will even pay a premium for—excellence.

Nancy Austin does not stand alone. You also can hear calls for excellence in education. We hear calls for excellence in science and technology. And excellence in the performance and administration of public policy is being renewed in halls of government as backlashes to the savings and loan debacle and the Congressional bank scandal are unfolding. With more than a third of Congressional seats up for election, it will not be business as usual in the fall elections.

But there is a confusing note to this universal call for excellence. It's as confusing as when I was in junior high school. The grading of work was by letters and not grade-point ratios as today.

In American history class, we were confronted with pursuing perfection or excellence. One day, our teacher returned our graded combination essay-and-multiple-choice tests. A group of us all had As, but some of the grades were followed with the word "perfect" and others were followed with the word "excellent." In our spirit of academic competitiveness (or was it jealousy?), we sought to find which was indeed the better grade. Our teacher focused her eyes clearly and, looking Solomon-like, stated, "Excellence and perfection are not synonymous. They each have their own distinct quality." She, of course, did not give us the answer that we had expected. Instead (as a good teacher so often does), she opened the door of learning ever so slightly, just enough to make us find the answer ourselves.

And it hasn't been easy to find that answer. In fact, it has been a bit like the fate of the Twenty-seventh Amendment to the Constitution—initiated in the eighteenth century and passed in the twentieth century.[1] But the distinction between excellence and perfection was finally made clear to me thirty-five years after that history class.

Psychiatrist Steve Wollin recently spoke to a meeting of the American Association for Marriage and Family Therapy, challenging the notion that all of us grow up needing to heal our wounded "inner child," and that we all grow up in dysfunctional families needing to set right the disease of childhood. Indeed, he dared to attack the very bread and butter of his audience by suggesting that we are a culture obsessed with blame before we begin to solve a problem. He concluded his presentation by stating, "As a profession, we need to accept that excellence doesn't mean perfection when it comes to parenting."

Mr. Webster states (in his collective wisdom called a dictionary): "To be perfect is to be complete. To meet all qualifications and expectations. Without fault." In this day of accountability and performance, it has been more than easy enough for social observers to cite the imperfections of American families. If, in the past, such observers found blame with undisciplined children who needed to be tamed by schools, parents, and churches in order to solve society's ills, the pendulum has now swung the other way.

Another speaker at the same conference chided professional therapists for being manipulated by hordes of "adult children" who have sought professional counseling in this decade because they feel incapable of leading satisfying lives due to what they perceive as inadequate or poor parenting by their mothers and fathers. "We let our clients spend more energy on blaming than problem solving; more time on delving into the past than re-constructing the present," that speaker said.

It wasn't long after that workshop that I received a phone call from a former parishioner whose son I had married some years earlier[2]. The son's marriage was a brief one, and he had remarried in another state where he now resided. By Christmas of that year, letters began to arrive addressed to Dad only. The son had entered therapy, and in the course of working out his therapeutic agenda, he expressed the feeling that he and his dad didn't have the same relationship as his two brothers had with his dad. His dad responded just as you would imagine—that is, if you have more than one child in your family.

But the letters of blame kept coming, to the point that Dad no longer opened them. So Mom tried to intercede on Dad's behalf, but it backfired. The son began to accuse Mom of abusive emotional behavior. And, as you probably can guess, the other two brothers and a sister caught wind of the letter writing. And they were outraged. Their brother had received no better or no worse from Mom and Dad than they had. Easter vacation that year was a disaster, to put it mildly. And the letters kept coming over the summer.

Then, almost a year later, Mom hit upon a stroke of wisdom. As she related to me over the phone—as she was wondering if she had acted appropriately—she had sent a one-page note to the effect of:

> *Dear Marty, We have been faithfully trying to respond to your letters and hoping that we were assisting in your therapy. I regret to say that while we didn't write what you wanted to hear, you didn't exactly write what we wanted to read, either. We finally figured out that we have tried to reason and apologize ourselves back into your love, and that it didn't work. We simply were not perfect parents; that much we acknowledge, but we think we had some excellent times with all four of you—but in different ways. We never expected perfection, why did you? We will not accept the blame for your unhappiness at thirty-two years of age. Love, Mom and Dad.*

No return letter has come, yet.

When did we ever raise in youth the expectation that perfect, completely functioning children are produced by perfect, completely functioning parents? What kind of human engineering do we think we can produce? The expectation that perfection is possible in most anything human is ludicrous from a theological standpoint. Perhaps the missed cue is our perceived perception of the biblical notion of perfection which is often discussed in the gospels. Today's reading from the Gospel of Matthew is a case in point. The translation seems too simple and straightforward. I learned it as a kid in church school from "Be Ye" posters plastered to the Sunday school's walls. "Be Ye Kind to One Another." "Be Ye Perfect Like Your Father in Heaven."

We do not take time to let our childhood simplicity evolve into an adult inquiry. If we would, we'd delve a bit deeper into this expectation that we must be as perfect as God. Examined more carefully, an equivalent understanding might be to approach or strive for perfection with God as your focus. In the Greek world of the early Christians, perfection was not understood as we might think it is in our twentieth century. In a way, not only contemporary sociology and psychology, but also contemporary theology have created an unreal cultural expectation of perfection as excellence.

Excellence was never expected to be perfection. Perfection is mechanical; excellence is dynamic. It is that spark—that little extra part—that will cover for and excuse what is not perfect.

Remember the papers in my history class? Now it's time for the rest of the story. We compared our papers. A few of the "excellent" papers actually had errors in spelling and grammar, marked in that ignoble red pencil. On the "perfect" papers, the red X marks were noticeably absent. But also absent were some exciting and motivating words like "well stated," "good point, great." There was flair about the excellent papers that was missing in the perfect ones.

It is love that makes us whole—not the mechanical accounting that all the Is have been dotted and all the Ts crossed. Perfection has its place, by all means. But those who pursue perfection as the key to living have missed the mark. The more excellent path to pursue in parenting—and in life in general—is love. Love, which forgives and forgets.

---

[1] Submitted to Congress in 1780, the Twenty-seventh Amendment took a record two hundred and two years, seven months, and twelve days to be ratified. It prohibits any law that changes the salary of members of Congress from taking effect until the start of the next term. It was eventually ratified as the result of an undergraduate student, Gregory Watson, who wrote a paper on it in 1982 (for which he received a C-). He started a successful letter-writing campaign that eventually led to the amendment's ratification.

[2] My father means "performed a marriage ceremony for." I always laughed when he introduced us to someone "he married." Taken literally, he would have had thousands of spouses of various genders in multiple states!

Concerning Prayer

6 [9] Pray then like this:

Our Father who art in heaven,
  hallowed be thy name.
[10] Thy kingdom come.
Thy will be done,
On earth as it is in heaven.
[11] Give us this day our daily bread;
[12] And forgive us our debts,
as we also have forgiven our debtors;
[13] And lead us not into temptation,
But deliver us from evil.

[14] For if you forgive men their trespasses, your heavenly Father also will forgive you;
[15] but if you do not forgive men their trespasses, neither will your Father forgive your trespasses.

Bible Version: Revised Standard Version (RSV)

Concerning prayer

Sermon by Richard Murdoch | Corfu, NY | 1970

"Our Father." Those words begin a form, a set order, a traditional prayer that is universally used by Christians of all churches. It probably is the one thing that all Christians can agree to without having to give up or give in to any other group of Christians.[1]

Much research has been done on the origins and meaning of this prayer. It is clear from the accounts in both the Gospel of Matthew and Gospel of Luke (the prayer is found in both books) that it was tied to a teaching mission of Jesus. It was part of the Sermon on the Mount in Matthew and the corresponding Sermon on the Plain in Luke. The question was asked of Jesus, "How ought we to pray?"

Those at the teaching session were of Jewish faith. At this time, Christianity was not separate from Judaism but merely one denomination in the spectrum of Judaism. Prayer was to be offered privately and publicly as a part of one's faith. Rabbinical tradition had it that the holy purpose of Judaism (as the light of the world) should be blessed in prayers, that God's will should be sought, and that obedience to the traditions of the Jewish fathers and prophets of Moses through Jonah be kept.

Jesus's answer reaffirmed the rabbinical tradition and then added a new dimension. He outlined what was okay to pray for and about:

- Prayer should have a direction that is to God: *Our Father, who art in heaven*
- There should be trust: *Hallowed be your name*
- It should point to the future: *Thy kingdom come*
- It should indicate acceptance of God's presence*: Thy will be done*
- and it should remember worldly concerns as well as spiritual concerns: *on earth as it is in heaven*
- It is okay to pray for survival needs*: Give us our daily bread*

- It must include our relationships with others and our treatment of them: *Forgive us our debts/trespasses as we forgive those who debt/trespass against us*
- It concerns judgments for our actions and our acceptance of responsibility: *Do not bring us to the test* (often stated as *Do not lead us into temptation*, which is an alternate translation of the original Greek πειρασμός).
- Finally, as a suitable ending when addressing a deity: *For yours is the kingdom* (found in the Gospel of Luke version only).

The prayer is a simple cataloguing of acceptable needs and desires on which we can form an acceptable relationship with God.

Much of Judaism in the time of Jesus was concerned with individual purity before God on the Judgment Day and the success of the Jewish nation of Israel. God was addressed as a mighty king, a God above all Gods, a great military commander who had the power to strike down those who did not follow in the way of the Torah. The word for God in Hebrew is unpronounceable. It is *Yod*, a *Heh*, a *Vav*, and a *Heh*—YHVH. It would be the same as if you put together the letters XYZ. You cannot pronounce the word. The word for God was then skipped when read because it was so holy that not even a pronounceable word was permitted. While reading the scripture aloud, when the word for God came up, a hand was held up, and the speaker paused, so that every worshipper could bow low.

You can readily see that, for Judaism in that time, God was awesome and unapproachable. Jesus preferred to portray a God that was personable—like a father—hence the "Our Father" form of the prayer became used. Jewish rabbis familiar with this new sect bitterly debated as to whether the familiar address of "father" was blasphemous or not. Finally, they let it pass with that old phrase, "If it be of God, it will survive; if it be not of God, it will die away."

Some people object to using familiar terms to address God, stating it is not respectable. We've gone through cycles of argument ever since the Our Father prayer was written. We've seen the magnificent cathedrals and their splendor, suggesting that God is to be worshipped as a king, and using a formal, kingly language of *thee* and *thou*. In Europe, "high" German was used to address God, kings, and lawyers, while "low" German was used to speak to those of humbler walks of life. And we have customs of nobility such as the removal of hats in church for men and the wearing of hats for women. We have traditions of dressing in fine clothes to worship. All of these various customs point to a respectful and awesome idea of God.

And then, each generation comes along with those who remind us that God is like a friend. Remember the hymn "What a Friend We Have in Jesus"? There are churches that became more relaxed architecturally, and congregations that accordingly relaxed their clothing styles.

There are all sorts of clues as to what kind of relationship is acceptable with our God. Based on the suggestion from Jesus to pray in private, the Quakers would never pray in public meetings—except in silent "quakes." But we also have the suggestion from the Apostle Paul that we must witness and pray before the world. And then we have churches where spotlights are brightened and dimmed theatrically during the pastor's long prayer, in hope that all will hear and come down to the stage to give their lives to Christ.

So, this is our experience as a Christian people—it is a multitude of experiences, all with a scriptural base, but varying depending on the needs of the times and the needs of the individual soul.

Praying one's own prayers requires focus—not merely a mumbling of words. It is one's feelings that must be communicated to God. In years gone by, there were classifications of prayers for different situations. Prayers of only a few words communicating feelings of despair or great joy—"Great God!" "My God!" "Oh Lord!" "Praise God!"—were known as ejaculatory prayers and repeated ten or twelve times in succession in order to evoke and "eject" the feelings of a person.[2]

There were travelers' prayers for passengers on ships, asking for safety on the voyage. The people petitioned God to slay the sea dragons and monsters. To induce courage, sometimes the prayer was addressed to the winds, asking the winds to be kind and secure in their powerful thrusts upon the ship's sails.

There were prayers to purge houses of evil spirits. These prayers communicated feelings of fear, which, once spoken, would cleanse the soul of fear. Similarly, think of the children's prayer that many of us were taught: "Now I lay me down to sleep, I pray the lord my soul to keep. If I should die before I wake, I pray the lord my soul to take."

We have the theological doctrine of omniscience that says that God knows all and sees all before we ask or have need of it. Why then the need for prayer? No need, if all we want to do is to ask for this and that, as children do with permissive parents who will give their child everything and anything her heart desires. But there is a need for prayer if you see prayer as the means toward a relationship.

Relationships are made not by guessing what someone likes about you or needs from you, but by communicating feelings. The same is true about God: A relationship must have feelings communicated. It is okay to tell God you're angry, upset, disappointed, or sick of things. You don't need to put on your pious face and pretend to be someone you aren't because you'd like to appear your best. That doesn't create an honest relationship, does it?

Being yourself before God means being consciously yourself and honest with yourself. Sometimes we will be our miserable selves and sometime our joyful selves—and this is okay. It's not about speaking the words someone wrote, or whether you pray on your knees, standing, sitting, or lying down. It's about communicating your feelings to God and yourself. That's prayer.

[1] Of course, all Christians do not agree on the exact wording of this prayer. An Internet search will bring up many different variations based on the translations of a seemingly endless number of Bibles. One notable difference is "Forgive us our debts" vs. "Forgive us our trespasses." Thus, when I'm at a wedding it's easy to tell the breakdown of the audience by denomination based on whether "debts" or "trespasses" is louder. I learned at my own wedding that we sure had a lot of Catholic friends! Interestingly, a Jewish friend of mine mentioned one day that he began spontaneously saying the Lord's Prayer in the mornings, which might seem odd to some Christians, until we remember that Jesus was Hebrew, so originally the prayer was to teach Hebrews how to pray to God.

[2] I paused when I read this! The use of the word "ejaculatory" in reference to prayer predates its usage as a sexual definition. So I had to clean up my thoughts there.

Man Born Blind Receives Sight

9 [1] As he walked along, he saw a man blind from birth. [2] His disciples asked him, "Rabbi, who sinned, this man or his parents, that he was born blind?" [3] Jesus answered, "Neither this man nor his parents sinned; he was born blind so that God's works might be revealed in him. [4] We must work the works of him who sent me while it is day; night is coming when no one can work. [5] As long as I am in the world, I am the light of the world."

[6] When he had said this, he spat on the ground and made mud with the saliva and spread the mud on the man's eyes, [7] saying to him, "Go, wash in the pool of Siloam" (which means Sent). Then he went and washed and came back able to see. [8] The neighbors and those who had seen him before as a beggar began to ask, "Is this not the man who used to sit and beg?" [9] Some were saying, "It is he." Others were saying, "No, but it is someone like him." He kept saying, "I am the man." [10] But they kept asking him, "Then how were your eyes opened?" [11] He answered, "The man called Jesus made mud, spread it on my eyes, and said to me, 'Go to Siloam and wash.'"

The sighted blind

Sermon by Richard Murdoch | Rye, NY | March 14, 1999

Language is like a kaleidoscope: Each decade gives its own turn to the cylinder, producing arrays of meanings. I had a great aunt who had one leg shorter than the other, because she had polio as a child. When I was young, we used to refer to Aunt Janette as a "cripple." It was not a pejorative word then. But when she retired early under Social Security, "cripple" somehow got changed to "disabled" in our family discussions. When she died some years later, her obituary referred to her as "handicapped." I guess that if she were alive today, sensitivity to politically correctness would describe her as "mobility challenged."

In today's politically correct world, we would be expected to refer to the biblical Bartimaeus as non-sighted or even visually challenged, because blind is too stark and harsh. It describes a physical condition which is neither easy to accept nor to explain. Blindness is failure—the failure of the human body to function correctly. In Jesus's day though, blindness was not only a physical failure—it was also a moral failure. In the story, Jesus is asked, "Whose sin caused this man's blindness—his or his parents'?"

Forthright, weren't they? There was clearly little attempt to soften feelings with political correctness in Jesus's day. But there was good reason. Today, we live in an era of self-assessment. We believe only what we experience and can remember. We forget the rawness with which life was often lived before our time, because that is not in our memory bank. Our technology protects us from much of the unpleasantness of our predecessors. We can cruise in comfort above the ocean and arrive in Europe in less than a half a day, whereas an earlier generation spent a month enduring the sea for a fresh start in the New World. Unlike yesterday's biblical world, when the blind were hidden at home or left to beg in the streets, today the non-sighted are often mainstreamed into the sighted world. Detailed instruction is provided to develop specialized coping skills, often with society's financial support.

There are opportunities for medical transplants to give sight to those who formerly saw only darkness.

In today's America, few of us have the daily experience of encountering the blind or non-sighted among us. Thus our lack of personal contact makes it difficult to understand—unless we have traveled to countries where the lack of any form of social assistance forces the blind to beg in the streets, or we have a non-sighted relative or friend.

In my childhood church, Mr. Hawthorn sat in the third row on the left on most Sundays. I remember him as a large man, over six feet tall and probably over two hundred pounds. He was not well dressed in Sunday clothing, but that had little to do with his economic situation. "Dress coveralls," as he called them, were easier to get into because of the brass button flap on the front bib. "Not easy for a blind man to tie a necktie," he would tell us when he was our substitute seventh-grade Sunday school teacher (although I remember my father remarking that any man could tie his own tie blindfolded!). Mr. Hawthorn's presence was unmistakable, as he refused the arm of an usher, and instead walked alone down the center aisle of the church accompanied by his white walking stick, thudding as it struck the carpet.

One Sunday school lesson that proved to be memorable was the lesson on Blind Bartimaeus—a blind man telling a blind man's story. Our Baptist Sunday school lesson had a ritual for the closing prayer, in which each student was obligated to pray in succession while seated in a circle of chairs. As I remember, each of us had been informed by our parents not to divulge family illness or failures because that might lead to public embarrassment. But about midway through the circle of those petitions—yes, you have guessed it—someone prayed for Jesus to heal Mr. Hawthorn that day. There was, as I remember, silence around the room. While we might all have thought the same thought, due to fear of embarrassment we did not have the courage to utter it aloud.

After Mr. Hawthorn had pronounced a concluding "Amen" after the succession of prayers—and probably having sensed the earlier embarrassed silence—he announced that he had something to say about one of the prayers. He began by saying that the world was much more complicated now than in Jesus's day, and that God had a lot more on his mind than healing someone like himself. He said furthermore that being blind had been very good for his business and, ultimately, for his family, so good that his children could both look forward to college and good jobs. He said that when he shook the hand of a customer as he made a deal in his furniture store, he couldn't tell what color it was. His reputation as a colorblind merchant in a segregated culture provided a special insight which earned him a unique place in that town that other merchants could not share. As he said, "I see what others can't see."

The biblical story of Bartimaeus (we know his name from the Gospel of Mark) serves as the occasion for Jesus to address the blindness of the people to the conditions around them. After his healing, Bartimaeus is shuttled between several rabbinical courts to certify him as a repentant sinner of whatever had caused his blindness. It was not enough for the practice of that day that he was physically healed, he must also be morally healed. Such certification did not come easy. No less than three appearances—including one by his parents—brought the accusers of Bartimaeus no closer to seeing that his blindness was nowhere close to their own blindness in understanding what they had seen.

Essential to the story of Bartimaeus is the prophet Isaiah's promise in Judaism for a messiah. One of the signs that Isaiah predicted would precede the true Messiah was that "the blind shall see and the lame walk"—hence the repeated references in the gospels to characters like Bartimaeus. However, the foci of these many references is not the miraculous nature of the healings of these individuals, but their insight. The difficulties of disability and impairment challenge them to perceive beyond the physical.

Thus many of us—and especially our children—must stretch to make this story "our story" because our culture and station in life protects us from the experience of blindness and thus from its insight. The shuttling movement of Bartimaeus from one place to another is a clue to the inability of those in authority to respond to anything that is outside their perceived boundaries. They do not look for new venues to understand God's activity in the world. Only that which has been by tradition or personally experienced can be trusted. They fail to respond to the contradiction which Bartimaeus represents: Those who are blind, can see; and those that can see are blind.

Jesus challenges his followers to see the world differently than it may appear. Just like those in the story, we have drawn our own boundaries in such a way that we are blind to God's working in and through our lives. For example, John Bayley, the Oxford University literary critic, has written recently about the challenge of his wife's Alzheimer's condition. You may recall that she, Iris Murdoch, Dame of the British Empire and an author with more than 26 novels to her credit, died just two weeks ago. Bayley speaks of their time together in the mornings when he and Iris Murdoch were seated—she like a preschooler—in front of their ancient television enjoying the show "Teletubbies." He describes what laughter and joy the four brightly colored and soft little creatures brought to Murdoch as they emerged into the sunlight from their subterranean abode.

Yet, the televangelist Rev. Jerry Falwell sees the Teletubbies—or at least one of them—as sinister creatures who should be banned from television. Falwell perceives the Teletubbies as an assault upon morality. If, as Christians, we believe the biblical view that God has created a world that is good, then why is it that some of those who claim to believe in God look at creation as if it is an assault upon God from which Christians must withdraw? Jesus calls his followers to see the world through different eyes. We are not blind to its potential for good.

If we believe that the world can provide a venue for goodness, then our behavior needs to follow it. It needs to be congruent. Those in the story were not only blind to God's good creation, they were also blind to the changed behavior. Their traditional legalism had no place for the outsider who might view the world differently than they.

Conversely, in an era before Civil Rights legislation, my Sunday school teacher, Mr. Hawthorn, believed that the world was a place which included God's goodness to all—even though the culture in which he lived did not exhibit such laws at the time. He behaved in such a way that outsiders and insiders both were welcomed and served by his furniture store. It took no changed legislation, no changed society. In his blindness to accepted cultural norms, he was free to show what Jesus would have done—had Jesus owned a furniture in the 1950s.

We are called to see differently from what may be seen by others, and to act accordingly. Our mission in the world is to imitate God's intention of love, mercy, justice, and hope. We cannot get wrapped up entirely in our own lives to such a point that the center of the world is *me, mine,* and *us,* while shutting out *you, ours,* and *them.* We are the sighted blind.

The Parable of the Good Samaritan

10 ²⁵ Just then a lawyer stood up to test Jesus. "Teacher," he said, "what must I do to inherit eternal life?" ²⁶ [Jesus] said to him, "What is written in the law? What do you read there?" ²⁷ [The lawyer] answered, "You shall love the Lord your God with all your heart, and with all your soul, and with all your strength, and with all your mind; and your neighbor as yourself." ²⁸ And [Jesus] said to him, "You have given the right answer; do this, and you will live."

²⁹ But wanting to justify himself, he asked Jesus, "And who is my neighbor?" ³⁰ Jesus replied, "A man was going down from Jerusalem to Jericho, and fell into the hands of robbers, who stripped him, beat him, and went away, leaving him half dead.

³¹ Now by chance a priest was going down that road; and when he saw him, he passed by on the other side. ³² So likewise a Levite, when he came to the place and saw him, passed by on the other side.

³³ But a Samaritan while traveling came near him; and when he saw him, he was moved with pity. ³⁴ He went to him and bandaged his wounds, having poured oil and wine on them. Then he put him on his own animal, brought him to an inn, and took care of him.

³⁵ The next day he took out two denarii, gave them to the innkeeper, and said, 'Take care of him; and when I come back, I will repay you whatever more you spend.' ³⁶ Which of these three, do you think, was a neighbor to the man who fell into the hands of the robbers?"

³⁷ [The lawyer] said, "The one who showed him mercy." Jesus said to him, "Go and do likewise."

When is enough, enough?

Sermon by Richard Murdoch | Rye, NY | April 9, 1995

The premise upon which Jesus's parable was constructed was not original with him. From the beginning of Judaism, acts of charity and mercy were not optional, but were obligatory for those who continued the religious faith of the patriarchs. Judaism was decidedly more than a religion of only ritual and creed; it was a religion that demonstrated God's ideal way of living. Hebrews believed that rituals and creeds of religion must be matched with corresponding behavior. So, acts of charity and mercy were deeply ingrained in the rituals, creeds, and behaviors of Judaism in the days of Jesus.

The occasion for the parable of the Good Samaritan was a question raised by people who were familiar with responding to the needs of others: "How far do I go with my charity and acts of mercy? When is enough, enough?" Jesus did not intend to portray either the priest or the Levite in his parable as being callous and unfeeling—as they are often portrayed in popular Bible commentaries which you might read. Neither does Jesus portray them as ignorant of the religious code of charity and mercy. Jesus intended this parable to be heard by his audience as a parable about boundaries of charity and mercy. When is enough, enough?

Both the priest and Levite found themselves in a moral dilemma. How much should they put themselves at risk in helping someone? If they stopped to assist the robbery victim, they would have each been vulnerable to trouble. Under the code of the temple, a priest would lose his vocation if he were guilty of touching a corpse—even one of his relatives—much less a complete stranger. Since the robbery victim was profusely bleeding and probably unconscious, the priest chose not to risk losing his livelihood and vocation by going further than the law required. The Levite found himself in a somewhat similar dilemma. Although the prohibition against the touching of a corpse would not have cost him his job, it would have presented a distinct problem. Had he touched the victim, he would have been subject to quarantine for a certain period of time, but then he could be restored to his place in the religious services of the temple.

According to the law, the Levite responded within established tradition because acts of charity were only obligatory with those who were "neighbors." The injured victim did not meet the test of being a neighbor to the Levite. First, he was not of his Levite tribe; secondly, the victim had no professional or economic ties to him. To assist the injured man was beyond the Levite's religious and moral boundaries. There would be no commendation or recognition forthcoming that overcame the potential risk. History would not dub him the Good Levite! So he—in the same way as the priest—stepped over the victim in the road and went his way.

The form in which the question is asked—"Who is my neighbor?"—becomes the focus of the parable, not the action of charity which was already established in Jewish scripture and tradition. I am confronted almost weekly with this question in my mail. A week does not go by that there is not an appeal for a very worthy charity. In fact, the current political climate of "de-governmentizing" the social "safety net" has created a significant increase in charity appeals. They come from local, independent, denominational, or interdenominational agencies that have grown up over the last twenty years in every state. They come because I am pastor of a Presbyterian Church and our zip code is 10580, a denomination and a zip code that assumes that there are significant resources to be shared. Those who appeal to me expect me to put words into actions: Show mercy; act charitably; be a Good Samaritan!

But who, really, is my neighbor? Does charity really begin at home? A couple of my colleagues restrict their charitable acts to our neighborhood. Another of my colleagues restricts his donations to his religious denomination. Yet another restricts hers to our county. And another tells me that enough is enough. He has refused to encourage any emergency social funding. "It's a drop in the bucket," he said. "It's money down the drain. The social calamities of a society should not be the exclusive responsibility of the religious sector. Why should our church fund the nation's social stability so the homeless don't riot while the roof of our church is leaking? I am tired of being told that the War on Poverty is my responsibility!"

His view reminds me of an article I read last November. A clergyman on Chicago's South Side stated that in the last ten years, their church budget had doubled, yet they could not afford a new heating system because they had reached a level of diminishing returns: The social needs of their community had grown faster than their income. Ten years ago, they fed fifty at their soup kitchen, now it's one hundred and fifty. Ten years ago, they had no homeless program, but now they house five families. Yet the very building in which they conducted these social programs would soon not be heated. He reported, "We can't continue this way much longer. What do we do? How do we decide who gets fed and who gets shelter?"

Who is your neighbor? Is Jesus suggesting that each and every human being in need is worthy of our aid? Is he suggesting that the priest and the Levite had an unacceptable boundary to define who is their neighbor? Is my neighbor the man who called me on Friday from Peekskill asking for one hundred and twenty-three dollars so that the gas would not be turned off? "Father, I used to live in your town. I'll pay you back. Help me." Or is my neighbor the woman who called on Thursday, seeking another year's contribution to a well-established migrant ministry in another country, whose recipients live in yet another country, but process the food that I eat in *this* country?

Does the parable of the Good Samaritan define my neighborhood as the world, and my neighbor as anyone who is in genuine need? Yes, that's clear from the story. There are no geographical, cultural, or religious boundaries in responding to human need. But the parable leaves silent the question of how much is enough. Jesus was not a legalist who defined charity in a mechanistic way. There is no number of Good Samaritan awards to be given to fulfill a believer's quota to either stay in the church or get kicked out. Being a Good Samaritan is a dilemma each time we are confronted with a need—can I risk it?

I cannot do everything for everyone, but I can do something for someone. That decision is not easily reached, but it should be seriously reflected upon because our response to the human needs presented before us by our neighbors will test the sincerity and boundaries of our faith in God.

The Rich Man

10 ¹⁷ As [Jesus] was setting out on a journey, a man ran up and knelt before him, and asked him, "Good Teacher, what must I do to inherit eternal life?" ¹⁸ Jesus said to him, "Why do you call me good? No one is good but God alone. ¹⁹ You know the commandments: 'You shall not murder; You shall not commit adultery; You shall not steal; You shall not bear false witness; You shall not defraud; Honor your father and mother.'"

²⁰ [The man] said to him, "Teacher, I have kept all these since my youth." ²¹ Jesus, looking at him, loved him and said, "You lack one thing; go, sell what you own, and give the money to the poor, and you will have treasure in heaven; then come, follow me." ²² When he heard this, he was shocked and went away grieving, for he had many possessions.

²³ Then Jesus looked around and said to his disciples, "How hard it will be for those who have wealth to enter the kingdom of God!" ²⁴ And the disciples were perplexed at these words. But Jesus said to them again, "Children, how hard it is to enter the kingdom of God! ²⁵ It is easier for a camel to go through the eye of a needle than for someone who is rich to enter the kingdom of God." ²⁶ They were greatly astounded and said to one another, "Then who can be saved?" ²⁷ Jesus looked at them and said, "For mortals it is impossible, but not for God, for God all things are possible."

²⁸ Peter began to say to him, "Look, we have left everything and followed you." ²⁹ Jesus said, "Truly I tell you, there is no one who has left house or brothers or sisters or mother or father or children or fields, for my sake and for the sake of the good news, ³⁰ who will not receive a hundredfold now in this age—houses, brothers and sisters, mothers and children, and fields, with persecutions—and in the age to come eternal life.

³¹ But many who are first will be last, and the last will be first."

The celestial garage sale

Sermon by Richard Murdoch | Omaha, NE | October 24, 1982

The gospel lesson for today is so familiar that often when we read it, it makes little impact upon us. But change the context and it can produce new insight. Imagine that when the young man comes to Jesus with his question, "What must I do to inherit eternal life?" Jesus answers, "Go home, and have a garage sale. Sell all you have, giving it to the poor!" Would you go away sorrowful because you have great possessions?

Garage sales have become a permanent fixture in American suburbia. Any Friday and Saturday will produce a cluster of signs gathered at every street corner inviting you to the best garage sales of the century—bargains that you cannot pass up! Garage sales are not merely a way to clean your home of cast-offs, but also a way to pass on almost brand-new articles that you aren't using. Jesus is talking not about a few outdated items here, but a celestial garage sale. Sell everything!

What would you think if you drove up to a garage sale and saw your neighbors—whom you have known for some years—conducting a garage sale, and displaying their mother's fine crystal, heirloom china, and sterling silver? On a side table is a collection of fine sporting guns lovingly collected by the husband. Sitting in the driveway is an assorted collection of first-rate furniture sprinkled with antique accent pieces. The kids' new ten-speed bikes are there. In fact, everything the family owns is there, waiting to be sold. "Have you taken leave of your senses?" you might inquire, most unbelievingly. "No," comes the reply, "we are having a celestial garage sale so we can inherit eternal life! All we make goes to the poor!" You would probably walk away in utter confusion. "That's taking religion too far," you might mutter to yourself.

That's exactly what the rich young ruler in the story did: shook his head and walked away. We cannot believe that Jesus would expect us to do that, can we? After all, we are not rich. That is someone else. "This verse applies to those who have more than I do, not me," we tell ourselves. "I am not rich."

So whose yardstick do we use to measure? If we carry that logic too far, everybody who makes less than me, will call me rich, wouldn't they? Wealth is relative, isn't it? We have to be careful about judging: "With what measure you judge, you shall be judged," the scriptures warn us. Few of us can really escape the designation of "rich" when compared to the standards of the rest of the world. We are indeed richer than two-thirds of the people of the world, simply because we happen to live in the United States of America. So we cannot excuse ourselves from reading this scripture for ourselves. It is meant to speak to us.

Would you have a celestial garage sale? No, because you're not rich enough? Then let's go to the second common excuse.

Jesus, of course, is speaking here to a select group of people who want to go the second mile. These are people who would be affectionately referred to by fundraisers as the "Advance Gifts" clients. The verses are for those who are fully committed to a program because they have some personal investment that causes them to go the second mile. They have limited needs and abundant resources.

Since we have spouses and children to care for, Jesus can't, of course, mean us. It would not be fair to put my family in jeopardy by disposing of all our assets. How can I treat my God-given family responsibility so lightly, in order to provide for the unfortunate, which my taxes and charity gifts already provide for? In our modern culture, this demand of Jesus is clearly out of date. The poor don't need any money, they have programs enough to support them. We live in a humane society. I am not expected to be a one-man welfare bureau.

Would you have a celestial garage sale? No, because you have family responsibilities? Then let's go on to excuse number three!

"I come to church to feel good about myself. I want to go away with a happy feeling. This kind of scripture reading is really unnecessary. I would much prefer that you kept the Bible readings on a happier level. Let's just close our eyes on this one!" you say. That's theological blackmail, isn't it? To claim that the Bible is God's word to us, and then to read only the comfortable parts doesn't say much for religious integrity, does it?

I am reminded of my uncle in his first church out of seminary. From time to time, he would find five or ten dollars missing from his paycheck (which was issued by the treasurer of the little country church he served). Thinking that the older gentleman had made a slip of memory, he let it go by several times. Finally, he felt it had gone far enough so he inquired. The treasurer replied, "Well, Reverend, the first time I deducted five dollars for the hymn we didn't know. The second time, I deducted five dollars for the Bible reading about the woman caught in adultery. I think that word should not be used in front of all those young children. It corrupts their morals. And the third time, I deducted ten dollars for the sermon you preached about the Ten Commandments. It's not what I think you should have said." My uncle stood quietly for a second, and then responded, "Sir, I do not think that God appointed you to be my judge, but I am willing to accept your mercy in the same way in which God may show you mercy for your intolerance." From that time, there were no further deductions!

Would you have a celestial garage sale? "No, it's not the kind of thing that makes me happy!"

Since we have three excuses for not having a celestial garage sale, what lesson may we glean from the lips of Jesus? Those who have entered the monastic orders have found these verses to be comforting. In politically charged years, many Christian socialists in Germany, Italy, and France also found these to be comforting words. Some Christian social reformers like Walter Raushenbush, the father of modern social reform in the 1920s, found these words to be a Christian's marching orders. But what about us? How can we, as middle-class capitalists, living in the 1980s during an era of accelerated technological and social change, respond to these words of the gospel?

When Jesus was teaching with these words, he was speaking with the backdrop of a Pharisaic teaching known to the audience. It was simply that God blessed the righteous with good things. The evidence of your piety was seen in the material status you enjoyed in life. It still happens today. An Arkansas layman once boasted to evangelist Charles Templeton that God had given him a Cadillac. Templeton answered him, "It's interesting that God gave you a Cadillac. He gave his only begotten son a cross. And he gave Paul—one of his first and strongest disciples—stoning, shipwreck, imprisonment, and all the other thousand troubles he faced."

Just what can we expect as a reward for righteousness? Suffering and martyrdom? Will that secure eternal life for us? There certainly have been days where this was faithfully believed. Renouncing all material goods and being martyred for the sake of Christ is documented in at least half the centuries of the Christian church's existence. We even say today that suffering builds character.

Jesus was first and foremost a prophet who was usually fair in his assessment of people. He had a quarrel with the Pharisees and their commandments. The Ten Commandments (or Decalogue) was only the heart of the matter. In today's story, Jesus inquired as to whether the man had kept the Law. He responded, "Yes!" And then he began to enumerate the laws as a reminder. The young ruler had been a model for his community. His parents' hearts and the local rabbi's hearts must have swelled with joy to see him succeed in a day of Roman influence. His references and his credentials were impeccable.

But Jesus confronted the man so abruptly that he could not even say, "No! I can't." He just walked away without a word—but his body language spoke it all. His countenance fell—you could see it in his face. He walked with his shoulders stooped. The meaning was clear: "I can't satisfy your expectations. I am good enough already! I'll do it on my own! My way!" But it wasn't a defiant, "I'll do it my way!" It was more of an inner groaning: "I will rely upon myself in my own way."

Self-reliance need not always be a sin. One of Ralph Waldo Emerson's greatest lines of poetry is captured in these words from his 1833 poem "Self-reliance":

> *Henceforth, please God, forever I forego*
> *the yoke of men's opinions. I will be*
> *light-hearted as a bird and live with God.*
> *I find him in the bottom of my heart,*
> *I hear continually his voice therein.*

Self-reliance—when it is grounded in God—is quite different from self-reliance grounded in the power of accumulated wealth, prestige, or power. In a moment, those can be swept away by financial reverses, employment changes, or ill health. They are not an eternal rock to which you may anchor any security. The rich, young ruler's wealth was not his problem, but his perception of it was!

"Wealth is not a right, but a privilege," Rabbi Mamenoides[1] penned years ago. And privilege carried with it a responsibility to the one who granted the privilege. Therefore, if the one who granted you the privilege to be wealthy asked you to forego that privilege, then you must not hold onto it because you have no control. The young ruler felt instead that wealth was a right. Therefore, he had to hold on to it until the bitter end—regardless of what it might do to him.

During newspaper reports of the recent Claus von Bulow[2] trials, the *San Francisco Chronicle* stated, in a featured article entitled "The Case of the Dying Socialite":

> *The characters in this story... Sunny, Claus and their friends... don't worry much about how to make the world nicer for other folks; they worry mainly how to preserve every cent they have inherited, how to increase their fortunes and how to have as much pleasure as possible. The trouble is, in the end none of it seems to have given them much pleasure.*

As long as our wealth is seen as a right, then we will never be ready to have a celestial garage sale. If we see our wealth as a privilege, we will know that celestial garage sales are a distinct possibility—if required by God who has granted us that privilege. But we hope he never ask us to. Meanwhile, on a smaller scale, we may open our wallets to those in need around us because of the influence of Jesus's encounter with the rich, young ruler.

[1] An important medieval Jewish philosopher, scholar, and physician.

[2] A British socialite accused of murdering his wife via an insulin overdose that left her in a persistent unaware state.

The Request of James and John

10 ³⁵ James and John, the sons of Zebedee, came forward to him and said to him, "Teacher, we want you to do for us whatever we ask of you." ³⁶ And he said to them, "What is it you want me to do for you?" ³⁷ And they said to him, "Grant us to sit, one at your right hand and one at your left, in your glory." ³⁸ But Jesus said to them, "You do not know what you are asking. Are you able to drink the cup that I drink, or be baptized with the baptism that I am baptized with?" ³⁹ They replied, "We are able." Then Jesus said to them, "The cup that I drink you will drink; and with the baptism with which I am baptized, you will be baptized; ⁴⁰ but to sit at my right hand or at my left is not mine to grant, but it is for those for whom it has been prepared."

⁴¹ When the ten [other disciples] heard this, they began to be angry with James and John. ⁴² So Jesus called them and said to them, "You know that among the Gentiles those whom they recognize as their rulers lord it over them, and their great ones are tyrants over them. ⁴³ But it is not so among you; but whoever wishes to become great among you must be your servant, ⁴⁴ and whoever wishes to be first among you must be slave of all. ⁴⁵ For the Son of Man came not to be served but to serve, and to give his life a ransom for many."

Trading stamps as a way of life

Sermon by Richard Murdoch | Corfu, NY | May 7, 1972

While going through the dark and dusty attic of Judy's grandmother's pre-revolutionary home in Pennsylvania, we found numerous bottles, old writing exercises from school, a Gramophone[1] horn, and much plaster dust. There were also two books of trading stamps[2] from the early 1900s. There was no date in them, but one book of stamps would probably buy an iron if you could still redeem them. Trading stamps from the Larkin Soap Company in Buffalo would get you Buffalo Pottery or sturdy maple furniture. Today, S&H Green Stamps and Plaid Stamps are saved and traded for merchandise. They can even be redeemed for church buses or kidney machines for patient care—if you can manage to save enough! Trading stamps are a bonus—a bonus for paying cash, it says on some—although we understand intuitively, you probably pay for them in some other way. But the incentive remains: you give something, you get something.

This reminds me of a book I read, entitled *Games People Play* by Eric Berne. In it, there is a game entitled *"Scratch My Back, and I'll Scratch Yours!"* The author/psychiatrist described this game of transactional analysis as used in businesses, marriages, families, community organizations, and politics. The "game" can be played easily except for one resulting problem: The person doing the scratching usually feels that he is given less scratching than he gave. That is the problem of fair balance: Do I get as much as I give?

The scripture lesson this morning mentions some back scratching among the disciples James and John, the sons of Zebedee. James and John were nicknamed "the sons of thunder" after their preaching ability—although I imagine this probably also described their temperament in general. I think it is of credit to the gospels that this bit of embarrassing backbiting—this rather petty problem—was not covered up. Even though, later in Christianity, the disciples will be put upon pedestals and halos will appear around their heads in stained-glass windows, they were indeed very much like all of us.

No doubt they felt as though they had enough "trading stamps" to redeem them for a gift. Indeed, had they not wholeheartedly served with Jesus? Had not they lived from hand to mouth? Had not they been ridiculed? It had been a risky business following Jesus, and, indeed, if this kingdom was really real, they had better trade their stamps in before someone else got there. Maybe it was the need for recognition or maybe it was the pull of human ambition to excel. Whatever the motivation was, the request was the same: "Lord may we have favored places in your kingdom, may we ascend to the power we deserve for patiently waiting. Lord let us be helpful and help you by being your closest instruments of service."

There is a philosophy that says that goodness is not its own reward, that token motivation is necessary. To get people to be good you must give them something. You in effect must give trading stamps. In my childhood church we received Sunday school pins for attending Sunday school. One friend I knew had ten pins trailing down his lapel, authenticating that he had not missed Sunday school in ten years. If you were part of a system that admired and accepted this type of token motivation, you would admire him and he would have a certain kind of status. It was ego building. To him, it was worth all those years of sitting in Sunday school to get that status. But if you were not a part of that system, it was a source of ridicule and foolishness to be dismissed.

Today, a new kind of religious outlook is marketing itself. A new expression of faith, which surfaces when people get tired of the sameness of traditional forms. That faith says that if a specific set of rules are followed you can get "heavenly green stamps." And this idea also appears in our businesses, schools, and communities.

It works this way in religion: "If you accept this religious set of principles and follow them, then success can be yours. And to guarantee it, we can show you examples of people who are prosperous, happy, model human beings. If you go halfway, God will come the other halfway, and showers of blessings shall be yours."

It works this way in business and education: "If you accept this way of doing things, the system will meet you halfway. Put your time in at work, and put your time in at school. We will meet you halfway and see that you are graduated or promoted, and the blessings shall be yours."

It works this way in community service: "You support my project and I will support yours—but don't stick your nose into my project and I won't stick my nose into your project. We will be happy as long as we meet halfway."

The trading stamp way of life trades one commodity for the next. If you want love, affection, acceptance, status, worth, or power, you must have the right number of credits saved up in the relationship and it will be redeemed.

But equity is an elusive commodity. Everything that is equal is not necessarily fair and just. And by the same token, everything that is legal is not necessarily moral. More relationships are broken by the strain of equality because that is the mechanism by which we measure when our lives have become impersonal. It's time we stop asking what we can *get* from our relationships, and instead look at what we can *give*— unmotivated by immediate rewards or the promise of future rewards.

---

[1] Before the MP3, CD, cassette tape, and eight-track there was the phonograph—commonly known as the record player. Gramophone was a trademark for the type that featured a large horn instead of modern speakers. The name came from the combination of the Greek words for "letter" and "sound."

[2] For those of you too young to remember trading stamps, they were the predecessor to today's loyalty reward points, earned for making purchases in certain stores. They were originally invented to reward users who paid for purchases in cash rather than on credit—and by credit, I mean store credit, or "running a tab," as there were no credit cards in the late 1800s. In the 1960s, S&H bragged that it printed more trading stamps than the U.S. Postal Service did postage stamps.

Jesus Curses the Fig Tree

21 ¹⁸ In the morning, as [Jesus] was returning to the city, he was hungry. ¹⁹ And seeing a fig tree by the wayside he went to it, and found nothing on it but leaves only. And he said to it, "May no fruit ever come from you again!" And the fig tree withered at once.

²⁰ When the disciples saw it they marveled, saying, "How did the fig tree wither at once?" ²¹ And Jesus answered them, "Truly, I say to you, if you have faith and never doubt, you will not only do what has been done to the fig tree, but even if you say to this mountain, 'Be taken up and cast into the sea,' it will be done.

²² And whatever you ask in prayer, you will receive, if you have faith."

Bible Version: Revised Standard Version (RSV)

Prayer
changes things

Sermon by Richard Murdoch | Corfu, NY | March 16, 1969

So many times I have seen this phrase: "Prayer changes things." It is a mistaken notion among American Christians. Prayer doesn't change things—prayer changes people, and people change things.

The scripture reading this morning involves a parable about faith that Jesus evidently taught. The author decided it needed a completing moral, so we have the phrase, "And whatever you ask in prayer, you will receive, if you have faith." In many of the early manuscripts, this phrase is missing, which points to the fact that the parable, which is about faith enough to move mountains, stood by itself without the appeal to prayer as a means to an end.

I have chosen this scripture because I believe that it generally describes our approach to the meaning of prayer. Prayer is basically a means by which gifts are asked for, when they are beyond our reach and human abilities. That, of course, leaves this kind of prayer to be possible only if we have faith.

This kind of approach to prayer—matching results with faith—is not specifically Christian. It is basically primitive. It is common to all of humanity: the bushmen of Australia, the Incas in the Andes Mountains, the American Western Indians, and the Druids of England. The Hebrews and the Persians have always included this kind of prayer. It was this kind of intercessory—or asking—prayer that formed the heart of prayer piety. This kind of prayer is a duty, not an opportunity.

This asking and receiving prayer—backed by faith for results—was the reason that some unnamed disciple said to Jesus one day, "Teach us how to pray rightly." The result was the form of prayer known as the Lord's Prayer.

But I think few of the gospel writers caught the real intent of Jesus's words about prayer. Most times prayer is mentioned—which isn't a lot— it is a petition, an asking prayer, expecting that faith be there for results.

In the Book of Acts and in the early church, prayer as asking was only part of it. Prayer was understood as a sacrament. A sacrament is something in which God meets us. It is an action that God begins and we finish. It is an action in which we remember what God has done. A sacrament is not a pious act that we do in order to gain favor with God. Prayer is not something we do to God, but rather it's an opportunity for what God does to us.

I am not saying that we sit back and let a robot by the name of God do our thing for us. Rather—in the understanding of the church—prayer is an openness to respond to God's will for us. If prayer is not seen as an opening to respond to God, then it becomes merely a rote ritual by which we salve our souls with beautiful words.

I can remember my style of praying for public worship in my seminary days. There was an adoration prayer that I edited from a book each week. The phrases were really wild. The adjectives went on and on, something like "Oh great God our Father, whose majesty fills the air, and whose glory covers the earth, and whose name praises," and on and on. One week, a dear lady remarked, "I just loved your adjectives today. That's what I have been teaching in my English class this week, the proper use of adjectives."

So long as prayers remain places for the use of proper English phrases to separate the divine from the human, we will not experience that openness—that giving ourselves to prayer. Perhaps that explains it: We are so accustomed to giving prayers that we are unable to give ourselves to prayer.

An example of giving ourselves to prayer is included in the new curriculum we've adopted for the preschool children at the church school. It includes fresh, delightful ways for prayers. One reads, "Thank you, God, for Timmy's chipmunk. He's so furry and soft. Thank you for furry and soft animals that make us happy. Amen." That's giving yourself to prayer, I think!

The early church broke with tradition, referring to God with the friendly, intimate form of Father. In Greek and Aramaic, the term used for our father—in the Lord's Prayer and others—is *Abba*. That is the word used for the family head by a child. It was comparable to Daddy, Pop, or Dad. Most people during that time would never dare to use such a friendly term to address the Almighty and powerful God. Even to this day, some Roman Catholic masses preface the Lord's Prayer with "We dare to be bold to say: Our Father, who art in heaven," which is a phrase from over two thousand years ago.

The use of The Abba (or Our Father) is the heart of what Jesus tried to teach about prayer. We must give ourselves to prayer—that is open ourselves to the possibility of self-renewal and change. You cannot earnestly pray when your mind is already fixed in one position. This is the meaning of the words, "Thy will be done." It doesn't mean that we go through the crossroads of life as though they were already predetermined. "Thy will be done" means to be open to a new reality, a new possibility, to be ready for someone else's idea instead of your own.

When the author of the Gospel of Matthew recorded that short parable about faith "enough to move mountains," he meant just that—in pictorial language. The word for "mountain" in Greek doesn't mean a physical pile of earth and rocks. It refers to the same kind of mountain we use to describe a pile of things we need to take care of: "I've got mountains of wash to do," or, as we say in business, "I've got mountains of paperwork." Somehow the mountain seems so high it's hard to get motivated enough to get going. There is always some kind of procrastination that lets us put it off. My mind says, "I must do it," and there it looms before me, but I'm unable to make a dent. We see the mountains of life as mountains instead of a collection of hills mounted on top of each other and overlapping. It would be best to start with a hill and move on to the next, thereby conquering the mountain. This is the meaning behind Jesus's words about mountains being moved by faith. Faith is best translated as "openness" in this place—being open to a motivation other than our own; to demands other than our own; and to God, rather than being closed within ourselves.

Prayer is openness to the presence of the divine. It is the kind of openness that comes with practice, not with memorization. It develops with trust, not with ritual duty. It dares to boldly say "Our Father" in the familiarity of a family—thereby trusting a fatherly relationship, not an austere majesty of adjectives.

Go ahead. Take the first step of prayer—the kind of prayer that changes people, so then people can change things.

The Parable of the Wedding Banquet

23 ²⁷ [Jesus said,] "Woe to you, scribes and Pharisees, hypocrites! For you are like whitewashed tombs, which on the outside look beautiful, but inside they are full of the bones of the dead and of all kinds of filth. ²⁸ So you also on the outside look righteous to others, but inside you are full of hypocrisy and lawlessness."

Humility

Sermon by Richard Murdoch | Rye, NY | August 20, 1995

Humility is usually considered the opposite of pride. Since pride is one of the Seven Deadly Sins, it would seem reasonable to think that humility would be listed as one of the Seven Virtues. Not so. Those seven are: prudence, temperance, courage, justice, faith, hope, and love. Humility is absent.

Humility defies objective definition; by definition, it is individual and therefore subjective. It's like the response of a shopper, who, when asked by a weary shopping companion, "What are you looking for?" says, "Well, I can't really describe it, but I'll know when I see it!"

It is most often defined as a *who*, not a *what*. How do you visualize humility? Who comes to mind when you are asked to think of someone who has humility? For many of us, humility brings up images of somebody "with hat in hand," or "Jesus, meek and mild," or "Caspar Milquetoast"[1], or even "eating humble pie."

On the one hand, humility brings us images of people with low self-esteem. Yet, on the other hand, it is said that pride can foster humility. There is a famous scene in Shakespeare's *Antony and Cleopatra*, in which Antony and Octavius exchange arrogant courtesies. After trading prideful taunts of each other's military and political self-worth, they bend to a calmer respect for one another.

On the shifting sands of cultural and political correctness, a call is heard to return to so-called time-honored virtues that will strengthen families, communities, and our nation. The news media is gearing up for the prelude to the fall elections. Pleas for a return to "normalcy" appear from village firehouse halls to professional meetings in city convention halls.

We hear that the permissiveness and excess of the last two decades have led to the 1990s being a decade of moral readjustment—a correction, if you will. It's supposedly a return to a time in which drugs, violence, and family breakups were not front-page news every day; a time in which jobs were plentiful, housing was cheap, and *Leave It to Beaver* dominated the early evening television slot; a time in which education did its job, individuals took responsibility for their own destiny, government worked well, and politicians were clear about their roles.

I was almost seduced into believing it all—until a week ago. I was reminded then of what I had forgotten and maybe of what I was too young to learn.

Let me explain. In our spare hours this summer, I have convinced my wife Judy to tour historic places with me. My children, however, are now free of such exercises in historical research. It was not until my two daughters were in college that they revealed to me that while traveling by car on vacation, they routinely would draw attention to some roadside scene on the opposite side of the road so that I wouldn't see the sign along I-80 announcing yet another stop to be explored on the old Oregon Trail.[2]

Two weeks ago, I fulfilled a childhood dream to visit Hyde Park, New York. As a first grader, I attended school in a Baltimore suburb, where the most important event of the week seemed to be the opportunity to buy Savings Stamps and hear the school report on the March of Dimes collection. I don't suppose that you could exactly say that we were traumatized by the war and polio, but both ongoing events did affect us because everybody had relatives in the Armed Forces and two children in our school had succumbed to polio.

When we heard the funeral train that bore FDR's body would be coming our way, some of the older children organized an expedition one afternoon to the tracks, unknown to our parents. We never saw the train, but that didn't deter young minds from offering all kinds of opinions about the details of the death of the President. "Why would they take him to Hide Park?" we wondered. It was a while before we knew that Hyde Park was spelled with a Y! I have now made it to Hyde Park. The displays in the Presidential Library make it apparent how fragile the victory of World War II was. Some of the history I had forgotten, and much of it I was too young to have learned. But the notion with which the next generation grew up—that victory was assured because "we were number one"—betrays the truth.

In 1820, C.C. Colton—in his *Lacon, or Many Things in Few Words*[3], a book that is addressed to those who think, wrote: "The greatest friend of truth is time, her greatest enemy is prejudice, and her constant companion is humility." But in the words of a contemporary sports icon,

"It's hard to be humble when you're as great as I am." The truth is, humility is easy when there is the right kind of pride. Today's scripture reading speaks to this. Jesus is speaking about the false humility that is exhibited by some Pharisees due to their misplaced sense of pride.

The Pharisees usually get a bad rap, even to the point of the English language's using the word "pharisaic" as a synonym for "hypocritical." In all honesty, the Pharisees really should not be so looked down upon. They represented the business and professional classes of their day, and were the moral/social reformers, with their feet planted firmly on the ground, so to speak. They prodded the other two main religious/political parties—the Sadducees (who were the landed gentry) and the Essenes (who were the isolationists)—to wake up to the reality of the world around them. Yet, for some of the Pharisees, their pride in their accomplishments dulled their sense of themselves. So busy were they with their appearances of charity and reform that their inner character rotted away, leaving them puffed up.

Puffed-up people are a bit hard to take, don't you think? Oftentimes, when the truth is out, puffed-up people have no self-esteem at all. It is the very absence of self-esteem or the right kind of pride that causes them to be puffed up. And, of course, those with low self-esteem are prime candidates for expecting people to be puffed up!

Years ago, when I was a young theologian, I was asked to make a call to the home of a certain Mrs. Jones. I was given the directions to her home. A small gravel path wound itself off the paved road, leading to a very modest house in a wooded glen. She met me at the door, accompanied by two large dogs who—peering through the screen at me—looked ready for a walk in the woods. Once the necessary formalities of introduction and greeting were over, she gathered a cape and a walking stick, and off into the woods we went, muddying our feet and sliding on the wet autumn leaves.

I judged my walking companion to be in her mid-seventies, although later I learned she was a good decade older. Her conversation revealed that she led a quiet life in the country with her two dogs during most of the year, but that she traveled on a regular basis to Manhattan for cello lessons, to have lunch, and occasionally go to the theater with old friends. "Do you get in to the theater?" she asked. A quick headshake answered "no" for me. She hinted that something should be done about that. "What led you to study for the ministry?" she asked. She then shared that while she was a member of a different church in another state, she had come on occasion to the church I had just joined.

She then revealed her agenda for our visit. It went something like this, "You're young and new. Churches have a way of keeping assistant ministers too busy for their own good, especially young ones. If you need a walk in the country to clear your head, here's the place. Just don't come on Thursdays, that's my cello day in the city." So I did, and occasionally a concert or theater ticket also came my way. Eventually, the grapevine let me know that she came from a prominent family and that her deceased husband was the longtime medical director for a large company. But during our meetings, little did I know of this. Nor, of course, did she speak of it.

Humility is a lifelong lesson. It is rarely acquired simply by skill. It is not made easier because of riches, nor is it made easier by poverty. You know humility when you see it, and when you feel it. There are those who, like the Pharisees in the story, are able to appear to possess humility, but truth seeks them out. Yet in their very appearance they have their reward. On the other hand, true humility goes unnoticed, but is truly rewarded.

[1] Caspar Milquetoast was a character from the 1920s cartoon *The Timid Soul*. Designed by H.T. Webster, the character eventually appeared in books, movies, radio, and television programs. For fun, search out the cartoons on the Internet.

[2] Recently, I dragged my own spouse along I-90 to retrace one of my childhood trips across South Dakota. And you bet I stopped at every brown historical landmarker—while my husband tried to distract me by pointing out instead each approaching Wall Drug sign. "Sow corn, grow corn," as they say.

[3] From this book also comes the quote, "Imitation is the sincerest [form] of flattery."

The Institution of the Lord's Supper / The Dispute about Greatness

22 ¹⁴ When the hour came, he [Jesus] took his place at the table, and the Apostles with him. ¹⁵ He said to them, "I have eagerly desired to eat this Passover with you before I suffer; ¹⁶ for I tell you, I will not eat it until it is fulfilled in the kingdom of God."

¹⁷ Then he took a cup, and after giving thanks he said, "Take this and divide it among yourselves; ¹⁸ for I tell you that from now on I will not drink of the fruit of the vine until the kingdom of God comes."

¹⁹ Then he took a loaf of bread, and when he had given thanks, he broke it and gave it to them, saying, "This is my body, which is given for you. Do this in remembrance of me."

²⁰ And he did the same with the cup after supper, saying, "This cup that is poured out for you is the new covenant in my blood. ²¹ But see, the one who betrays me is with me, and his hand is on the table. ²² For the Son of Man is going as it has been determined, but woe to that one by whom he is betrayed!" ²³ Then they began to ask one another which one of them it could be who would do this.

²⁴ A dispute also arose among them as to which one of them was to be regarded as the greatest. ²⁵ But he said to them, "The kings of the Gentiles lord it over them; and those in authority over them are called benefactors. ²⁶ But not so with you; rather the greatest among you must become like the youngest, and the leader like one who serves. ²⁷ For who is greater, the one who is at the table or the one who serves? Is it not the one at the table? But I am among you as one who serves."

²⁸ "You are those who have stood by me in my trials; ²⁹ and I confer on you, just as my Father has conferred on me, a kingdom, ³⁰ so that you may eat and drink at my table in my kingdom, and you will sit on thrones judging the twelve tribes of Israel."

Greatness reversed

Sermon by Richard Murdoch | Omaha, NE | March 23, 1980

In today's gospel reading, we find another instance in which the words are not necessarily what we might expect: The one who serves is greater than the one who is served. So let's dive in a little deeper.

It is a fair assumption to say that when you go out to dinner, you—the customer—are the object of attention. A waiter or waitress is there to attend to your needs and see that your dinner is properly ordered, served, and cleared. If any of those functions are not properly performed to your liking, it is expected that you—the one paying for the meal—have the greater advantage in seeing that the waiter will correct any defects brought to his attention. In other words, the power of the one who dines is greater than the power of the one who serves. And, of course, the waiter knows that the size of the tip he or she may receive is up to you, so you hold the ultimate power.

Jesus suggests, however, that the roles are reversed: The waiter is greater than the one who dines. I am told that a good waiter can be made through good training, some experience, and developing a sensitivity to people. But a great waiter is one who has dined extensively. In other words, by reversing the roles, a person who has had the pleasure of dining will know specifically what should be done in order to make the meal well attended. Such a waiter is indeed greater than the one who dines!

One of our elders was traveling recently and attended worship at a local church. In his description of the church, he included the fact that the ushers were dressed in grey striped trousers and morning coats—formal attire. This custom is a vestige from days gone by, not because it looks impressive, but because it sends a message. In the past, every large Presbyterian church in established cities provided a wardrobe of morning coats, white gloves, and white spats for its deacons. Since deacons were to serve in the church, they were to attire themselves in formal serving attire that was not unlike that of a butler. The words of the Psalm 84 come to mind: "I would rather be a doorkeeper in the house of my God than live in the tents of wickedness."

It was the proper duty of a deacon to shed the role of everyday business owner, landowner, lawyer, physician, or industrialist at least once a month and become a servant rather than a master. When one was shown to a pew by a deacon like Andrew Carnegie, Andrew Mellon, or a similar "man of greatness" the words of Jesus took on new meaning. Here was a demonstration of what it meant to be a servant—it was meant to be a humbling experience. But, like so many things, the custom lost its message in the passing years, and only remains today as part of the tradition.

Experiences that cause us to become a servant are not only humbling experiences, but also strip away layers of assumptions, bringing us to new insights about ourselves.

For example, three weeks ago, my family and I sat down to supper in our usual fashion. In front of each place—in addition to our filled plates and our usual beverages—there was a small glass of cranberry juice and a small square of bread carefully buttered. Actually, it was one slice of bread, cut into four equal pieces and distributed to each of us by Amy, our six-year-old. In my usual way, I gulped down the juice, thinking it was an appetizer, and popped the bread into my mouth. Amy looked aghast at me. "What's wrong?" I asked. Very quietly and clearly disappointed, she said, "It's for after supper." Quizzically, I asked, "So?" She responded, "You know, like we do at church to remember Jesus." (It dawned on me that she was recalling a recent Family Communion Workshop where we had reserved a bit of bread and juice for the Lord's Supper in the same way the early Christians had done.) At that moment, I realized the reams of paper used to write about how children can't understand communion are just scrap paper. Children can comprehend what adults would like to think they can't. Lofty arguments about the transubstantiation[1] and consubstantiation[2] of the Communion elements become mere drivel in the face of a child who just wants to remember Jesus.

For many of us, "servitude" is a derogatory word. It conveys captivity, low status, direction by an authority, and seems anti-democratic. In America, we have developed an economic system in which no one is a servant in the traditional sense of the term. We have in our history the examples of house servants of Virginia plantations, butlers of New England industrialists, bond servants of craft shops, and slaves of Southern cotton fields. In our contemporary world, we have no such examples. Rather, we have feelings about what it would be like to be a servant. Simply put, a servant does what you tell him or her to do without questioning your integrity or your request. The servant (in return) anticipates that what will be done by him or her will enable the master to accomplish work that he or she alone could not do. In other words, the relationship—although hierarchical—is also reciprocal.

While we have no current models, we do have the *concept* of servitude that can help us understand how we are to be disciples for serving rather than for being served. We consider ourselves to be customers of Christianity. We ask the question, "What can it do for us?" This week, I was in Wichita for several days, teaching at a workshop for families and the church. One of the keynote speakers centered his speech on what churches can do for people. He said, "It can enhance your personal life; it can strengthen your family life; it can help you in your business and professional life," and on the advertising campaign went. People oftentimes take the same tact, telling their listeners what Christ can do for them in their lives. That's all well and good, but that's not the whole story, is it? What about the reciprocal side of the question? The Gospel of Luke states that the one who sits down to dinner is not greater than the one who serves.

Do you anticipate the ways in which you might be of service? Or do you let someone else take the initiative and merely wait to give a response? Service is merely the rent we pay for the space that we occupy in God's kingdom. Be of service.

---

[1] Transubstantiation describes a Communion doctrine in which the bread and wine are believed to actually "become" the body and blood of Christ.

2 Consubstantiation describes Communion in metaphysical terms, suggesting that the body and blood of Christ appear "next to" the physical bread and wine.

The Crucifixion of Jesus

19 ¹⁶ Then he handed him over to them to be crucified.

¹⁷ So they took Jesus, and he went out, bearing his own cross, to the place called the place of a skull, which is called in Hebrew Gol'gotha. ¹⁸ There they crucified him, and with him two others, one on either side, and Jesus between them. ¹⁹ Pilate also wrote a title and put it on the cross; it read, "Jesus of Nazareth, the King of the Jews." ²⁰ Many of the Jews read this title, for the place where Jesus was crucified was near the city; and it was written in Hebrew, in Latin, and in Greek. ²¹ The chief priests of the Jews then said to Pilate, "Do not write, 'The King of the Jews,' but, 'This man said, I am King of the Jews.'" ²² Pilate answered, "What I have written I have written."

²³ When the soldiers had crucified Jesus they took his garments and made four parts, one for each soldier; also his tunic. But the tunic was without seam, woven from top to bottom; ²⁴ so they said to one another, "Let us not tear it, but cast lots for it to see whose it shall be." This was to fulfill the scripture,

"They parted my garments among them,
and for my clothing they cast lots."

²⁵ So the soldiers did this. But standing by the cross of Jesus were his mother, and his mother's sister, Mary the wife of Clopas, and Mary Mag'dalene. ²⁶ When Jesus saw his mother, and the disciple whom he loved standing near, he said to his mother, "Woman, behold, your son!" ²⁷ Then he said to the disciple, "Behold, your mother!" And from that hour the disciple took her to his own home.

²⁸ After this Jesus, knowing that all was now finished, said (to fulfill the scripture), "I thirst." ²⁹ A bowl full of vinegar stood there; so they put a sponge full of the vinegar on hyssop and held it to his mouth.

Bible Version: Revised Standard Version (RSV)

I thirst

Sermon by Richard Murdoch | Corfu, NY | March 8, 1970

For what have you thirsted this past week? A little bit of silence? An income tax refund check? Or maybe for spring to break through? I've got it... a little more time to do the things you want to? Or perhaps a little less pressure?

We thirst because we feel we are dry in some way, similar to a man with a dry mouth who needs a drink to quench his thirst. Thus, to be thirsty can have a double meaning. And so, if we take Jesus's words only literally, we entirely miss the significance of the shortest—but possibly most profound—verse in the Bible: "I thirst."

It is profound because of what lies behind the words—the echo of Psalm 69, the Prayer for Deliverance from Persecution:

> *Save me, O God,*
> > *for the waters have come up to my neck.*
> *I sink in deep mire,*
> > *where there is no foothold;*
> *I have come into deep waters,*
> > *and the flood sweeps over me.*
> *I am weary with my crying;*
> > *my throat is parched.*
> *My eyes grow dim*
> > *with waiting for my God.*

Does it strike you as odd that a person who speaks about the waters coming up to his neck also complains about being thirsty? That a man who complains that the floods have swept over him says his throat is parched from crying? It's not odd if you realize he doesn't have a biological thirst, he has a spiritual thirst. He has a need to quench his dry spirit, which has been drained by his experiences.

Many people had placed Jesus on a pedestal, thinking his strength could heal their weaknesses. Jesus's admission—through both the biological and spiritual meaning of his words—brings forth his honesty and humanity.

There are still people today who think that human problems can most easily be solved by weak persons latching onto strong personalities. They think that the image of the strong one will inspire them to do, or be, better. Quite often this is the role of the teacher, pastor, physician, therapist, or social worker. There was a time when we expected people in these roles to keep their humanity to themselves—to remain professional. We needed models and heroes on pedestals to inspire us.

But as Jesus shows us through his very brief words, the pedestal must be broken. Traditional roles must be shattered for something new to happen. The words and feelings inherent in them change the relationship from one of students and teacher to a more personal one. Instead of instructing, he shares.

What can sharing do? It bridges the loneliness of thinking that only you exist in your world. And it can fill your spirit.

The man who ran to find something to quench Jesus's thirst was unable to understand the thirst of the spirit—he was simply solving the literal need. But the disciples, hidden among the crowd, knew what the thirst of the spirit was. They longed to reach out to Jesus, to support his courage. But none could take the chance of being caught and charged as a co-conspirator.

And so Jesus died, thirsty in spirit, having drained himself for others. And then in the moment of death, he gave a glimpse of what it meant to lose courage in a human kind of way. Through his thirst, he built a bridge.

Across the East River in New York City spans the Manhattan Bridge. It is a fairly new bridge—as bridges go—being built in the 1920s. And it bears a tremendous load of traffic daily. The approaches are massive. Huge stone colonnades decorate the entrance to this bridge as well as hide its less attractive iron girders. Engineers say that these massive stone approaches to the bridge will provide many more years of life for the bridge that brings together Brooklyn and Manhattan. The approaches serve as a spring board, allowing the steel structure to bounce with the traffic—to be flexible—and therefore not crack under the strain.

We need strong approaches to ourselves, to support us when the traffic becomes heavy. If the strong approaches are there, we know that we will bounce back. But if there are not strong approaches—like the support of friends, family, and a faith in God—our supports will crack under this strain.

When we thirst, if we have strong approaches, then we can create a sturdy bridge to them, to fill our spirits. Let us recognize the thirst in ourselves, and let us not be ashamed to show it or to quench it.

The Crucifixion of Jesus

19 ³⁰ When Jesus had received the wine, he said, "It is finished." Then he bowed his head and gave up his spirit.

It is
finished

Sermon by Richard Murdoch | Corfu, NY | March 15, 1970

Have you ever had the sensation that something is finished before it has even begun? It seems to be that way with Jesus. On the cross, he is said to have stated, "It is finished." But a thorough reading of the activities preceding this statement make a good case that it really was finished much earlier in the week.

Back in 1965, Hugh Schonfield wrote a highly controversial book, *The Passover Plot*, which quickly became a bestseller. In it, Dr. Schonfield puts forth the thesis that Jesus was an extraordinary organizer who wanted to reform the Jewish state and religion. He proposes that Jesus and his disciples organized—to the very last detail—each movement and method of Jesus's two and a half years in Galilee, including the move into Jerusalem (since he was unable to transform the establishment in Galilee).

Every move, every attempt was made to encourage the people of Jerusalem to take upon themselves the task of reforming their institutions. Dr. Shonfield states when reform didn't happen, Jesus and his disciples arranged a way by which Jesus would become the symbol for the start of such a reform—in a dramatic way. Crucifixion would be the symbol. Hence, Easter week honors the greatest single revolutionary symbol ever designed and carried out—eventually leading to the downfall of the Roman Empire.

While Dr. Shonfield's book is probably more fiction than fact, he does capture the vibrancy of Jesus's character. Somehow the idea has persisted that Jesus was a somewhat dull man who got caught in a power play between the temple and the government. They both used him as a scapegoat, and he was not aware enough to see how he was being used. Yet, I believe that Jesus was an eccentric, vibrant, and sensitive man who was intelligent to the world around him.

People often laugh at eccentrics. But they also often listen to those who speak about their own deep feelings. Jesus did exactly that. He didn't ignore what was going on in the world around him or try to brush it under the carpet. He knew of people's suffering and the injustice happening at the hands of the appointed rulers. These appointed rulers constantly reminded the people that they ruled by the will of God, which was their authority. But Jesus thought that the will of God was about more than ruling people. The will of God was intensely personal, part of a person's inner experience. And, Jesus thought, it was also interpreted by groups of people as they saw God acting in their world. Jesus wanted to reform the temple to incorporate these ideas— not destroy it or the Roman government. He wanted to call people to the tradition of Moses, Abraham, and the prophets.

But he knew it was finished. He knew that it was the beginning of the end on Palm Sunday. Why? Because many disciples evidently didn't go along with the Palm Sunday festivities—some did, but others didn't (according to the various writers). Some thought Jesus's act of destroying the bankers' tables was a destruction of personal property, inconsistent with his teaching of peace. Palm Sunday was the dividing line.

Jesus's Jerusalem ministry was quite different from his Galilean ministry. There was little emphasis on peace, quietness, and love in Jerusalem. There was a decided interest in getting the seat of power to listen to the problems of the people. Jesus, and the disciples who continued to follow him, thought that personal faith carried with it a responsibility to change the things they were seeing that they did not think were in accordance with God's will.

But it was finished, not long after it had begun. There are times in our life, too, when we know we are finished before we have barely begun. There are decisions that must be made, perhaps ones which we have put off too long, and we miss the opportunity to begin. We put off making decisions because we are afraid we will lose support, or be cut off from those we love or care about. But we must look out beyond the present, because there is hope in the wider purpose.

The Resurrection of Jesus / Jesus Appears to Mary Magdalene

20 ¹ Now on the first day of the week Mary Mag'dalene came to the tomb early, while it was still dark, and saw that the stone had been taken away from the tomb. ² So she ran, and went to Simon Peter and the other disciple, the one whom Jesus loved, and said to them, "They have taken the Lord out of the tomb, and we do not know where they have laid him."

³ Peter then came out with the other disciple, and they went toward the tomb. ⁴ They both ran, but the other disciple outran Peter and reached the tomb first; ⁵ and stooping to look in, he saw the linen cloths lying there, but he did not go in.

⁶ Then Simon Peter came, following him, and went into the tomb; he saw the linen cloths lying, ⁷ and the napkin, which had been on his head, not lying with the linen cloths but rolled up in a place by itself. ⁸ Then the other disciple, who reached the tomb first, also went in, and he saw and believed; ⁹ for as yet they did not know the scripture, that he must rise from the dead. ¹⁰ Then the disciples went back to their homes.

¹¹ But Mary stood weeping outside the tomb, and as she wept she stooped to look into the tomb; ¹² and she saw two angels in white, sitting where the body of Jesus had lain, one at the head and one at the feet. ¹³ They said to her, "Woman, why are you weeping?" She said to them, "Because they have taken away my Lord, and I do not know where they have laid him." ¹⁴ Saying this, she turned round and saw Jesus standing, but she did not know that it was Jesus.

¹⁵ Jesus said to her, "Woman, why are you weeping? Whom do you seek?" Supposing him to be the gardener, she said to him, "Sir, if you have carried him away, tell me where you have laid him, and I will take him away." ¹⁶ Jesus said to her, "Mary." She turned and said to him in Hebrew, "Rab-bo'ni!" (which means Teacher).

Bible Version: Revised Standard Version (RSV)

Resurrection:
Reaction and response

Sermon by Richard Murdoch | East Lansing, MI | March 30, 1997

There is a lot of motion in the scene that is painted for us in the Gospel of John. In contrast with our rather regular and orderly Easter, the Easter described is a frantic one. One simple observation by a woman creates a chain reaction.

Mary Magdalene went to the cemetery in the pre-dawn darkness. She found the stone—which the Roman soldiers had sealed against the cave-like tomb's entrance—ajar. It was rolled away from the entrance of the place where the family of Joseph of Arimathea—and then Jesus—was buried. There was an empty niche in the wall where Jesus had been. Mary let out a scream. And away she ran. She reacted with despair. Grave robbers! Was nothing sacred anymore? What was this world coming to? Just because Jesus was in a rich man's tomb didn't mean it rubbed off on him. Surely, everybody knew he was just a poor prophet, didn't they? Well, Mary wasn't going to handle this by herself. She looked for Simon Peter.

She found Peter as well as John. And that produced the second reaction: Peter ran. He didn't ask any details, and Mary didn't give him any except, "They've taken him!" If Peter had taken a moment to consider this, he could have asked some questions like: "Who is 'they,' Mary?" "When did you discover this?" "Who was with you?" "Who else have you told?" But there was no time for any careful detective work! He just took off and ran, presumably in the direction of the cemetery located outside of town—a distance of miles, not yards. (If the Apostles were in Bethany at the home of Lazarus, as is supposed.) Mary, having already run those miles, was a distant third in this marathon to the tomb.

The trio—huffing and puffing—caught up with each other at the cemetery. Peter, being the acknowledged leader, entered first. There, up on the ledge carved from the rock, where the body of Jesus had been lovingly placed, ready to receive the ointments and preservatives that were customary for a wrapped corpse, Peter saw a strange sight: All of the wrappings were right there, in perfect order, as if the body had evaporated from them. The Gospel of John is very specific about this scene. Each piece of grave clothing was lying exactly where it would have been if a body was still there—but the body wasn't there. That's the point of Verse 7: "...and the napkin, which had been on his head, not lying with the linen cloths, but rolled up in a place by itself." If Jesus had gotten up and taken off the grave clothing, which consisted of wrappings of three- or four-inch linen strips, he would have likely unwrapped himself, leaving the strips in a heap on the floor with the square piece of linen that covered his face on top of the little heap. But there was no heap of clothes on the floor. Now a third event in this chain reaction happened: Peter, John, and Mary ran back home, "For as yet they did not know the scripture, that he must rise from the dead!"

Glory be! They didn't know the scripture? Come now! Jesus had told them over and over in the teachings of the previous week how he would die and be raised again. He had even compared the building and the destruction of the very temple under whose shadow they met as to be like his body! They might not have believed it was going to happen, but they sure knew the words about it! This rather incongruous and incredible revelation gives us the real clue as to what is going on in the Easter morning scene among three of Jesus's most faithful followers.

The word "know" has more meanings than simply cognitive learning. In Greek, it is an expansive word that has a variety of meanings relating to the cognition of facts, emotions, and perceptions. No doubt, these three followers cognitively knew the words about resurrection. But there was no way they were able to connect what they saw before them with what it might mean. They could not believe simply because they had seen. Now that's a bit strange for us, because we are indeed slaves to that adage "Seeing is believing!" However, consider it a bit further: We really do not believe simply because we see either. Consider these thoughts of theological ethicist Richard Niebuhr in his book, *Experiential Religion*:

> *Believing does not belong to the realm of words, nor does it mean giving logical assent to what one sees alone. The moral energy it takes to believe is fundamental; it is tiring. But it creates much more which is beautiful, coherent and purposeful in our human*

world. A person acquires personhood by believing. No institution, no system, no book can instill belief. It is an energy which once tapped fosters more and more until the whole person struggles to become one. It requires judging, inquiring, and experiencing. No one can believe for you, but someone can witness to what he or she has believed. A witness can provide a clue by which another might come to his or her belief, people must be set free to believe; they cannot be forced to assent to that which their heart cannot validate. The heart may not let the soul believe what the eye has seen, until it too can feel the impact of the vision.

I would like to think that Niebuhr's idea explains the reason that the other two left, leaving Mary alone to deal with her heart, head, and eyes. They had all reacted. They could not respond. *Responding* is one of the shades of that Greek word *to know*. It makes sense now, doesn't it? They were busy reacting, but they did not know or respond.

I also want to make a distinction today about reaction and response. I am not using response in the way that a behaviorist uses it, as in a stimulus-response model. I want you to think about response in terms of its dictionary meaning, which describes it from the French, meaning: "to answer back; to give an indication of will."

I can briefly describe the difference between reaction and response in a personal incident. My wife Judy taught third grade in a public school last year in Omaha, Nebraska. She came home one evening rather upset. One of her students had brought a gun to school and pulled it out in front of her. "What did you do?" I asked. "Well, I just told him to give it to me!" she said. I replied with something like, "That's crazy, it's a good thing he didn't think 'give it to me' meant shoot you!" She defended herself, "I didn't have time to think. I just said it."

She only had time to react in the moment. She didn't have time to process what might have happened and what kind of response to formulate. For her to get the gun was the most important thing. While she reacted, I could respond. I had the information, the time, and the objectiveness to consider the event from a safe distance. I could say things like, "Now when this happens next time, what will you do? What is your strategy? How can you protect yourself from this happening again? Can you get the child transferred?" All she could do was react at the moment. Later, she could respond.

Likewise, the three morning tomb visitors had spent all their energy reacting—they could not respond. Two went to their homes. Mary sat down in the cemetery and wept, uncontrollably. Actually, it was wailing in the old-world style and so loud it frightened up two angels and a gardener, each of whom enhanced Mary's ability to move from reaction to response. She did as Niebuhr said in his book. Instead of being awed by the angel, she spoke directly to him. She didn't run away this time. As if interviewing her for a newspaper, the angel asked, "And what, how, when, where, and why are you here, Mary?"

Mary replied, "They took him away, my master. I want to know more information about where his body has gone." She took charge of herself, ready to go after that information, as Niebuhr suggests. Up popped a gardener, and she put the question to him—perhaps not as nicely by this time, but with the respect due the sexton of the cemetery. "Sir, tell me what you've done with him—and I'll take him off your hands."

At each step, Mary moved from reacting to the situation to responding to the situation. Slowly, she assimilated what was going on around her. She put the pieces of the puzzle together between her head, her heart, and her eyes. And she concluded with a response that she recounted to the Twelve Apostles, "I have seen the Lord and he has told me these things." In Niebuhr's words, she reached a belief to replace her reaction. This belief became acted upon as she declared that Jesus was present for her. She could not believe for the other disciples. They were still reacting to the event. They needed to begin to work out a response also, if that morning was going to last beyond simply the phenomenon of an empty tomb.

Christians around the world react each Easter to the phenomenon of the empty tomb. Our reactions cover the ranges, from awe and respect to wonder and amazement. Those reactions are punctuated with appreciation for spring weather, warm-weather clothing, the fragrance of lilies, as well as the enjoyment of family and friends around festive tables. The season of Easter and signs of spring gave Christians and non-Christians alike a reason to react with joyful praise. And that was how it should be.

But we can't let it stop there. Our reaction must lead to a response if Easter is not to be forgotten, to become just one more day gone by in the march of calendar days. Truly, we must see Mary Magdalene as a model for our response. We should strive to reach those same words: "I have truly seen." An empty tomb gets a reaction. A working of faith gets a response.

This next story has been around for a few generations. But it captures a relevant response for this day: There was a man who stretched a cable across the Niagara Gorge above the whirlpool rapids. He announced that he would be pushing a wheelbarrow before him as he walked across the cable from one side to the other side. A large crowd gathered. People came to watch the spectacle of the death-defying walk. Slowly, he inched his way across. A cheer went up from the other side as the wheelbarrow touched the ground. It was then that he announced that on the next day, he would push a man in the wheelbarrow across the cable. People said that it couldn't be done. The next day, another large crowd had gathered in anticipation of the event, even larger than the day before. Again, people expressed their doubts at such a great death-defying event. But a boy was heard to say, "Oh, I know he can do it. He has a steady eye!" Just then, a man stepped beside the boy. "Do you really think it can be done?" the man asked. "Oh, without a doubt," the boy answered. The man then said, "I am glad to hear you say that, for I am the man who is going to push that wheelbarrow today. I have not yet found a man who is willing to ride. Come, let us go!"

Permit a bit of allegory in this story: The cable across the whirlpool of life is faith; the wheelbarrow stands for the Easter event; the man pushing, of course, is God; the crowd is humanity. The great majority of us react with amazement to the feat; but few respond with faith like the small boy: "He has a steady eye. I know he can do it." And so he goes!

Today, don't just react; make a response in faith that God's steady eye will see you through the whirlpool of life.

Jesus Appears to His Disciples / The Ascension of Jesus

24 ³⁶ While [the disciples] were talking about this, Jesus himself stood among them and said to them, "Peace be with you." ³⁷ They were startled and terrified, and thought that they were seeing a ghost. ³⁸ He said to them, "Why are you frightened, and why do doubts arise in your hearts? ³⁹ Look at my hands and my feet; see that it is I myself. Touch me and see; for a ghost does not have flesh and bones as you see that I have." ⁴⁰ And when he had said this, he showed them his hands and his feet. ⁴¹ While in their joy they were disbelieving and still wondering, he said to them, "Have you anything here to eat?" ⁴² They gave him a piece of broiled fish, ⁴³ and he took it and ate in their presence.

⁴⁴ Then he said to them, "These are my words that I spoke to you while I was still with you—that everything written about me in the law of Moses, the prophets, and the psalms must be fulfilled." ⁴⁵ Then he opened their minds to understand the scriptures, ⁴⁶ and he said to them, "Thus it is written, that the Messiah is to suffer and to rise from the dead on the third day, ⁴⁷ and that repentance and forgiveness of sins is to be proclaimed in his name to all nations, beginning from Jerusalem. ⁴⁸ You are witnesses of these things. ⁴⁹ And see, I am sending upon you what my Father promised; so stay here in the city until you have been clothed with power from on high."

⁵⁰ Then he led them out as far as Bethany, and, lifting up his hands, he blessed them. ⁵¹ While he was blessing them, he withdrew from them and was carried up into heaven. ⁵² And they worshiped him, and returned to Jerusalem with great joy; ⁵³ and they were continually in the temple blessing God.

Void
if detached

Sermon by Richard Murdoch | Omaha, NE | April 25, 1982

A thing will often lose its value, if it is detached. Airline tickets expressly state that if the coupon is detached from the whole by an unauthorized person, this will result in cancellation. Legal contracts can have items attached which, if detached, will render them null and void. The value of a lamp is worthless when it is detached from the wall outlet that provides it with electrical current. It simply cannot light on its own power without being attached to its source of power.

In the scriptures, there are less than a half dozen appearances of the risen Christ to his followers. Most appearances are individual and quite unique. The gospels do not agree on any of their details. But the intent of the resurrection appearances are all the same, to connect the community of Apostles and disciples with the power of God, enabling them to continue their function, even though their leader is gone.[1] In each and every case, the Apostles and disciples are scattered and discouraged because the years of their lives spent following Jesus had been washed down the drain. Even the word of his resurrection seems to be impotent. The news of a resurrection confuses and frustrates them. In today's reading, we note that "while in their joy they were disbelieving and still wondering." Confusion, conflicting reports, and inaccurate assumptions seem to have prevailed. But in their confusion, the Twelve Apostles (now, of course, reduced to eleven with the demise of Judas[2]) stayed in Jerusalem to ponder their course—stay together or scatter?

You can well imagine in your mind the conversation in that upper room—the same room that they had rented for the Passover weekend before Jesus's death. Perhaps they said, "Well, I think we ought to return to our villages, and then meet here at Pentecost Festival. We'll all be back in town and then we'll have a little time to think about things." Or: "We are all quite emotional now, we can't make good decisions." And then: "Well, from what the women said, I think we ought to just stick tight and wait here, something is bound to happen." Which may have been opposed by: "No, I think we ought to get busy about the master's work. There are people who need us out there." Isn't it too bad we don't have a recording of the very human and ordinary concerns that must have been present then?

And wouldn't it be helpful to have a record of their theological conversation? We can probably guess quite accurately what they were thinking and saying. "If God is good, then why did he let this terrible thing happen to our master?" That's a question asked over and over through the centuries by people. That question caused the story of Job to be included in the canon. That same question prompted a rabbi in Massachusetts named Harold Kushner to write a little essay that turned into a book entitled, *When Bad Things Happen to Good People*. It's at the number three spot of the bestseller list this week.

Why do we know this is the question that was being discussed? Because of Jesus's answer: "Thus it is written, that the Messiah is to suffer and to rise from the dead on the third day." A suffering and crucified messiah—even though it had been discussed by Jesus in his ministry—was not in their scenario. They were very much like us. The Apostles heard what they wanted to hear. And they chose not to hear that suffering was part of the redemption story. They were looking for the glamour, the power, the easy way to religious recognition. This humiliation of death was not in their plan. Everyone knew then—as indeed many people still think today—that God gave blessings to the righteous and gave suffering to the sinful. Success belongs to the good and failure to the evil. Or, to put it another way, some credit God with success and Satan with failure.

And Jesus comes to stand among them as the Messiah who suffered (as Isaiah had said) and who was raised by God (as Hosea had said) and was now among them. There in the upper room, where they celebrated the Last Supper, they now celebrated their first supper.

What source could those eleven Apostles and other disciples tap in the discussion of their future course? Jesus attempts to nurture them in the fact that a miracle—if that's how they looked at the resurrection—had no meaning apart from what went before. The resurrection is the result of faith, not the beginning of faith. It is a logical conclusion of believing in God's power. It's not the beginning. You cannot detach suffering from resurrection, or actions from faith.

We like to do that, don't we? A good friend of mine who is a physician and an elder once related to me the fickleness of humans when it comes to religious faith. He had spent his younger years in a small town. His father had died and his mother had raised the children by taking in washing and doing other small jobs. He worked his way through medical school. He could have easily specialized in a more exotic skill, but instead became a country doctor. He always considered his medical skills and profession as a calling. Somehow, he kept good humor around him, but at times, it was sorely tried.

He had referred a patient with a malignancy to an oncologist in a neighboring city. She didn't care to travel that far and suggested that if he was a *real* doctor why he couldn't cure it. He patiently explained that he could perform surgery, but he couldn't know everything about everything. He could diagnose, but he would prefer her treatment be with a specialist. She reluctantly agreed.

After eight months of surgery and therapy, she returned to his office with the good news that she was in remission. But she had some bad news. Her neighbor had a similar problem, she thought. The neighbor went to the hospital for only a week and had a miracle happen to her— God healed her right away through prayer. "My," said the country doctor, "that was amazing, wasn't it?" The woman replied, "Yes, and if you were more of a Christian, you could have done the same for me in one week instead of eight months!" He scratched his head and said gently, "Well, you know, God doesn't always like healing by himself, that's why he uses us doctors every once in a while. When he's had a busy week, we're kind of his assistants. Assistants aren't always as fast, but they do the same job. I'm glad both you and your friend are healed. Good day!"

The physician believed that the power to heal did not come totally from his own skill and knowledge. God had given him a brain to learn, hands to move, and motivation to help others. He had developed his potential to the best of his ability, and he trusted God totally to see him through. But somehow, the patient was seeing the physician's skill as separate from his source, which left her living in a divided world, separated from the very source of power she craved to have. She found it impossible to see God permeating the world with his spirit through people. Instead, she wanted God to be a giant doctor this week, a giant father the next, a giant soldier the week after that. She didn't like the idea of people being instruments of God's grace and healing; she wanted only the original source, so that way she would be special.

Jesus tells the Apostles that their power—their source—will come to allow them to continue their life. But they must remain in Jerusalem for a while. They must work out for themselves the style of the ministry and community. During his ministry, Jesus had done and directed their work for them. Now it was time for them to do it themselves, without his physical presence. They would be the instruments of his grace. They would not do it on their own. They were extensions of what he had already begun. But they could not do what they needed to do unless they remembered and tapped into his power.

While you may tap the source, and while you may access the power of God, you cannot have everything. God is not a "gimme God." He is not a permissive parent who gives you everything your heart desires. God is not an endless bank account, nor is he a charge account without a credit limit. But it is true that we can do one thing at a time. And that is exactly what the Apostles experienced: One thing at a time began to be resolved and done, until fifty days later they all came together.

There's a saying, "You can have an expensive gold watch with a perfect assembly of pieces, but it is worthless if the mainspring is broken." Likewise, it was with the Apostles. They had all the parts, but their mainspring was gone. Yet once they recognized the mainspring was still among them, life began to work again for them. And it is that way with us, isn't it? We fail to recognize the mainspring of our lives and expect somehow the pieces will work if we utter religious words and perform pious actions. But words and actions are usually void, if they are detached from their source.

[1] So what's the difference between a disciple and an apostle? Sometimes the terms are used interchangeably. "Disciple" refers to a follower or learner, so all of those following Jesus were disciples. The references to disciples can get confusing. Sometimes it refers to all the disciples in the movement, and sometimes only "the Twelve." The term "apostle" comes from the Greek word meaning *to send out*. In the Books of Mark and John, Jesus chooses twelve of his many disciples to send out

into the world to spread the news; thus they become the Apostles. (I could argue that the seventy-two disciples sent out to preach by Jesus were technically also apostles, but it is usually just the inner circle of twelve that are referred to as the Apostles.)

I love this particular definition: Disciples are called; apostles are sent. All apostles are disciples; not all disciples become apostles.

[2] Oh, the controversial Judas. Did he hang himself after betraying Jesus (as noted in the Book of Matthew)? Did he instead buy a field, fall in it, and have all his "bowels gush out" (as noted in Acts of the Apostles)? What about the idea that he was a willing participant acting an important part in Jesus's grand plan (as noted in some non-canonical works)? Just like exactly how many licks it takes to get to the Tootsie Roll center of a Tootsie Pop, "The world may never know."

Context:
History of the Faith & Church

"Christianity is not so much the religion of Jesus (the religion that he himself proclaimed) as the religion about Jesus (the religion that is based on his death and resurrection)," states the biblical scholar Bart Ehrman.

And this can be seen clearly in the books of the Bible that follow the gospels, as well as in the diversity of non-canonical writings during the decades (and centuries) after Jesus's death. In fact, the word "Christianity" is not used in the Bible until well into the eleventh chapter of the Acts of the Apostles.

Jesus was Jewish, and his early followers were a combination of both Jewish as well as non-Jewish women and men. After his death, there was confusion about what his life (and death) had meant. How should his followers continue the ministry, now that their leader was gone? Was the kingdom of God coming now? Or would it come later?

So, many paths developed at the same time. But, contrary to popular belief, there was not a single "Jesus Movement" that developed into one form of Christianity, which later split into many denominations. There have always been different denominations and differences of opinion about Jesus.

Remember the Nag Hammadi find? Well, once those writings were discovered in 1945, scholars learned just how much variety there was. In biblical study, you'll hear references to these groups, including the Nazareans, Docetists, Ebionites, Marcionites, Johannines, Gnostics, and so on. All these groups were practicing forms of early Christianities.

Each community believed different things about who Jesus was, what he had said, what actions he had taken, and what the resurrection meant. They also differed in their opinions about the Christology of Jesus: Was he human, divine, or both? And they differed in their rituals, practices, and just how closely they were aligned with the ideas and laws of the Jewish faith.

In fact, the majority of books usually contained in the Christian "New Testament"—twenty-one of the twenty-seven—deal with trying to answer many of these questions, first through the historical narrative of the Acts of the Apostles, and then through a series of letters.

I think it is important to note that what we find in the Christian Bible is not a true history of all of early Christian thought and activity, but rather the polished history of one path of early Christianity—what we might call the "winning one" since it was ultimately canonized.

Early Christianity didn't really make world news. The vast majority of the writings that have survived from the first few centuries after Jesus's death were overwhelmingly about political, military, or secular news. Even Roman history makes little mention of Christianity till well after this Apostolic Age.

Most of the Apostles were busy traveling, preaching, forming congregations, and resolving conflicts, rather than documenting their own history so we would be able to read it today. And the majority of them would likely not have been able to read or write, and neither would their audiences. Literacy just wasn't widespread then. (A study by professor of Jewish studies at the University of London, Catherine Hezser, estimates that only 3 percent of Jewish people during the early years of the first century CE were literate. What about non-Jewish people? Columbia professor William Harris, in his book *Ancient Literacy*, estimates only 10 percent of the entire ancient population could read, and this was mostly restricted to the upper classes.)

So just how did Christianity spread so well? The Apostles shared their message at the great cities along well-established trade routes. Then their converts would travel outwards, establishing new congregations in the ancient suburbs. And *their* converts would do the same to the remote villages, and so on.

In some ways, Judaism had been constrained by its ethnicity and geography (proximity to the temple in Jerusalem). Although this had lessened after the Exiles, and people of Jewish faith were living in many different areas, the land of milk and honey still factored strongly into the tradition.

In contrast, the path of Christianity described in the Christian Bible rather quickly decided to open its message to a wider group, when the initial reaction to the message was lukewarm in most Jewish communities. This evolution and other tactics are described in the first biblical book following the Gospels: The Acts of the Apostles (which perhaps would be better described as: The Acts of *Some* of the Apostles Plus This New Guy Named Paul).

The Acts of the Apostles

Together with its "Part One" (aka the Gospel of Luke), the Acts of the Apostles makes up about twenty-five percent of the New Testament. Agewise, it is dated to approximately 80-85 CE. Contentwise, the book provides a historical narrative about the geographical spread of Jesus's ministry, based primarily on speeches that were most likely created by the author. (It was common during this era for authors to create speeches based on what a deceased or absent person *would have* said, or what people told the author *had been* said.)

The Acts of the Apostles begins with Jesus's appearances to his disciples and his direction for them to stay put in Jerusalem until they feel the power of the Holy Spirit upon them. According to Acts, as the book is known, the Holy Spirit arrived on Pentecost, a Jewish agricultural festival that is celebrated fifty days after Passover. The spirit worked miracles, and it was said that thousands of people now "believed" (in the Resurrection story). The Twelve Apostles were busy turning the movement into a more structured organization. They were also suffering persecution. Stephen, a deacon in the early church in Jerusalem, was stoned to death (and is considered the first Christian martyr). In Sunday school, when I was a child, I rarely heard—or comprehended—the brutality of what happened to the early Christians. But Acts provides a literal blow by blow.

About a third of the way into the book, we meet a new player, Saul, one of the main persecutors. But he has a conversion experience—being temporarily blinded in the process—and becomes the main character for the remainder of the book, with the new name of Paul. As you'd expect, the book includes some disagreements between this new convert and the original Apostles. In a sort of two-week "Meeting of the Apostolic Minds," Paul meets with Peter, and then James, who are building the growing Jerusalem church. They come to an agreement so that Paul can head out to spread the word throughout Cyprus, Greece, and Asia Minor.

What about the other Apostles? Though the Bible does not delve deeply into their journeys, extra-biblical writings—and more often church tradition—provide some suggestions. For example, Peter spent a good deal of time in the Jerusalem church, eventually ending up in Rome (where Roman Catholics point to him as the first Pope). James also spent time at the Jerusalem church before beginning his missionary travels. He's reported by some as ending up in Spain, but scholars are divided on whether this is fact or legend. John headed over to Asia, ministering to many new fledgling congregations, making Ephesus (Turkey) his home, and eventually spending some exile time away on the penal colony of Patmos.

It's remarkable how far some of the Apostles traveled, especially when considering how rough, dangerous, and unpredictable travel—and politics—could be during these days. Andrew preached in Turkey, Greece, and as far as what is now Russia. A few claim he made it as far as Scotland. Simon ("the Zealot") traveled to Persia, Egypt, and North Africa. Some claim he made it up to Britain once he finished in Africa.

Matthew headed to Persia, Egypt, and Ethiopia. Philip was nearby in Carthage (North Africa). Some later traditions even put him in Gaul (France). Bartholomew was a busy guy, including India, Ethiopia, Southern Arabia, and Armenia (with Jude Thaddeus), on his journeys. In fact, Armenia was the first Christian country in the world. In 301 CE, Christianity was declared the national religion—seventy-nine years before Constantine did the same in Rome.

Thomas headed out as far as India. The rich (but non-canonized) Gospel of Thomas carries an Eastern flair, comprised of 114 sayings attributed to Jesus (similar to the Dhammapada's sayings of the Buddha). The Acts of Thomas provides stories about his missions. Scholars have spent a lot of time commenting on both of these books in recent years.

And everywhere the Apostles went, they spread the word about Jesus and their perspective on what it meant. Hands down, though, we know the most about the travels of Paul. There is no doubt that Paul was instrumental in spreading the religion of Christianity through his missionary trips. Paul had never actually met Jesus, and his ministry was much less about what Jesus said or did. It was more about what Jesus's death and resurrection meant for individuals and communities. Which brings us to the epistles, or letters.

Epistles: Romans – 1 Corinthians – 2 Corinthians
Galatians – Ephesians – Philippians – Colossians
1 Thessalonians – 2 Thessalonians – 1 Timothy – 2 Timothy
Titus – Philemon – Hebrews – James – 1 Peter – 2 Peter
1 John – 2 John – 3 John – Jude

In early Christianity, churches did not look like ours do today. There was no stained glass or raised wooden pulpit, no Sunday school or choir room, and no stage for a band or sound system. Actual church buildings weren't created until at least two centuries after Christianity started. Churches instead were "house churches." Wealthier members of a group would agree to hold the gatherings in their homes.

And when these house churches had questions, they couldn't pick up an official version of the Christian Bible to try to find an answer—it didn't exist yet. So instead they did business the way most people in the ancient world did—through letter writing. Copies of these letters were then given to other churches as reference materials. When the canon was developed, many of these letters were included in the Bible, since they often answered questions that were applicable to all the developing churches.

Some of the letters have a number in front of them. Unlike in the Hebrew scriptures—when the numbers one and two referred to the parts of a scroll that had been split—the numbers here actually denote different letters. And they are tricky to read, because it is like hearing only one side of a phone conversation since either the original or the reply letter is missing. In most cases, the letters are named for the people who are receiving them (for example, the Epistle to the Romans.) The exceptions are James, Peter, John, and Jude. Their letters are named for their writers (for example, the First Epistle of James).

So, for the first group, who wrote the letters? The majority have been attributed to Paul. However, some of those have come into dispute by scholars. Most scholars agree that Romans, 1 and 2 Corinthians, Galatians, Philippians, 1 Thessalonians, and Philemon were written by Paul. The scholars are not so aligned on Ephesians, Colossians, 2 Thessalonians, 1 and 2 Timothy, and Titus.

Each community had its specific concerns, as you'll see in the sermons that follow. What can be learned from these letters is that the details of the Christian faith were slowly being figured out along the way through these letters, plus numerous other letters that we don't have.

Also, there is a fascinating document, called the Didache, which scholars date to this same time period. Beginning "Teaching of the Lord to the Gentiles (or Nations) by the Twelve Apostles," it's a detailed handbook that provides a rich look into the inner workings of early Christianity, including prayers, fast day schedules, ethical codes, instructions for rituals, and so on. Like many other writings, it lost the battle of canonization. But we can still learn a lot from it, too.

As the organization of the Christian church as a whole continued to develop, numerous councils would begin to answer the questions: "As Christians, what do we believe? And how do we act?"

The answers sometimes unified—but other times divided—the faith.

Meanwhile...

Up north in Scandinavia, the Goths crossed the Baltic Sea into what would eventually become Poland. Their religion emphasized linkage to ancestors, the presence of spirits in the land, and drew heavily on the Norse gods, especially Mars. It would be another few centuries before they made it into the Roman Empire, but when they did, it would have a dramatic effect.

Over in Asia, the Mahayana school of Buddhism was on the rise— focusing on the belief that all beings have a Buddha nature, and thus should aspire to Buddhahood. Via the Silk Road, this form of Buddhism reached China. Confucianism was now the official religion of China. But, Buddhism was getting a toehold, with the building of the White Horse Temple, the first Buddhist temple in the area. And Buddhist monks in Sri Lanka began to write down the Buddha's teachings, creating the Pali canon.

As trade and travel increased, Eastern and Western thought intermingled and influenced each other. Cross-pollination between different religions and philosophies abounded. A variety of early Christian paths referred to as Gnostics, held strong parallels to Hindu and Buddhist ideas. The Gospel of Thomas in particular contains striking similarities with Hinduism. Another group, the Essenes, practiced an asceticism similar to that of Buddhist monks.

In Rome, after Caesar Augustus's death, the Roman Empire continued to display more and more power via emperors Tiberius, Caligula, Claudius, and Nero. Moving north into Britain during the Gallic Wars, the Empire established rule in the southern part of the island, known as *Britannia*, where it would rule until 410 CE. There seemed no end to Rome's continued expansion.

The Coming of the Holy Spirit / Peter Addresses the Crowd

2 [1] When the day of Pentecost had come, [the disciples] were all together in one place. [2] And suddenly from heaven there came a sound like the rush of a violent wind, and it filled the entire house where they were sitting. [3] Divided tongues, as of fire, appeared among them, and a tongue rested on each of them. [4] All of them were filled with the Holy Spirit and began to speak in other languages, as the Spirit gave them ability.

[5] Now there were devout Jews from every nation under heaven living in Jerusalem. [6] And at this sound the crowd gathered and was bewildered, because each one heard them speaking in the native language of each.

[7] Amazed and astonished, they asked, "Are not all these who are speaking Galileans? [8] And how is it that we hear, each of us, in our own native language? [9] Parthians, Medes, Elamites, and residents of Mesopotamia, Judea and Cappadocia, Pontus and Asia, [10] Phrygia and Pamphylia, Egypt and the parts of Libya belonging to Cyrene, and visitors from Rome, both Jews and proselytes, [11] Cretans and Arabs—in our own languages we hear them speaking about God's deeds of power." [12] All were amazed and perplexed, saying to one another, "What does this mean?" [13] But others sneered and said, "They arefilled with new wine."

[14] But Peter, standing with the eleven, raised his voice and addressed them, "Men of Judea and all who live in Jerusalem, let this be known to you, and listen to what I say. [15] Indeed, these are not drunk, as you suppose, for it is only nine o'clock in the morning. [16] No, this is what was spoken through the prophet Joel:

[17] 'In the last days it will be, God declares,
that I will pour out my Spirit upon all flesh,
  and your sons and your daughters shall prophesy,
and your young men shall see visions,
  and your old men shall dream dreams.
[18] Even upon my slaves, both men and women,
in those days I will pour out my Spirit;
  and they shall prophesy.'"

What dreams!?
What visions?

Sermon by Richard Murdoch | Rye, NY | May 26, 1996

In the evolution of the Christian church's calendar, Easter is the premier holy day. Among Christians of every belief, the great festival of Easter is the best-attended religious service of the year. No one disputes its theological significance. Early in the first century CE, two more holy days joined Easter as significant church festivals: Pentecost and Epiphany. Two hundred more years passed before Christmas—the fourth and last of the great feast days of the church—completed the traditional Christian calendar. Christmas, like Easter, has few detractors. But if you ask the average person on the street to name the four great festival days of Christians, Easter and Christmas probably will be named, maybe with Epiphany tagging along. However, Pentecost will more than likely be omitted.

Today, Pentecost is a distant cousin to the other three holy days. Over four hundred years ago, Protestant reformers like Calvin, Bucer, and Zwingli eschewed the pomp and circumstance of special worship on holy days and preferred to practice the theological belief that each Sabbath worship was equal before God and beautiful in its simplicity. Easter was retained as the only church festival—a minimum concession to popular cultural needs. Today, Pentecost is lost not because of theological reasons, but simply because of the calendar. It is lost in the celebration of a civil holiday like Memorial Day, a cultural holiday like Mother's Day, or a family event like graduation weekend. Pentecost just can't compete with these important days of our secular calendar. So, preachers must make a choice about whether to preach about the sacred or secular. But I will attempt to bridge both.

Now, permit this digression: I am one of those people who doesn't take well to theological jargon. Too much of it was forced upon me as a child. I know, of course, that every profession, job, or sport has its jargon. Jargon has its place. All of us use it. And when we change from one setting to another, we usually shift gears and learn the jargon of the new setting.

For example, consider this story: Several summers in college, I worked as a carpenter's helper, roughing out houses in developments throughout Rochester, New York. Back then, houses were built the old-fashioned way. When building an outside wall or room partition, the two-by-four studs were arranged on the floor deck and toenailed to each other. Then sheets of plywood were nailed on top, and finally windows and doorways were cut out. When this was completed, it was time to "fly the wall." The first time the crew leader yelled these words, my imagination went wild! What was next: helicopters, boomerangs, or wings? Yet all we did was lift and push the wall into place. I was a newcomer from academia. As a summer carpenter, I had to learn a new language—a jargon that initiated me as a member of a group of workmen who had a common task. A specialized language helped not only build a bond of mutuality, but allowed us to communicate in a shorthand. Sometimes it also separated us from others.

We can see this separation in religion as well. Stories about the events of Jesus and the Apostles began to be spread in simple everyday conversations in Aramaic. When a later generation recorded these conversations, they were written in a very simple international language of the marketplace: Koine Greek. Unfortunately, after twenty centuries, what began in secular, everyday language has been transformed into sacred, theological language, thereby creating an unnatural chasm in our minds between the sacred and the secular.

Today, the story of Pentecost tells—in sacred language—the empowering of the Apostles by the Holy Spirit. Originally, the story was told in a secular setting, free of theological jargon: "Your young men shall see visions and your old men shall dream dreams." Pentecost is a story about the winds of change that blow through human history. It is a particular story about a particular people: a group of Jewish people who believed God was doing something new in the world—just as Memorial Day and Independence Day, civil holidays in our secular calendar, are particular stories about a particular people called Americans, who responded to the winds of change that blew through human history two hundred rather than two thousand years ago.

There is a curious, yet distinctive point being made in the text of Acts 2:17 that purposely transposes "dreams" and "visions." In the thinking of the ancient world, young men were supposed to dream dreams and old men were supposed to see visions. A vision requires mature experience and wisdom. It is a blueprint for future actions that come as either a self-revelation or a revelation received from another— usually divine—source. It is a prediction based upon data. A vision has substance that motivates others to action. And visions usually occur in the daylight.

On the other hand, dreams are not derived from wisdom and experience, but instead, come from unconscious longings from the recesses of the mind. Dreams can be fantasy, entertaining the possibility of the impossible. A dream is usually individually operative. That is not to say that a dream is not real or not motivating. But a dream usually is directed to a future goal upon which an individual will act. Dreams happen to the young and inexperienced. As quoted from the prophet Joel, the text describes a time of change in which the established order is upset. Pentecost is such a time, believes the author of the Acts of the Apostles.

Instead of the normal order of young men with dreams and old men with visions, the time is at hand that the young will have visions and the old will dream. The consequence of such a disruption in the usual expectation of things marks the beginning of a new way in the world. Instead of the Apostles working within the framework of Judaism in Palestine, the Apostles must break out of their ethnicity and accept the fact that their faith is both outside as well as inside Palestine. It is a faith rooted in its Jewish past, but it must accommodate itself to a world that speaks a multitude of languages and is transcultural.

Likewise, Memorial Day is a story of remembering that self-determination in governance is not limited and can survive only within the boundaries of our nation with a global perspective. The winds of change that blew in 1776 are challenged to blow again in different generations. And with change comes conflict—conflict of values and cultures which necessitates defending democracies against autocracies at a high price. Memorial Day is a retelling of the risks incurred when the winds of change blow.

When I was but a first-grader during World War II, I clearly remember the red/white/blue cover of *LIFE* magazine that my mother kept on the coffee table about the Sullivan brothers from Waterloo, Iowa. She was from Iowa and she took pride in the five brothers. A couple of years ago, a television journalist returned to Waterloo, asking passersby in that small city, "Who are the Sullivan Brothers?" Only one in ten was able to answer. For some years after the war, the Sullivans' house and their parents had been icons of patriotism. But alas, even though a memorial was placed in a city park, few townspeople could recall just who inspired that memorial. Nor could they remember that because of the Sullivan brothers, the Navy changed its practice to assigning no more than two blood relatives to the same ship.

All five Sullivan brothers made recruitment history when they volunteered for the war. Having come from a close-knit family, they requested (and were given permission) to train together and then go to sea together. Midway through the war, the ship on which they were stationed was torpedoed by the Axis powers in the Pacific. All five sons were lost, leaving their parents childless. A nation's sympathy went out to them; a grateful city erected a memorial, but fifty years later only one in ten in their hometown had any recollection of what price freedom for the nation had cost the Sullivan family.

"Young men shall see visions and old men shall dream dreams." The vitality of both the church and the nation depends upon visions, not dreams. Memorial Day celebrates the vision of a nation; Pentecost the vision of the Christian church. Visions are never static; they are always changing and adjusting, always open to receiving more wisdom. Visions are powerful because they motivate energies and hopes of people who are committed to more than themselves as individuals. They, like the Sullivan brothers, are committed to an ideal which is enduring beyond the present time.

But visions bring conflict in times of change when the young, who are expected to dream, see a vision, and the old, who are expected to see visions, are told to be content with dreaming. On the eve of the twenty-first century, the younger generation is fashioning a vision in both the church and the nation that is challenging the vision of a generation more secure in the twentieth century. Words like "loyalty," "commitment," "family values," "work," "money," "parenting," and "spirituality" are clues in visions about the individual dreams of different generations as they perceive what is best for the church and the nation. Behind these vision statements stand perceptions about solutions to human existence and paths to fulfillment.

Memorial Day is a confirmation by ritual of the vision statement of a nation: that certain freedoms require sacrifices, if not by all, then by some, like the Sullivan Brothers. Pentecost is the confirmation of a vision statement of the Christian faith that it will not be controlled by the boundaries of any nation alone, nor by those of any single race or culture. Be vigilant. Without constant attention, visions such as these are in danger of being reduced to only dreams.

✟ Acts 6:1-7 ✟

Seven Chosen to Serve

6 ¹ Now in these days when the disciples were increasing in number, the Hellenists murmured against the Hebrews because their widows were neglected in the daily distribution.

² And the twelve summoned the body of the disciples and said, "It is not right that we should give up preaching the word of God to serve tables. ³ Therefore, brethren, pick out from among you seven men of good repute, full of the Spirit and of wisdom, whom we may appoint to this duty. ⁴ But we will devote ourselves to prayer and to the ministry of the word."

⁵ And what they said pleased the whole multitude, and they chose Stephen, a man full of faith and of the Holy Spirit, and Philip, and Proch'orus, and Nica'nor, and Timon, and Par'menas, and Nicola'us, a proselyte of Antioch. ⁶ These they set before the Apostles, and they prayed and laid their hands upon them.

⁷ And the word of God increased; and the number of the disciples multiplied greatly in Jerusalem, and a great many of the priests were obedient to the faith.

Bible Version: Revised Standard Version (RSV)

When Christians murmur

Sermon by Richard Murdoch | East Lansing, MI | April 21, 1991

"Ain't it awful?" a non-attending church member complained to the pastor. "Politics in church! You'd think that at least in church, politics could be avoided. That's why we don't go anymore after what the deacons did to Pastor Bob."

According to the 1989 Gallup Poll survey of religious habits and perceptions of Americans, one out of three non-attenders faulted church politics as the reason for disinterest. Those surveyed did not describe themselves as non-believers in God, but simply as suffering from burnout or being burned up by the results of internal church power struggles.

Politics mean conflict; politics mean accusations; politics mean negotiating, politics mean wounded feelings. Politics often have the aroma of dirty laundry. Life without politics would be bliss, but life without politics would be literally, a world without people. The Greek word *polis* is the root of our English words, "politics" and "population." Its narrow definition is "city or gathering of people." Using some simple logic, we can assume that politics are present when two or more people are gathered together. And politics increase in direct proportion to the magnification of the *polis* or the gathering of people. The more people in a social system, the more politics will be present.

Is it surprising to find that just a few months after Jesus's crucifixion, death, and resurrection—and just weeks after the fire of Pentecost had invigorated the discouraged Apostles with a passion for evangelism—we hear about church politics? The incident is painfully clear. Those newly converted Christians in Jerusalem who came from Jewish (read: ethnic and more conservative) synagogues were receiving better treatment than those newly converted Christians from the Hellenistic (read: ethnically mixed and more progressive) synagogues.

In those days, children were a parent's old age insurance. It was customary that widows, who had no children to support them, were supported by the synagogue, which became their extended family. In exchange for food and shelter, these widows often performed tasks for the synagogue. (Some church historians suggest that this tradition became the foundation for nuns.) The early Christian church relied heavily upon the synagogue and temple structure for its survival until Rome destroyed the Jerusalem temple and its organization in 70 CE.

The theme of today's story from the Acts of the Apostles deals with unfulfilled expectations, expressed as a charge of unfairness. The more progressive Hellenistic members thought that they were being short-changed by the Apostles, who seemed to spend more time meeting the needs of the more conservative Jewish group. So church politics began between progressives and conservatives.

It is clear from the story that the Apostles, who became a kind of board of directors for the church, did not refute the charge of unfairness. They stated the problem as not having enough time to do everything that needed to be done. With teaching, preaching, and administering, they didn't always make it to the traditional dinners on time. As the demand on their time increased, shortcuts were inevitable. They simply slighted the widows they didn't know well—which were the Hellenists. The Twelve called together the larger body of disciples to announce their solution to the charge of unfairness—the delegation of responsibility.

The body of disciples, sometimes called the Seventy-Two, was to select seven to serve the tables, creating a new level of leadership (referred as *diakonia* or deacons). This allowed the Apostles to remain free to travel, preach, and administrate. The method of selection was the nomination of a slate and then the casting of lots, which would have entailed casting special religious dice (*urim* and *thummim*) to discern God's will—that is, if the Hebrew way were followed. Or if the Greek way had been followed, each voter would be given white and black balls to deposit in a box and be counted as each candidate's name was called. Any candidate receiving a black ball would have been disqualified.

The Apostles—while refraining from suggesting names—are clear about qualifications: "Select from among you seven men of good standing, full of the Spirit and of wisdom." These are not the usual words associated with an election, are they? We would expect to hear about loyalty and trust, respect and honesty, faithfulness and truth. Instead, the two criteria for those to be elected were spirit and wisdom (or in Greek: *pneuma* and *sophia*), two rather specialized and technical words. Why not reasonableness and honesty? But I suspect it was too late for negotiation. The situation was beyond simple consensus, because the word "murmur" was used.

What a word! It is in the Book of Exodus that we first come upon the word. There, the reader finds the Israelites murmuring against Moses because he has led them into the wilderness without any food to fill their hungry bellies, water to quench their thirst, shade to cool them from the desert sun, or blankets to warm them from the desert nights. The Israelites' expectation was freedom without inconvenience.

The major New Testament reference for "murmur" is here in the Acts of the Apostles. In the infancy of Christianity, the equality of Jewish and Greek, slave and free, male and female was highly touted by Paul. Converts had the expectation that these words would be transformed into actions. When the Apostles themselves didn't meet these expectations, disappointment turned into resentment.

"Murmur" is a strong and emotional word. It expresses physical disappointment. It is used when things are ugly and angry. It is a word that already accepts that rumors are flying fast and hard. It is the word of last resort before outright rebellion. It is a word that stirs people to immediate decision-making. So the Apostles, recognizing the immediate crisis, made their decision quickly, realizing if they were to name people, they would be accused of unfairness again. So they left the selection to the Seventy-Two, giving two guidelines: spirit and wisdom.

The election resulted in the choice of two with Hebrew names (Stephen and Phillip) and five with Greek or Hellenist names (Prochorus, Nicanor, Timon, Parmenas, and Nicolaus—who is noted as being from Antioch, suggesting that although he has a Greek name, his background is Aramaic). However, the solution worked only temporarily. The Book of Acts tells us that in short time two of the disciples (Stephen and Phillip) quit serving tables and begin to preach, teach, and administrate just as the Twelve were doing. Stephen was martyred for his preaching and Phillip went to Ethiopia. So much for the poor Hellenist widows, who were left to be served by their own Hellenist four.

Is it possible that the Twelve Apostles expected too much and the Seven Deacons promised too much? Was it reasonable to expect spirit and wisdom in the same person? How many individuals do you know whom you admire for both their spirit and wisdom? Probably very few.

But, in any group, there are often individuals who clearly exhibit one or another of these characteristics, thus enabling the group to accomplish what sole individuals cannot.

The Twelve Apostles soon found that even though they might be admired as saints (because they were intimately connected with Jesus) they were not carbon copies of Jesus. In their enthusiasm, they sought to fulfill all expectations by themselves and (worst of all) they allowed the Seventy-Two to believe and expect the same.

Church leaders are often seduced into thinking that they can meet all of their congregation's needs and desires, healing all wounds and creating peace among all peoples. Church members often allow church leaders to be unrealistic as well. We often believe that the church is an institution of divine origin, and thus it should possess divine wisdom while eliminating the need for politics.

Politics happen everywhere there are people who have expectations to be met: in churches, in legislatures, and in companies. Unfortunately, not all expectations can be met. In reality, only a few can be negotiated or reached in consensus. Does that mean that we stop stating our expectations? Does it mean that we avoid discussing our needs? Does it mean we stop complaining when we see injustice? By no means! It simply means that churches are not divine institutions with divine power to right all of the ills of life. Churches are gatherings of people who come together to do as best they can within their limited wisdom and charisma. There are some expectations which can be met, other expectations which need to be delegated, and still other expectations which will not be met and thus will remain dreams for the future.

We can learn from the Acts story that the solution to unfulfilled expectations is not murmuring or gossiping. The solution is a group effort within which wisdom and spirit can be found in individuals who are collectively delegated tasks of ministry. It is a hard pill for us to swallow that we cannot fulfill all expectations for all people. It is just as hard a pill to swallow that every church, as a gathering of people, is always subject to politics and capable of erring. But while our churches may disappoint us, our true faith is in God, not in his church.

James Killed and Peter Imprisoned / Peter Delivered from Prison

12 ¹ About that time King Herod laid violent hands upon some who belonged to the church. ² He had James, the brother of John, killed with the sword.

⁴ When he had seized [Peter], he put him in prison and handed him over to four squads of soldiers to guard him, intending to bring him out to the people after the Passover. ⁵ While Peter was kept in prison, the church prayed fervently to God for him.

⁶ The very night before Herod was going to bring him out, Peter, bound with two chains, was sleeping between two soldiers, while guards in front of the door were keeping watch over the prison. ⁷ Suddenly an angel of the Lord appeared and a light shone in the cell. He tapped Peter on the side and woke him, saying, "Get up quickly." And the chains fell off his wrists. ⁸ The angel said to him, "Fasten your belt and put on your sandals." He did so. Then he said to him, "Wrap your cloak around you and follow me." ⁹ Peter went out and followed him; he did not realize that what was happening with the angel's help was real; he thought he was seeing a vision. ¹⁰ After they had passed the first and the second guard, they came before the iron gate leading into the city. It opened for them of its own accord, and they went outside and walked along a lane, when suddenly the angel left him. ¹¹ Then Peter came to himself and said, "Now I am sure that the Lord has sent his angel and rescued me from the hands of Herod and from all that the Jewish people were expecting."

¹² As soon as he realized this, he went to the house of Mary, the mother of John whose other name was Mark, where many had gathered and were praying. ¹³ When he knocked at the outer gate, a maid named Rhoda came to answer. ¹⁴ On recognizing Peter's voice, she was so overjoyed that, instead of opening the gate, she ran in and announced that Peter was standing at the gate. ¹⁵ They said to her, "You are out of your mind!" But she insisted that it was so. They said, "It is his angel." ¹⁶ Meanwhile Peter continued knocking; and when they opened the gate, they saw him and were amazed. ¹⁷ He motioned to them with his hand to be silent, and described for them how the Lord had brought him out of the prison. And he added, "Tell this to James and to the believers." Then he left and went to another place.

To pray...

Sermon by Richard Murdoch | Omaha, NE | July 18, 1982

This story comes from Mark Twain's *Huckleberry Finn*:

> *Then Miss Watson she took me in the closet and prayed, but nothing come of it. She told me to pray every day, and whatever I asked for I would get it. But it warn't so. I tried it. Once I got a fish-line, but no hooks. It warn't any good to me without hooks. I tried for the hooks three or four times, but somehow I couldn't make it work. By and by, one day, I asked Miss Watson to try for me, but she said I was a fool. She never told me why, and I couldn't make it out no way. I set down one time back in the woods, and had a long think about it. I says to myself, if a body can get anything they pray for, why don't Deacon Winn get back the money he lost on pork? Why can't the widow get back her silver snuffbox that was stole? Why can't Miss Watson fat up? No, says I to myself, there ain't nothing in it.*

Children have a way of cutting though all the niceties of life and bringing us to the point of reality, don't they? Miss Watson bluntly tells poor Huck to fit in to her neat little Mississippi River world. And Huck tries to do just that, but somehow it doesn't work for him. Miss Watson, instead of dealing with the real issue, just blames Huck for not understanding. "Just a fool," she says. It's so easy for adults to avoid the real issue.

Prayer as a religious ritual is shared by the whole world. It may surprise some of you to know that prayer is not an exclusive Christian invention. Prayer is defined in the dictionary as "the act of asking for some petition, usually of a divine being." Muslim people pray, Jewish people pray, Hindu people pray. It is certainly a human activity. But it seems to have a further dimension than the dictionary states: Certainly we consider prayer as more than just asking.

Prayer is something that people expect as part of both public worship and private devotion. Prayer is a human activity that has divine consequences. In the scripture lesson for today, Peter was released from prison in a miraculous way because "many had gathered and were praying." While it was fervent, it also seems to have been a ritual because not too much was expected from it. The account states that Rhoda jumped up to go answer the outer door to the villa when it rang. She yelled to the others that it was Peter, but they answered back from across the courtyard that it was impossible—and, yet, they were praying for the very same! It is a sobering fact that not all early Christians and disciples were perfect, isn't it? They shared the same humanness that we do. No doubt they bickered awhile while trying to decide whether it was the real Peter, just an impostor, or maybe his ghost. Imagine poor Peter standing outside, nervous about being discovered, while his Christian brothers and sisters inside discussed whether to let him in! It is possible for an answered prayer to present as much of a problem as an unanswered prayer, I suppose.

There are probably more books written on the subject of prayer than anyone can count. Each and every one has its own point. Each has a technique unique to itself. Some have copious Bible passages to support their ideas about prayer. Many claim a how-to approach that works to satisfy mind, body, and spirit. And most tackle the problem of unanswered prayer. I have reread a half dozen such books this week to refresh my thoughts. It struck me how heady these books all are.

Regardless of the theological point of the author, the main bulk of the books was on verbal, articulated prayer—the kind of prayer that stresses words to communicate with God about praise, sin, thankfulness, self-wants, and others' needs. We have names for all of these types of prayers, of course: prayers of petition, prayers of adoration, prayers of confession, prayers of thankfulness, prayers of intercession. Most praying seems to be talking to God, with very little time spent listening to God. In other words, most prayer is one-sided. We're so busy telling God what we want, need, and think that there's little time for God to speak to us. It is rather amazing that we humans haven't noticed that God gave us two ears and one mouth. The implication of that, according to one of my teachers, was "so that you will listen twice as much as you talk in my classroom."

A woman told me recently that for several months she had been considering a job transfer. It was an attractive one. She kept praying about it, going over in her mind its positive and negative aspects before God. But she never seemed to be able to reach a conclusion. When she finally had run out of words to say in her prayers, she was reduced to quiet listening and meditation. Then the conclusion came to her: "I haven't done much listening to God, all I've done is the talking."

Jesus encountered this reality in his ministry. He reminded some of his listeners that they should not be like the hypocrites who pray daily in front of great audiences. Instead, he recommended his followers enter into their closets and pray in quietness. I have lived long enough (and have been in the religious current deep enough) to gather a perspective on prayer in our culture. Great religious leaders have inspired people, motivated hymn writers, and counseled congregations to discover prayer in the still, quiet places of contemplation. Their wisdom was to listen for God in the "rustling of the grass," in the "sweet hour of prayer," and "in the sweet by and by," as suggested by the late Victorian hymn writers.

But those days are gone. We are counseled by each paperback self-help book to assert ourselves and ask for what we want: "For if you ask of your father in heaven, it will be granted to those who have faith." Popular religious leaders of today give accounts over and over of God's blessings upon those who have asked—from healing cancer to winning a horse race, from getting a date to having a bank loan approved. There seems to be no end to what God will do for those who ask in the right way. The current has changed course. Now, it is not the quiet time of prayer which brings results by listening, but the articulated prayer unashamedly asking for anything we cannot get for ourselves on our own.

Now, I know you're all thinking, somewhere in your mind: "Which is right prayer? Maybe this is a trick and neither is correct." Unsolicited advice is always received, as it is given—prejudicial to your own life's outlook as if you lived in another's shoes. And yet, to provide no direction is to be awash on the sea of indecision, being washed here, and washed there. Jesus suggested a form of prayer through a pattern that could be used by his disciples and followers. It was carefully constructed in order to show the flow of prayer. You'll find his suggestion, the Lord's Prayer, in Matthew 6:9-15. We often rush over it so quickly that we don't see the direction it takes. It provides not only a technique nor words, but also an attitude, a stance for prayer.

In the Acts account of Peter's deliverance from prison, the scripture makes the point that a number of people were at prayer. We are not told specifically what the words were—but we are told of an attitude or a stance. To be at prayer does not mean specifically to be kneeling and uttering words at each moment to God. To be at prayer is to be in contact with a divine understanding—ready to listen, to act, to be at ease, and to be summoned as one contemplates one's life's pleasures, joys, and needs. Prayer is both an active and passive process. It can be terribly draining, terribly frustrating, terribly joyful. But one thing can be assured: Too many words will clutter the scene.

Not too long ago, I was with a group of clergy at a seminar meeting. A question was asked about clergy lifestyles: How much time do we each spend in prayer? Typical of America's materialistic culture, the responses came in as "ten minutes a day," "fifteen minutes," "when I feel like it," "when I need to." I was somewhat embarrassed when my time came to answer: "Thirty-five to forty-five minutes a day." Of course, I had won the prize, so to speak, for being the most righteous. That is, until one person asked, "How do you find the time?" I answered, "When I jog each morning." He replied, "Oh, well, that's not real prayer." By his judgment, perhaps not, but by mine, yes! It is real prayer! It is in that time alone that I can put body, mind, and soul together to thank God for another day, a beautiful sunrise, a crisp morning. It's time to reflect upon the needs of myself and others for the day. Unfettered by telephones, people, and schedules, I can be at ease with God, both speaking and listening, but listening more than speaking. And I sincerely believe that to be at prayer is something that happens *with* God, not always something that is said *to* God.

For many, prayer is a talisman, something to ward off the bad things of life. For many, prayer is the power of positive thinking: Ask and you shall receive. For many, prayer is a beautiful religious ritual.

But for those gathered in the home of John Mark's mother—guided by the example of Jesus—prayer is an attitude, a stance through which we are with God. It can be spoken or it can be in meditation. It can happen while kneeling, standing, or jogging. It can be speaking with God, but most of the time it must be listening to the presence of God which surrounds us.

The Gift of Love

13 [1] If I speak in the tongues of mortals and of angels, but do not have love, I am a noisy gong or a clanging cymbal. [2] And if I have prophetic powers, and understand all mysteries and all knowledge, and if I have all faith, so as to remove mountains, but do not have love, I am nothing. [3] If I give away all my possessions, and if I hand over my body so that I may boast, but do not have love, I gain nothing.

[4] Love is patient; love is kind; love is not envious or boastful or arrogant [5] or rude. It does not insist on its own way; it is not irritable or resentful; [6] it does not rejoice in wrongdoing, but rejoices in the truth. [7] It bears all things, believes all things, hopes all things, endures all things.

[8] Love never ends. But as for prophecies, they will come to an end; as for tongues, they will cease; as for knowledge, it will come to an end. [9] For we know only in part, and we prophesy only in part; [10] but when the complete comes, the partial will come to an end. [11] When I was a child, I spoke like a child, I thought like a child, I reasoned like a child; when I became an adult, I put an end to childish ways. [12] For now we see in a mirror, dimly, but then we will see face to face. Now I know only in part; then I will know fully, even as I have been fully known. [13] And now faith, hope, and love abide, these three; and the greatest of these is love.

Faith, hope and... love

Sermon by Richard Murdoch | East Lansing, MI | October 21, 1988

Translations of the Bible differ sometimes because there are often times no clear equivalents for the Greek or Hebrew word in question. For example, in the First Letter to the Corinthians 13:13 we see the following example. Translations of the Greek word μένει (transliterated as *menei*) vary: abide, endure, stand, remain, constant. But the word which makes the most sense contextually is some form of *remain*. I think that probably *remains constant* might convey the sense of what Paul is saying.

I came upon this conclusion in the dark of night somewhere in Kentucky, driving back from funeral services for another one of my aunts—the last of my mother's sisters—all four of whom have died in the last sixteen months. Being the eldest surviving grandson in my mother's family, much responsibility has fallen upon me when it comes to the widowed and childless sisters. In fact, so much of my energy has been consumed these past months that one of the church staff greeted me upon my return with, "You're about to run out of aunts one of these days!"

Regardless of whether death comes to a family member or a friend, whether it is a surprise or expected, and whether you are young or old, grieving takes more than the form of sadness. It takes on the form of debriefing a bit of your computer brain space. I found myself thinking as far back as I could about Aunt "Do," as we called her in our younger years because calling her Dora was too hard for us. I first met Aunt Do at a train when I was four, at the 30th Street Station in Philadelphia. I was more interested in the great electric train than I was in her. I can remember it now. It backed into the great glass-covered station. I pulled my Dad along to the front, so I could see the engine. Thus began a child's love affair with trains. Saturday mornings were special days when my Dad and I would take a trolley car to the station to watch the trains. Until I was eleven, I knew I would be an engineer! (Later someone would squash this dream.)

My last memory of Aunt Do is from just this past summer. In her younger years, she taught home economics at the University of Georgia and supervised for the state education department. For the past five years, she had lived in a nursing home in the red hills of Georgia outside Athens. I visited her just a week after her eighty-ninth birthday, and just several weeks after my forty-ninth. As many of you know, conversation among the infirm is often limited to informing. I noted that next year she would be ninety and I would be fifty. With a smile of recognition, she said, "But you're going to have more fun than I am." With her bit of humor released, she lapsed back into unrecognition.

In between my initial and my final remembrance of Aunt Do, my brain has stored a lot of information—information about precious gifts—especially my first leather suitcase, which she gave me for my graduation gift from high school—and about trips—especially when I turned fourteen, got my driver's license, and accompanied her to Iowa in a new green and white 1953 Chrysler Newport coupe with automatic transmission and tailfins! And about holiday dinners—especially her Lane cakes (which we teetotaling Southern Baptists affectionately called "drunk cakes" because they had a lot of booze inside, but that was "okay since she was Lutheran").

I remember what she taught me about life—especially the stories about the back-road hotels of little Georgia towns, when she would push the dresser against the door for safety since "men were rough and tumble in those days if you had a Yankee accent." I remember her small home, decorated with the antiques she collected in Savannah or New York (before it was fashionable to do such). And I remember her silk clothing. We had never known anyone who wore silk. Everyone we knew wore cotton dresses. But she was practical. "In the South, it is so hot in the summer, only silk will keep you cool and fresh," she said, although I think the perfume we smelled must have helped as well.

When I went to the nursing home to gather up her "effects" (as we euphemistically call final possessions), the maintenance supervisor presented me with four plastic bags of clothing, a box of tissues, a telephone, a television, and a small bag of snapshots and greeting cards. These were her minimum needs for five years. The first two were necessary for personal survival and the last three for contact with the outside world. In addition to my memories, what remained of Aunt Do's eighty-nine years of living was compressed into my car trunk as I drove away.

But with one glaring exception: There remained love. Those who came to the memorial service testified to it. There was a woman who was beholden to Aunt Do for her first position at the university. There were also those who had been supervised by her; people from her small and struggling Lutheran church, the city government, and the university administration; there was her college classmate; and there were her nephews. But most importantly, there was a friend who I met for the first time.

Shirley was a woman about my age, whose name I had heard but we had never met. She told me that for the past three years, three times a week, she had stopped to visit Aunt Dora. In fact, two months ago, when my aunt had endured a series of capillary strokes that set in one after another, the nursing home asked if Shirley might come feed my aunt, because Dora had refused food. Shirley came. My aunt recovered enough to qualify for physical and speech therapy. I was curious about why Shirley had been so committed to my aunt, and asked her about it. She replied, "I am a Stephen minister at our church."

Briefly, Shirley related to me how twelve laypeople in that congregation of less than two hundred members had been trained to give a kind of specific pastoral support that the pastor was unable to give as personally as individuals could. Two gave support to the recently bereaved, three to the recently divorced, three to those in transitional phases in and out of the local university, one to those in legal difficulties, and three to the infirm.

But what was most significant to me was when she explained the Stephen ministering process. Shirley said, "I have certainly received back more than I have ever given. I am a busy woman, with a job in the university, two children in college, and a mother-in-law in a Wisconsin nursing home. But the time I have spent with Miss Dora has made me feel, think, and act more humanely in my own life. Life passes too quickly when we focus exclusively on our own survival. I live life much more easily now that I have accepted that much of love is self-giving without expecting a reward. I was raised to believe that if love was real you stuck it out to the end, because you'd get something back.

I invested a lot in my kids, and got rather angry when I didn't get back from them as much as I thought I should for all my parental love. Now that I went through the Stephen process and am involved in it, what is called self-giving love makes a lot more sense to me. Love's not so much a burden or something I ought to do, but an opportunity to experience being human."

Shirley gave me a personal perspective—not from the side of a professional managing an adequate level of pastoral care coverage, but from the experience of a person who has grown in her spiritual journey by being a part of a ministry. Her point was simply that in caring for each other, we become more aware of our values and experience them more deeply and personally.

What remains for Shirley—and for me—of Aunt Dora is more than just simply memories and a few survival items. Her life extends beyond this time and place. That is exactly what Paul means in 1 Corinthians 13 through his definition of love. His audience was expecting the *eschaton*, the end of the world. Paul believed very sincerely that Jesus Christ would come again in his lifetime to gather up the Apostles and disciples into a heavenly kingdom of peace and love. But Paul grew older, and the time for Jesus's return got shorter and shorter. Paul rethought his faith and his hopes for it. While our faith and hope may end with this life, our love continues on into the next dimension of our lives. Love remains constant in this life and the next.

Being Subject to Authorities

13 [1] Let every person be subject to the governing authorities; for there is no authority except from God, and those authorities that exist have been instituted by God. [2] Therefore whoever resists authority resists what God has appointed, and those who resist will incur judgment.

[3] For rulers are not a terror to good conduct, but to bad. Do you wish to have no fear of the authority? Then do what is good, and you will receive its approval; [4] for it is God's servant for your good. But if you do what is wrong, you should be afraid, for the authority does not bear the sword in vain! It is the servant of God to execute wrath on the wrongdoer.

[5] Therefore one must be subject, not only because of wrath but also because of conscience. [6] For the same reason you also pay taxes, for the authorities are God's servants, busy with this very thing. [7] Pay to all what is due them— taxes to whom taxes are due, revenue to whom revenue is due, respect to whom respect is due, honor to whom honor is due.

Flags, flags, and more flags

Sermon by Richard Murdoch | Rye, NY | July 2, 1995

Of all of the weeks of the year, this is the one when you will see the most flags displayed. Each village, city, business establishment, and public park will be awash in the red, white, and blue. In fact—courtesy of many fashion designers—you can even dress in the same theme for your Fourth of July celebrations. Although, I hasten to add, a little more than a generation ago, that would not have been an option. More than one court case during the protests of the Viet Nam era highlighted not only the appropriate and inappropriate uses of the flag, but also the constitutional and unconstitutional uses as well. Clothing made with an actual flag was prohibited, but clothing with a flag design was not— even though both were cloth. (And did the Supreme Court justices dance merrily around that one!)

Flags, of course, have been around a very long time. They are part and parcel of human celebrations, a county's patriotism, and symbols of authority for rulers. What makes our experience as Americans particularly delicate is that our loyalty to our country is expressed in a Pledge of Allegiance that is made not to a person, or a constitution, or even a homeland, but to a piece of cloth. And even that piece of cloth has an uncertain origin. Instead of one, more than a half dozen flags evolved out of the Revolution. Betsy Ross's design was a late entry in the flag sweepstakes, which included the Bennington, Guilford, Continental, Serapis, and Washington flags.[1] But what is even more unique is the fact that the pledge itself is barely a hundred years old and has no connection to the founding fathers or their final decision for Betsy Ross's design of stars and stripes that waves today.

Today's almost sacrosanct Pledge of Allegiance was written and suggested as a marketing piece for a Boston magazine for young readers. Francis Bellamy, circulation manager for *The Youth's Companion,* composed a few words for students to repeat on Columbus Day, October 12, 1892. In that year, the four-hundredth anniversary of the "discovery" of America by Christopher Columbus was being celebrated at an exhibition in Chicago. Thousands of pamphlets were printed and distributed to schools around the country—along with a free copy of *The Youth's Companion*—thus beginning a patriotic ritual which today not only youth but even adults repeat. However, it was not until 1942 that Congress officially recognized the words of the Pledge of Allegiance and cast them into stone.[2]

It was barely a decade later (1954) that a change was made to insert the words "under God" at the urging of President Dwight D. Eisenhower. He stated: "In this way, we are reaffirming the transcendence of religious faith in America's heritage and future; in this way, we shall constantly strengthen those spiritual weapons which forever will be our country's most powerful resource in peace and war." (And this was stated by a president who—in that same year—joined a church and was baptized as a Christian for the first time.)

I remember well the change, because many of us in our small elementary school near Annapolis, Maryland, stumbled over the Pledge when it came to the new words, because we had learned to say it in a sing-song child's manner. Any deviation meant we had to start the recitation over again.

But one classmate didn't confront our problem. John was a Jehovah's Witness. He always stood silently during the recitation. Strange it is how memories from childhood remain sharp years later. My memory is still clear about the PTA gossip from my parents' discussion about the change. All the parents felt that John's parents should certainly make him repeat the Pledge of Allegiance now that God was in it. But the PTA parents had missed the point. The issue was not the pledge, it was any allegiance that was to any other than God alone.

In a way, Christian patriotism is a contradictory term, an oxymoron. For some, these are two words that cannot be used together; each cancels out the other. Jehovah's Witnesses believe that to be a Christian means it is impossible to be a patriot. They petitioned the Congress and received an exception for military service in World War II (other groups were unsuccessful in this). Their members could be excluded from any patriotic duty, including military service. But they were not so different from many Christians in the church's two-thousand-year history. They believed that the New Testament stated that a true believer in Christ is a member of God's kingdom, not this world. Thus, Christians can acknowledge no leader and no government that is not of God.

With the fall of the Roman Empire in the fourth century, the church embarked upon making the world exactly that: God's kingdom. Parish churches incorporated the local courts and administration into their own. All land was held in trust for God alone; owned not by individual citizens, but by the church. Marriages were regulated by the church. Medicine and law were regulated by the church. And finally, all commerce carried a tax for the church. Five hundred years later, by the arrival of the first millennium, the Christian church had brought a moral order to the world, but had exacted a great price. Popes crowned and uncrowned kings, archbishops regulated all land and commerce, and bishops directed all education. And as the Inquisition displayed so vividly, anyone who disagreed with the church's law and order was subject to be charged with treason against the King, which brought death. The state was the church; the church was the state.

Among those who settled America were refugees of the Old World. They came seeking a New World. Many were religious refugees who were wary of the entangling alliances of church and world. Some (such as the Puritans) wanted simply to purify the Old World, and created an environment that was even more restrictive, more oppressive than the old one. Others wanted no involvement of religion in the affairs of government and were labeled "freethinkers." Had the Pledge of Allegiance to the flag even been suggested in the first hundred years of our country's history, it would have been soundly defeated. Those who seize the offensive need no Pledge of Allegiance to a flag to bolster their patriotism; the passion of patriotism is its own energy. It is when we lose the passion of the revolution that loyalty must be engendered with pledges of allegiance.

In today's reading, Paul calls upon the Christians in Rome to obey the Roman authorities regardless of whether they conform to Christian principles or not. It is kind of a get-along/go-along philosophy. The struggling church of the first century existed in contradiction to Rome's demand for full allegiance. Paul's viewpoint has been quoted in different religious contexts over the centuries and even today. It has even been interpreted to mean an evil government can exist in the permission of God. The leaders of the Lutheran Church of Germany used it to justify letting the Nazi regime incorporate itself into its social fabric, although a few refused.

They became known as the "Confessing Church" and opposed vehemently the Nazi takeover of the churches, saying it was incompatible with God's kingdom. When the leaders of the established Lutheran Church cited Paul, the leaders of the Confessing Church cited when Jesus upset the government-supported moneychanger's tables in the temple as being in conflict with God's kingdom. Theirs (like Jesus's) was a summary justice; there were no papers brought against regulatory agencies, no consumer fraud, and no breach of religious or civil rights—just clear and unambiguous justice on the spot.

Christian patriots often come in these two varieties, but they both claim the same biblical authority. Patriotism, for a Christian, thus becomes an examination of the causes as well as one's own faith journey. For some, it has meant martyrdom, for others, it has not. For some, it has meant leaving their native land and starting out new in another one. Or it has meant a loss of stature and fortune, or civil disobedience, or holding public office—or for some people, none of those things.

The road of patriotism is not a well-marked one that has specific road signs. Instead, it requires accountability of one's faith with one's own call from God. Our particular nation has seen Christian patriots of both varieties—those who have felt called to follow Paul's words and those who follow Jesus's words. It is not an easy decision, but without those two choices, this nation would not be what it strives to be: the land of the free, and the home of the brave.

[1] These flags are worth a quick search online. In today's world of "design by committee," when everyone has an opinion (or a blog!) about logo design, it is thought-provoking to see the flag versions that didn't win.

[2] Interestingly, the original 1892 pledge read, "I pledge allegiance to *my flag*." The National Flag Conference changed this in 1923 to "I pledge allegiance to *the flag of the United States of America*." Why? Because new immigrants were confusing loyalties between the U.S. flag and the flags of their countries of birth.

14 ¹⁷ Now this I say and testify in the Lord, that you must no longer walk as the Gentiles do, in the futility of their minds. ¹⁸ They are darkened in their understanding, alienated from the life of God because of the ignorance that is
in them, due to their hardness of heart. ¹⁹ They have become callous and have given themselves up to sensuality, greedy to practice every kind of impurity.

²⁰ But that is not the way you learned Christ!—²¹ assuming that you have heard about him and were taught in him, as the truth is in Jesus, ²² to put off your old self, which belongs to your former manner of life and is corrupt through deceitful desires, ²³ and to be renewed in the spirit of your minds, ²⁴ and to put on the new self, created after the likeness of God in true righteousness and holiness.

Bible Version: English Standard Version (ESV)

How are your callouses?

Sermon by Richard Murdoch | Omaha, NE | August 8, 1982

There is a funny story about a preacher who went out to make some house calls one afternoon. When he knocked at one screen door, no one answered, but the inside door was ajar. After he knocked several more times, a voice responded back: "Come in, come in!" He opened the screen door, and entered a hallway. The voice came again from what seemed to be the far end of the hallway: "Come in, come in!" He entered the kitchen, only to be accosted by a large, ferocious dog that pinned him against the wall, between the table and chairs. Caught by surprise, the preacher panicked. He looked around for a way out or for protection. It was then that he spied the source of the invitation to enter: a parrot in a cage joyfully saying, "Come in, come in!" The preacher bellowed, "You stupid parrot, see what a mess you've gotten me in. Can't you say anything else besides 'come in'?" The inflection in his voice was effective. The parrot gleefully changed his words to "Sic 'em, sic 'em!"

The seeming callousness of the parrot reminds me of a newspaper report I read recently. Mike, a seventeen-year-old youth, stood at the edge of a high building in the Lower East Side of Manhattan, ready to jump. The reporter stated that Mike's family had disintegrated around him, and he was despondent about the death of his mother, the incarceration of his brother, and the alcoholism of his father. The report went on to say that the crowd that had gathered below began to chant, "Jump! Jump! Jump!" They were encouraging self-destructive behavior for their own twisted pleasure—not unlike the parrot with its "Sic 'em, sic 'em!"

Callous behavior abounds around us each day. For example, are you following the continuing saga in *The New York Times* of Mattie Dudley? She is sixty-seven years of age and sells newspapers for $5 a week from her wheelchair in Charlottesville, Virginia. Recently, she has become a national figure due to the rules and regulations of government agencies.

Physically challenged from birth, Miss Dudley must look after herself. There is no one else to help her, and she has no means of support except for a Supplemental Security Income payment of $284.30 a month. Using her newspaper earnings, she bought a contract with a local mortuary for $1,000, so that she would be assured of a decent burial with a headstone of her choosing. However, when local officials discovered she had such a contract, it was ruled as an asset and its interest made her exceed the available limit to receive SSI and Medicare, which has paid for portions of her disability medical care.

As with every issue, there certainly is another side to this story, one which we don't know, but the point has been made that certain rules and regulations appear to be callous when a burial certificate—by which an elderly woman tries to take care of herself—winds up being a detriment to her own survival. The rules are telling her, either give up your funds for living or your funds for burial. You can't have both.

However, there is a happy ending to both of these stories. For Mike, there was a reporter who climbed up the fire escape from the crowd and talked for an hour and a half to him. The reporter persuaded Mike that his life was valuable and worth saving, and invited him into his own home. He had no son of his own and said he would accept Mike as his own. The *New York Daily News* reported just this spring that Mike has been adopted by the reporter and his family. No callousness there!

Miss Dudley received calls from as far away as Alberta, Canada, where office workers were shelling out to buy a burial certificate in her name. A New Jersey couple wanted to set up a trust to guarantee $1,500 for her funeral expenses. A Florida woman sent her $1,000. A woman in Los Angeles wrote and asked where her neighborhood could send funds to help. No callousness there!

This word, "callous," appears in the letter to the Ephesians:

> *They are darkened in their understanding,*
> *...alienated from the life of God*
> *...due to their hardness of heart*
> *They have become callous.*

The "they" spoken about are the Gentiles, for that is the culture and community in which the hearers of this letter lived. There they were,

Gentile Christians raised in a society that claimed something else other than what they believed. (There were not many Jewish Christians in Ephesus). It was so easy to be tempted back to the old ways when the going got tough in the early church.

Some people like to dismiss much of the culture in which Paul lived as simply immoral. But in actuality, the culprit was not sexual immorality, but rather greed and the misuse of power—in the marketplace, in the center of governments, and in the rising technological advances. In a world in which goods were produced more rapidly than ever before, the word "covetousness" had a prime focus in several of Paul's letters.

For example, the average family in Ephesus had inherited their two-room home from the previous generation. They probably possessed a half dozen storage pots, a few implements of iron, no more than two changes of clothing. Almost all furniture was in some way built into the walls of the home. They may have owned some beast of burden, but that was rare. Except for the extremely powerful, the net worth of a typical free family of two generations was equivalent to your car filled by you, your family, and whatever possessions you could fit in between the passengers. That was it. To covet another's success was a real temptation. Like a child who has been to camp for a week and has not had a hamburger, fries, pizza, or soda, the urge to gorge oneself all at one time in the nearest fast-food restaurant is almost unbearable.

In a world of newfound materialism and consumerism, the Christians of Ephesus found it difficult to limit their appetite, whether it be for the newest clothing, the newest sexual passion, or the newest storage jar. Reading between the lines, you can almost hear Paul echoing the words of the Sermon on the Mount: "Why do you fret about what you want to eat, or what you shall wear, or how to amuse yourself in your leisure time? Put off your old nature, which belongs to your former manner of living, and be renewed in the spirit of your minds. Put on the new nature, created after the likeness of God in true righteousness and wholeness."

It is so easy to see the plight of the Ephesian Christians as they tried to cope in their world. They just simply did not fit in anymore with their new nature. They were always against the grain. Who cares if a few thousand slaves were sacrificed in an Ephesian silver mine in order to bring forth new jewelry for the next season? That's progress. Unless, of course, you are the jeweler. Who cares if the granaries are empty for the people on the west side of the city? That's war. They'll just have to starve. Unless, of course, it is your cousin. Who cares if a woman loses her means to a decent burial? Rules must be followed for the good of all. Unless, of course, it is your aunt. Who cares if a seventeen-year-old wants to jump? It's his life anyway. Unless, of course, it is your son. It's so easy to become calloused—unless it hits you personally.

After all, physical calluses do have a positive aspect. A callus protects you from pain. I was reminded of that last month as I picked up part of a hoe from the field beside my great-grandfather's abandoned home. I mused over the thousands of times his hands had gripped the hoe handle as he wore it thin in the cotton and corn. I remembered that for two weeks each spring, I couldn't wait to build up calluses on the palms of my hands so that when I gripped the hoe for eight hours a day it would not rub my hands raw chopping cotton.

Those calluses on your feet—the ones you expose at the pool or on your patio as you delight in barefoot summer days—protect your feet from the pain of shoes that are too short, too narrow, or too thin. The more the shoe rubs, the more your foot builds up its defense with layers of skin. Calluses are natural defenses against legitimate pain.

But spiritual "callouses" (from callousness), as Paul notes, have a way of alienating us from the life of God by creating a hardness of heart. The issue is certainly not one of callouses or no callouses. We can never respond to all the employment injustices, all the Mattie Dudleys, and all the Mikes—the guilt would be overwhelming. No, the issue is clearly that of the Ephesians. Do I join in and yell? Or do I remember that I am created in the likeness of God (*imago dei*), and refuse to yell "Sic 'em" or "Jump!"? As I look at the world around me, do I remember that righteousness will cause me pain? Do I merely read through the accounts of war saying, "Glad it's not me," or do I utter a soft prayer that one day young men will no longer fight old men's wars? When government policy changes place feeding the hungry back on local communities, do I give a little more to the food pantry? Or do I merely pay lip service? It's not easy to maintain yourself in a calloused world, but there are rays of hope, shafts of light. We go against the grain of our world.

Several years ago, there was a terrible earthquake in Alaska. Anchorage was devastated. A number of people wrote to the governor and demanded that he do certain things for them. They outlined the suffering they had endured and demanded the government take responsibility. Later the governor appeared on television and reported that among all the demands he had received in the mail was a message from a boy, on a plain notecard with two nickels taped to it. The boy had written these words: "Use this wherever it is needed. If you need more, let me know."

No spiritual callouses there! How are yours? Do they protect from legitimate pain, or do they alienate you from the life of God by creating a hardness of heart?

1 ²² If I am to live in the flesh, that means fruitful labor for me; and I do not know which I prefer. ²³ I am hard pressed between the two: my desire is to depart and be with Christ, for that is far better; ²⁴ but to remain in the flesh is more necessary for you.

²⁵ Since I am convinced of this, I know that I will remain and continue with all of you for your progress and joy in faith, ²⁶ so that I may share abundantly in your boasting in Christ Jesus when I come to you again.

²⁷ Only, live your life in a manner worthy of the gospel of Christ, so that, whether I come and see you or am absent and hear about you, I will know that you are standing firm in one spirit, striving side by side with one mind for the faith of the gospel.

Are we worth more dead than alive?

Sermon by Richard Murdoch | East Lansing, MI | September 30, 1990

At certain times in our lives, we are worth more dead than alive. However, it's not a physical worth. I remember the amazement of our high school chemistry class, when our teacher revealed that the chemicals in our bodies were worth a mere eight dollars and twenty-one cents. I imagine that has risen a bit with inflation, but it's still a paltry sum.[1] No, it's not the physical and chemical reductions that people often use to measure our worth, but the social inventions of life insurance and death benefits.

Upon our death, our mortgages can be paid off, leaving a home free and clear; salary continuances and employee continuances offer substantial sums of money that can be invested, as well as life insurance. A management journal recently suggested that few employed men and women of childbearing age would fall below their normal income if one of two employed spouses should die, since most insurance benefits are planned to replace lost income. But there is an added financial boost— because the principal from which the income was derived is still intact and could be divided at a later time.

In other words, adults are worth more dead than alive due to the financial safety nets we have created among the middle-class worker. The corollary is also true. At other times, this does not apply. For example, students have their whole earning potential ahead with no insurance yet, and older adults have term insurance that decreases with age or termination of employment.

We are talking, of course, about security of the financial type. Finances aside, adult-aged surviving children will tell you that the emotional security of a parent is worth far more. They would rather have their mother or father alive (without financial security) than dead (with financial security). Many surviving adult children can tell you of the nightmares of parental absence. They will tell you of the years spent reconstructing the past, which has been hidden by well-intentioned relatives. It has conditioned their ability to trust, to hope, even to perceive. No matter how incompetent a parent might be, most surviving adult children—if given the choice—would opt for the security of a parent over the security of a bank account.

Paul, when writing to the Christians in Philippi, confronted the same dilemma. At this point in his life, he was really worth more dead than he was alive. Early post-apostolic Hellenistic Christianity often softened the moral and ethical emphasis of its religious parent, Judaism. In the world in which Paul traveled, things were changing as fast as they are in ours. Borders of countries were changing, economies were changing, Roman cultural values and philosophies were changing. As Pax Romana spread its arms further and further, embracing more and more people in the eastern area cultured by Greece, Roman lifestyles began to change on the frontiers. In the Hellenistic areas, life after death was worth more than life now. Moving from a republic to an empire, as well as moving from the confines of Italy to the outreaches of the Mediterranean Sea, brought enormous changes in culture.

A good parallel might be found in the change in our culture brought by the Interstate highway systems—or, as they are officially known in the enabling legislation, National Defense Highways. At the age of fourteen, I accompanied my Aunt Dora on her annual auto trip to share the driving. It took us two nights and the better part of three days to travel a distance of eleven hundred miles. I still have the diary that I kept then. Each part of the country had its own flavor. Finding a place to eat and sleep was a real chore and often an embarrassment. Aunt Dora was a professor and director of the home economics division of the University of Georgia. She had a ritual of inspecting the kitchen of an establishment before eating. On several occasions, we exited the restaurant without eating, after she had pronounced it to be "a greasy spoon."

Aunt Dora would check the tourist cabins, the tourist homes, and the newly sprung up Holiday Motel chain for bedbugs and cockroaches. On more than one occasion, we left red-faced because she had pronounced the place to be "a fleabag." I learned that screen doors were a necessity in the Paducah, Kentucky, heat. I learned to carry ice in a chest because the sulfur water was disagreeable in Missouri. Each town we drove through imparted a bit of its wisdom and way of life. I learned about "Blacks-only" and "Gentiles-only" tourist homes. In Illinois, the

Staley Corn Syrup towns differed from the coal mining towns. In Iowa, the water towers in one town differed from those in another, as did the silos, depending on the company that owned the territory. In some places, we ate at cafés on the town square; in other places, those same types of eateries were called diners.

In my adult years, I have traveled that same route many times on the Interstates. Now I see chains of motels and restaurants that are national—not local—extensions of culture. Each has a certain sameness, which I have come to expect. Country Kitchens, Denny's, and McDonald's have the same menus whether I begin the trip in Omaha or end near Atlanta.

Along the countryside of the roadways, I can point out stretches of Route I80 in Nebraska that look the same as a stretch on Route I70 in Missouri or Route I40 in Tennessee. If you do not read the road signs, you would be at a loss to identify through which state you were passing. With the sameness has come a nationalization of culture at the intersections. But a mile or two back, off the Interstate is that same small town withdrawing into itself, while the highway—just beyond its reach—passes away into the nearby urban culture.

Now, that's Philippi. Philippi was the scene of a decisive victory in 42 BCE. Cassius and Brutus battled with Mark Antony and Octavian. Antony renamed the town (as a symbol of victory) for the father of Alexander the Great. The Via Egnatia (the great Roman Interstate between Rome and Asia) was rebuilt by Antony to pass near this town. It became a thriving commercial center, as would an intersection on one of our Interstates. From its humble origins on the hill above, it developed into a cosmopolitan atmosphere. But if a traveler would venture to the River Gangites, back off the Great Interstate, you would observe the small rural Greek mentality that was exclusive of the Roman occupants and citizens who gave it its cosmopolitan appearance. With the overthrow of Antony and transferal of Roman military by Octavian (now known as Caesar Augustus) to Neapolis (which was at the next interchange), Philippi slipped back in time as far as Roman influence was concerned.

Paul sailed across the Aegean Sea from Ephesus, making Philippi his first stop from the seacoast in Europe as he approached the East-West Interstate. Thessalonica was to his right and Athens was to his left. His relationship with the church, established at the villa of a wealthy cloth merchant named Lydia, was the most consistent of all his settlings. Over the years, the church maintained regular communications with Paul, regardless of where he might be traveling. The bishops and deacons of the church took a personal interest by sending letters and money while Paul was in prison. No theological arguments seemed to interest the Philippians, who seemed to be more concerned with Paul's welfare than with his theological words. They were more concerned with their own economic survival than with power politics.

Paul addressed them not as children, which he did in several letters to other churches, but as brothers/sisters, signifying the level of this relationship. They were beyond petty disagreements. Martyrdom was easy for him to accept, and he cautioned them to not be worried, because actually it would have been better off had he been martyred. He reasoned that without the visibility that he received (by his confrontation with Roman authorities), Christians might have been accepted in the very tolerant atmosphere of the Roman Empire. In many ways, if he were dead, their security would have been enhanced. But he reasoned that he had an obligation to live as long as he could, having appealed his justice to the highest court of the Empire, Rome itself. Paul had always prided himself on being a Roman of free birth, which granted him privileges of the Roman citizenship—but he was now being denied those privileges.

It surprises many people that Paul's strategy—which landed him in prison on more than one occasion—was to employ the judicial system of the state, giving him entry to levels of audiences for his theological message which otherwise would have been beyond his reach. The appeal system that had brought him to Rome, first under house arrest and then actual prison, was slow to work. Paul was finding his exit painfully slow. He knew his eventual fate.

His friends in Philippi knew it too. But like adult children, wanting to delay that moment of eventuality as long as possible, they sent Epaphroditus with encouragement and money. The trip was long to Rome from Philippi and required both sea and land transportation for more than eight hundred miles, in which only fifteen miles was considered a good day overland and fifty miles at sea was thought favorable. Epaphroditus arrived in Rome sick. He almost died. Paul found that he must muster the courage to encourage him. He forgot his own dilemma of whether to seek martyrdom or to live. He knew he was worth more alive than dead to the Philippians, so he should continue his appeal in the courts. He knew he must not give up now. He had come so far; he had gained access to the Roman establishment with the gospel. He wanted Christianity to have a universal hearing instead of a narrow following. Those who knew him must also have known that death and life have equal worth, that heavenly reward is of no more value than a productive earthly life.

There is no additional security or reward for faith, whether one lives for it or dies for it. They are of equal value. Contrary to popular opinion, those who die for their faith have no more advantage than those who live for it. Christianity is a faith for life and for death. Paul knew it and struggled; we know it and struggle. Are we worth more dead than alive? No, we are worth the same before God.

---

[1] Using a U.S. inflation calculator, I determined that $8.21 would have been equal to $39.89 in 1990 when the sermon was written. In 2016, it would be $72.83. However, that wasn't accounting for the black market on body parts I discovered when researching this question! A recent article in *Wired* magazine tabulated that a body is worth up to $45 million if you include bone marrow, organs, and DNA. But Dad was simply referring to the cost of the specific chemicals that make up our body parts. DataGenetics currently tabulates this to be about $160.

Thanksgiving and Encouragement

1 ³ I am grateful to God—whom I worship with a clear conscience, as my ancestors did—when I remember you constantly in my prayers night and day. ⁴ Recalling your tears, I long to see you so that I may be filled with joy. ⁵ I am reminded of your sincere faith, a faith that lived first in your grandmother Lois and your mother Eunice and now, I am sure, lives in you. ⁶ For this reason I remind you to rekindle the gift of God that is within you through the laying on of my hands; ⁷ for God did not give us a spirit of cowardice, but rather a spirit of power and of love and of self-discipline.

⁸ Do not be ashamed, then, of the testimony about our Lord or of me his prisoner, but join with me in suffering for the gospel, relying on the power of God, ⁹ who saved us and called us with a holy calling, not according to our works but according to his own purpose and grace. This grace was given to us in Christ Jesus before the ages began, ¹⁰ but it has now been revealed through the appearing of our Savior Christ Jesus, who abolished death and brought life and immortality to light through the gospel. ¹¹ For this gospel I was appointed a herald and an apostle and a teacher, ¹² and for this reason I suffer as I do. But I am not ashamed, for I know the one in whom I have put my trust, and I am sure that he is able to guard until that day what I have entrusted to him.

¹³ Hold to the standard of sound teaching that you have heard from me, in the faith and love that are in Christ Jesus. ¹⁴ Guard the good treasure entrusted to you, with the help of the Holy Spirit living in us.

When you rekindle the fires

Sermon by Richard Murdoch | Omaha, NE | October 16, 1983

We often have unreal perceptions of biblical figures. We somehow suspect that they were a different kind of being. In fact, we even honor that in our artistic representations of them by placing halos around their heads. But the story of Timothy shares with us that common malady known as burnout. And the scripture is not embarrassed to report such to the world. Timothy was weary. He remembered what it was like to have been excited about faith. But now that had eluded him. It is comforting to know that even a saint like Timothy had to rekindle his fire.

You can identify with his feelings, can't you? These feelings come not only in terms of faith, but in all areas of life—job, marriage, parenting, friends. These feelings come at various stages of our lives, don't they? Timothy was a relatively young man, in his late twenties or early thirties. But burnout happens during many cycles of life, the most definable one being what we know as the midlife crisis—you'll recognize that as the time when your forty-five-year-old neighbor down the street walked out of his house, got on a motorcycle, and left for places unknown because he just didn't feel the way he used to. And then the tongues began to wag.

But there is hardly any part of life—or any person—that's immune from the feeling that Timothy expresses. And burnout doesn't just occur a day at a time, and isn't simply a case of being down in the dumps. Timothy, like many of us, had good reasons for his dissatisfaction with life. And Timothy, like many of us, could have wallowed in his self-pity. I suspect he did for a while before he wrote to Paul.

Paul answered Timothy's letter gently. He didn't castigate or intimidate him for his lack of faith. He could have said what we often do: "Work harder!" But you know what that does to someone who got burned out by working hard in the first place. No help there! Instead, Paul said, "I remind you." Isn't that a wise thing to say? Paul's saying "Let me remind you of your roots" called Timothy back to pleasant experiences in the past. Paul called Timothy to get in touch with some significant experiences that centered on his mother and grandmother.

In the experience of remembrance, there is great power. Jesus knew that when he instituted communion—a means by which his disciples could experience a continual nurturing of faith through remembrance. Likewise, nations also know about the power of remembrance. We erect memorials on behalf of famous people, so that we can derive confidence from the remembrance of their words.

I was reminded of that again this week when I visited the Lincoln Memorial in Washington, DC. Reading the words of the Gettysburg Address and the Second Inaugural Address inscribed on the walls of that Grecian temple, I found that those words of wisdom inspire confidence today as much as they did one hundred and twenty-five years ago—and as much as they will a hundred years from now. Justice and forgiveness in the face of conflict has never been easy—now or then. The victors yelled for revenge, but President Lincoln sought justice.

By heeding Paul's calling for remembrance, and by embracing those wonderful experiences of the times in his life when he felt alive, Timothy was able to rekindle the fire from the glowing coals that lay there under protective ash. He had not lost the fire—it was always there.

Think of a banked fire. It was a necessity when I lived with a wood heater. In the evening before bed, we went to the woodstove and carefully covered up the live coals after the fire burned down. The fire never really went out, and the next morning we could take three slivers of pine and begin the fire again. Coals never would produce the heat necessary to cook. But without coals, you could not produce the initial heat to begin the process. You never lose the fire; it is always there in its potentiality.

Timothy did not lose his fire, it just didn't flame like it used to do, nor was it as exciting as it used to be. So what would be the result of blowing upon these coals? Paul said that the gifts of God would be renewed—those individualized gifts through which Timothy had enhanced the lives of many.

The Greek word for gifts is *charisma*. You know what that is. It is the very presence of a person. We all have charisma, but some people seem to show it more than others do. Charisma is tied to being, not doing. That's our first clue about the good news that Paul brought to Timothy.

When you experience burnout or you wear something out, you have overdone the doing and forgotten the being. No wonder Timothy was so tired.

My friend Jim told the following personal story. His young son Bobby wanted Jim to play with him, but Jim was busy doing the work of a pastor in his first church. It was a small parish, and Jim had to do everything, from being part-time sexton, to part-time secretary, to full-time pastor. His son repeatedly asked him to play at the most inconvenient times, so it seemed. Jim usually brushed him off as nicely as he could, especially on Saturday afternoons, his sermon writing day. But then things changed. One day Jim gave Bobby the usual, "I can't play with you now, I have to get ready to preach tomorrow!" And then the door to the upstairs porch slammed shut, as Bobby stomped down the steps, muttering loudly, "Too much doing preaching, not enough being Daddy!"

Likewise, Timothy had been doing too much disciplining and not enough being a disciple. It's easy to get into a trap like that. Since we think busyness is next to godliness, we are especially vulnerable. Too busy doing the things of marriage, we lose being married. Too busy doing things to keep friendships from falling apart, we don't have time to be friends. Too busy doing our jobs, we lose the joy of working. So we need to heed Paul's first suggestion: When you're burned out, feeling down in the dumps, or dead-ended, see if your doing has cancelled your being.

Paul's second suggestion was not to dilly-dally around too long. The word for timidity in Greek is *didala*, from which we get our English equivalent, dilly-dally. We all know what that means. No one has to explain it. Paul simply says, "God has not given us a spirit of timidity." We can dilly-dally around so long in analysis and self-pity that we enter analysis paralysis. We need to get on with it. Having majored in the minors and minored on the majors, we dilly-dally in our spirit, afraid to go on to what we need to be.

Paul gave a third and final suggestion for Timothy: The spirit that we can release from our remembrance is a spirit of power, love, and self-control. These words pale in English translation. Their Greek versions are strong, vital, and living words. The word for power is *dynamis,* from which we get dynamite. No need to say more about that! The word for love is *agape*, which is self-giving love. The word for self-control is *sophronismas,* and that means moderation. Literally, it means to keep a sound mind. It was used extensively in the Greek ideal of the "middle way" or the Golden Mean. Finding the middle way has fallen into disrepute in our culture in recent years. Loyalty to the left or the right, seeing issues as black or white, and standing up for our principles are all part of a reaction against the situational ethics of a generation ago, which is now seen as wishy-washy and unstable.[1]

Now, imagine what can happen to Timothy. He can climb out of his malaise by getting in touch with his remembrance of his root experiences of faith with Lois and Eunice. He can call upon the ritual of laying-on of hands in blessing, which Paul had performed. He doesn't have to dilly-dally around, because the spirit God gives us is as powerful as dynamite. It is expansive and giving. It is secure and sensible, guiding itself neither left nor right, while avoiding the politics of loyalties.

Timothy can feel rekindled through that which is within him, and which never left him. Timothy can feel alive again! He can embrace the future through embracing the past. He is useful; he is necessary; he is good. He does have gifts to share with the world. They are not useless gifts, for they are from God and for the world. Self-giving love goes before Timothy. His charisma is dynamic, loving, and sensible. What better good news could he have expected to hear from his old mentor, Paul? And what better news do we need to hear—and be—than exactly the same? Rekindle the gift of God that is within you!

---

[1] Interestingly, since the time my father wrote this, the middle way has been making a strong comeback as people embrace Buddhism and Eastern thought. According to *Dharma World* magazine, there has been a fifteen-fold dramatic increase in Buddhists in America since the 1960s. Three million Americans claim to be Buddhists, and another twenty-seven million are "strongly influenced" by Buddhism.

Context: Revelation

I once saw this on a t-shirt: "Jesus was the first zombie." It caught my eye because I love zombies. And until I started researching this book, I thought the t-shirt was pretty darn clever. But I learned, thanks to Dad's sermons, that, according to the Hebrew and Christian scriptures, many people were thought to have been raised from the dead before Jesus—and not in a horror movie kind of way. So I'm not going to get the t-shirt.

In addition to my love of zombie movies, I'm a huge fan of teenage apocalyptic novels. My favorite bookstore has an entire wall of them, and I can't get enough. Post-exilic people of many faiths were big fans of apocalyptic literature too. The Book of Daniel is one example. So are the non-canonical Christian books: the Apocalypse of Peter, the Apocalypse of Paul, and the Shepherd (of Hermas).

And, of course, there is the Revelation of John in the Bible. When I found out its Greek title was *Apokalypsis Ioannou* (John's Apocalypse), I dove a little deeper into the history of the word "apocalypse." I found out it doesn't always mean what I thought it did. Apocalypse doesn't actually mean the end (as we use it today), it simply means "revealed" or "uncovering." And what was being revealed was a prophecy about the end of the world and the beginning of a new one.

This type of apocalyptic world view was common in times of despair and suffering. Jesus, Paul, and the early Christians had all preached that the end of the world was near, so this idea was not new when Revelation was written sometime around 65 CE to 90 CE by the prophet John of Patmos. (Tradition often attributes this book to the Apostle John of gospel fame, but scholars now think it is unlikely the two books were written by the same John, or that Revelation was written by the Apostle John, son of Zebedee).

Revelation is full of graphic, fantastic imagery and symbolism about the play between good and evil. A series of three sets of major disasters are detailed, with rich descriptions of destruction, false prophets, the antichrist, and a final judgment. This is followed by a stunning vision of the new utopian heaven.

Throughout the ages, people have used this book to point to the end of the world in their own time period. However, scholars think it is most likely a description of how the author thought God would overthrow the emperor, and the Roman Empire would be destroyed. Its words were meant to promote hope during a time of oppression and despair.

Meanwhile...

Around the Mediterranean, the original Apostles died. Tradition provides gruesome details, which run the full gamut. Apostles were stabbed, stoned, beheaded, crucified, flayed, or filled with arrows. Only John is said to have died in old age of natural causes. The internments of each Apostles' remains are claimed by churches in Spain (James), Sicily (Matthew), Germany (Matthias), Greece (Andrew), India (Thomas), Turkey (John and Phillip), and the remainder in Rome.

The Jewish/Roman Wars were underway, as the Jewish people tried to reinstate an independent Judean state that was out from under Rome's oppressive thumb. The Second Temple in Jerusalem was destroyed, and a Roman temple placed at its former spot. The Jewish people lost their homeland. (Six hundred years later, an Islamic shrine, named the Dome of the Rock, was built on the original Temple Mount, creating a real estate feud that still rages on today.)

A destructive earthquake hit the Roman cities of Pompeii and Herculaneum. A mere seventeen years later Mount Vesuvius, the only active volcano in mainland Europe, erupted in a twenty-one-mile high cloud of gas and ash. Both cities were destroyed.

Enormous displays of Roman authority continued, including the completion of the Coliseum. Its dedication included 100 consecutive days of gladiator combat, interspersed with hunting wild animals and executing Christians. According to an inscription on its wall, the building materials included war spoils—possibly including those from the Jerusalem temple.

It would be two hundred bleak and deadly years for the Christians before the 311 CE edict allowing the practice of the Christian religion in the Roman Empire. Over the next eighty years, Christianity would increase in popularity, and eventually, Emperor Constantine would declare it the official state religion. As the number of followers grew, and the centuries passed, the clashes between Christianity and other religions would grow. No longer a persecuted religion, it often would wield its power to be the persecutor, causing the oppression and despair it had itself tried to be free from.

Luckily, in many denominations there now has been a call to return to the messages within Christianity that can most benefit humanity as a whole, especially valuing neighborly love over power.

The more people of all faiths can embrace love over power—love of each other and love of our planet—the less likely we are to end up bringing on the end of our own world. We'd be wise to remember the revelation of the English poet Robert Browning: "Without love, our earth is a tomb."

The New Heaven and the New Earth

21 ¹ Then I saw a new heaven and a new earth; for the first heaven and the first earth had passed away, and the sea was no more. ² And I saw the holy city, the new Jerusalem, coming down out of heaven from God, prepared as a bride adorned for her husband. ³ And I heard a loud voice from the throne saying,

"See, the home of God is among mortals.
He will dwell with them;
they will be his peoples,
and God himself will be with them;
⁴ he will wipe every tear from their eyes.
Death will be no more;
mourning and crying and pain will be no more,
for the first things have passed away."

Will my dog go to heaven?

Sermon by Richard Murdoch | East Lansing, MI | June 13, 1993

"Will my dog go to heaven?" Little did the young girl know the depth of the simple question which she had asked. Even less did she know to what extent her Sunday school teacher would research her question, because he too, as a child, had wondered about his own dog. "I'm not quite sure, but let me think about it," the teacher replied.

That very Sunday afternoon, he began his assignment in the church's library. He first pulled out the *Dictionary of Theological Words* and turned to the entry for "heaven." He read that heaven is not a uniquely Christian concept. It is shared by many different religious traditions.

The notions of a heaven in the Bible seem to have two sources: the exile to Egypt in the fourteenth century BCE and the Babylonian exile in the sixth century BCE. A Christian interpretation of heaven is most noted in the Book of Revelation, authored on a Greek island in the Aegean Sea sometime between the first and second centuries CE, thousands of miles away from Babylon of the sixth century BCE.

The teacher went on to the *Dictionary of Biblical Words*. The word "heaven" is closely connected to height or highest in the languages of the Bible. In fact, Genesis refers to the upper part of the ocean of vapors which envelope the earth. And as the teacher read, to his mind came that marvelous twentieth-century photograph of our earth taken by the space explorers, showing a blue-green globe enveloped with swirling clouds. And he wondered aloud about the similarity of past "myths" of Genesis and present "facts" of science. Wow!

But this dictionary led the teacher into even deeper waters. He found in Hebrew scriptures, heaven was portrayed in no less than eight metaphors that included a mirror, curtain, dressing robe, and window. Then, in a gospel, he found that heaven seemed to indicate not only an idealized morality that reflected God's moral values, but also a defined space, which was idealized as paradise—the perfect or complete existence.

But it was in Revelation that the teacher found heaven as a defined afterlife, in which God (and those who believed in God) would dwell forever. He read about streets paved with gold and beautiful buildings made of gemstones. He read about the promise for no more sorrow, no more pain, no more tears. He read about trappings of royalty and power. He read and read, but in no place did he find that any dogs—or, for that matter, any animals—were included in this paradise, this perfect existence where all were joyful.

Armed with this arsenal of information from scholars and students of the Bible, the teacher began to reflect on how he would break the news to the distraught little girl. "No, Virginia, dogs don't go to heaven. The Bible tells me so." Simple and to the point. That's that! She might as well learn the hard facts of life now. He could soften the blow, he thought, by saying something like, "But Virginia, since we don't remember anything about this life in heaven, don't worry, it won't make you sad." But then he thought to himself, "What's the point of that? Memories are what life is all about. Do we start new memories over again in heaven? No, that's too much for even me to think about. Better leave that one alone."

But something continued to haunt him in his memory: the story about another little girl named Virginia and Santa Claus. In 1897, a little girl named Virginia wrote a letter to the *New York Sun* newspaper's editor because the existence of someone very special to her, Santa Claus, was denied. It seemed that both her childhood friends and the adults she knew didn't believe in her favorite person because they had more facts than she did. And they told her so. Heartbroken, she wrote a letter to someone who should know: the editor of a newspaper. And newsman Francis Pharcellus Church's poignant response included the following:

> *Virginia, your little friends are wrong. They have been affected by the skepticism of a skeptical age. They do not believe except they see. They think that nothing can be which is not comprehensible by their little minds. All minds, Virginia, whether they be men's or children's, are little. In this great universe of ours man is a mere insect, an ant, in his intellect, as compared with the boundless world about him, as measured by the intelligence capable of grasping the whole of truth and knowledge.*[1]

The gears of the teacher's brain began to engage themselves. If God created this boundless world in stages of days, as Genesis described, and pronounced each day's creation as good and pleasing, then why would he not include the same elements of creation in heaven? Secondly, if creation "groans," as Paul says in Romans, to be accepted to its fullness, then all of creation will be redeemed and saved, not just a portion of it, right? And thirdly, if heaven is a state of existence which begins now with moral reflection of God (a mirror) and extends beyond this life so that we can see more of God's goodness...

Virginia truly loved and took care of her dog. The dog was a companion upon which she lavished the same kind of feelings that adults do on other adults and children. Of course, the teacher thought, "If heaven is God's happiness with us, and that happiness has been shown through God's creation, then all parts of that creation will be present and continuing."

So the next Sunday came. The moment arrived. The teacher was satisfied that he could relieve the heavy burden of grief for the little girl. "Virginia, I have thought about your question about whether dogs go to heaven when they die," the teacher said. "You know, I think they do, because heaven is when we feel God very near. Heaven is when we feel happy, safe, friendly, and loved. Sometimes we feel that way right now. But sometimes something comes along and we feel sad and hurt. Heaven is a place where that will never happen, and it might be a long way off. God's happiness never ends, even though we might die and leave our family, friends, and pets. But sometimes they leave us first, like your dog. I think God has a special place for our pets because they are very special to us. Does that help you in your sadness?"

Wow, he thought, I got through it. Not a bad job, I guess? Then he looked inquiringly into the little girl's eyes to see how much of the theology had been absorbed. The little girl returned his glance without so much as a reflective "ah-ha" expression. She glibly replied, "Mr. Murdoch, my dog didn't die. I was just wondering."

---

[1] I highly recommend reading the full text of Francis Pharcellus Church's letter to Virginia. Simply do an Internet search for "Yes, Virginia, there is a Santa Claus."

Who speaks for God?

Sermon by Richard Murdoch | East Lansing, MI | February 16, 1986

When I was but a recently graduated seminary student, I served a congregation lodged in a historic, Colonial, white-framed church building.
Beside it was a Revolutionary-era cemetery in which several notable
persons were buried. To take a shortcut from the church to the social
hall, most everyone made a mad dash through the grave markers to get
to coffee hour, which was attended by both adults and children.

On one particular Sunday, I had dressed in a bathrobe and white
beard to relate a children's story about St. Paul. Midway along the path to
the social hall, I exited for the church school building and encountered
several small children wandering through the graveyard. As they saw me
rounding the corner, a look of amazement came over their faces. Quickly,
they ran inside the social hall's door for which they had been headed.

At coffee hour that day, a smiling mother greeted me with, "Well,
you gave our church school class a scare today! Several have the habit
of being tardy. Today they ran in breathlessly and announced that they
saw God coming through the cemetery! I knew they probably had timed
it right and had seen you. So I corrected them by telling them that you
were not God, but that you did speak for God."

Need I tell you that I was overcome with awe that a child would hold
me in such reverence? Yet, I also felt a great disappointment that the
teacher was not better prepared to interpret the finer points of theology.
Who does speak for God? Do I? Really?

Many claim to speak for God. Many claim to know the mind of God.
Do you remember the embarrassing incident several years ago when
the then-president of a local organization made the assertion in a public meeting that God does not hear the prayer of a Jewish person? Such
a statement in this quarter of the twentieth century evoked gasps of
unbelief from the secular press and quick apologies by embarrassed
preachers and members of the associated churches.

But he stuck by his words, on the basis of his theology—only God's elect and saved people (those with personal conversion experiences in line with the Acts of the Apostles) could be heard by God. "The Bible said so," he insisted; and he quoted jot and tittle for those who questioned his ability to speak for God.

"God's Word," as a written word in our Bible, can be traced back as far as the third century. Before the Council of Constantinople in 382 CE, the written Word of God was circulated in individual letter and scroll form. For nearly two thousand years previous, it was an oral tradition. It was passed by memory from generation to generation of the Twelve Tribes of the ancient Israelites—from father to son, priest to priest, and prophet to prophet. Each person who repeated the words spoke with the force of God himself.

Moses spoke with the force of God himself, not unlike his predecessors, the patriarchs Abraham, Isaac, Jacob, and Joseph. The great reformers Ezra and Nehemiah spoke the word with much the same credibility. The word they spoke was God's word. King David—who was both a secular and religious ruler—ruled by divine right. God's spoken word became the rule of a nation. David's enemies resisted Israel's move toward a monarchy. Only those with a religious vocation were worthy of speaking for God.

David secularized religion, much to the despair of the traditionalists—but alas, the world was changing! "The only thing we can be sure of in this world is change!" David spoke for God as did Solomon, and all the monarchs, until the kingdoms were divided and the monarchies fell. Then those who spoke for God were the prophets of the Exile—Isaiah, Jeremiah, and Ezekiel; Daniel, Hosea, and Amos.

But soon these prophets passed from the scene, and the local rabbis and the temple priests assumed the power of the Word of God. They spoke for God, said the people.

But with the successive invasions by outsiders, the political leaders began to speak for God. The Sanhedrin was the place in Jesus's day, where politicians spoke for God—the Sadducees and Pharisees.

A few wandering prophets tried to speak as well, but were hardly heard. John the Baptizer was one, but he deferred to his cousin Jesus, as were the Essenes, a semi-monastic community by the sea.

Jesus stood up in the synagogue in his hometown of Nazareth sometime around his thirtieth birthday—which, in that day, was somewhere beyond middle age—claiming to speak and act on behalf of God. He informed the hearers of the Isaiah passage that he was its fulfillment. The Apostles also claimed to speak for God, when their master Jesus was no longer present to speak.

After the Apostles had faded from the Earth, the bishops spoke for God. And one of them became a primary spokesperson in an era when people were looking for order. He was affectionately addressed as *Il Pappa,* the Holy Father, or the Pope.

In the Dark Ages of Europe, late in the first millennium, monasteries and their abbots, rather than the Pope or church councils, spoke for God. Monks were considered to be unspoiled by the world, therefore they could speak for God with a purer voice.

Then Reformers also spoke for God. Like the prophets Ezra and Nehemiah, Luther and Calvin railed against the corruption they saw in the faith. They—like David—secularized the church by suggesting that non-ordained persons might speak for God. John Calvin—the father of the Reformed and Presbyterian churches—never conducted a baptismal or a communion service, nor did he "marry or bury." He refused ordination to dramatize the idea that clergy were not the exclusive spokespeople for God. But laypeople went too far. Martin Luther criticized laypeople who spoke for God by using the written word, the Bible. He accused them of creating a "paper Pope," which he thought was no better than a human Pope.

And then monarchs began to speak for God again, in the tradition of King David. King Henry the Eighth of England claimed to speak for God. He refused to listen to the Pope. The Bible spoke to him plainly. Since the Sabbath was made for man, and not man for the Sabbath, according to the scriptures, then the same could be said for marriage, King Henry believed. So Henry the Eighth made sacred serial polygamy, the taking of a series of wives, one at a time in order, to maintain the succession of the throne by divine right.

In the 1700s, Czar Peter the Great sparred with the patriarchs of the Russian Orthodox Church. He ruled by divine right and spoke for God. God wanted Russia brought into the modern age, he announced, even though all religious persons opposed him.

But then democracy burst upon the scene, right upon the heels of capitalism, which offered profits and prosperity for all. Then church meetings began to speak for God. The majority rules in democracy, so it was obvious that God ruled by the majority too. Soon presidents and prime ministers began to claim again that through the majority election they ruled by the grace of God. President Lincoln claimed by virtue of his underdog election to have a divine mission to abolish slavery in a peaceful way.

But other prophets reveled in exposing social injustices like slavery. Sojourner Truth, a freed slave, proclaimed a divine mission, speaking for God to undo the wrongs of the centuries. As did the monks of the past, prophets spoke for God through the thunder of righteousness and the claim of individual morality to bring women's suffrage, Prohibition, Social Security, and the League of Nations.

Individual preachers who traveled on horseback through the western frontier claimed to speak for God because they could read the Word of God, while the unschooled could only hear it.

And then the minority claimed that it spoke for the God. In the tradition of the Israelite remnant, the minority was holy, not the majority. Think of Dr. Martin Luther King, who advocated peaceful non-compliance against the segregation laws. The minority movements took up the charge to be speaking for God through the support of the written word.

Conflict in one church is no different from conflict in any church. Conflict over social, moral, and theological questions—when reduced to its lowest common denominator—seems to be simply one of power: "Who speaks for God?"

But of those who speak for God, who has the right answer?

So...
do preachers' kids
have no religion?

"One should not think, 'My religion alone is the right path and
other religions are false.' God can be realized by means of all paths."
—from *Râmakrishna: His Life and Sayings (1898)*

"I'm going to need another bookshelf," I professed to my husband, Sean. Little brown book packets were arriving from all over the globe daily—thanks to the Amazon app on my phone. It seemed that I did indeed have religion... all of them.

My spiritual journey had bypassed the rest stops of religious exclusivity and mere religious tolerance, plowing instead straight onto the interstate of interspirituality. What an interesting outcome for someone who, as a teenager, had proudly—albeit briefly—declared myself an atheist and anarchist to Canadian customs officials, when questioned about a "Thank God I'm an Anarchist" sticker applied to the rear window of my Ford Fiesta.

Rabbi Jonathan Sack's description of atheists in his book, *The Great Partnership: Science, Religion, and the Search for Meaning,* pegs my teenage misstep well: "Atheism deserves better than the new atheists, whose methodology consists of criticizing religion without understanding it; quoting texts without contexts; taking exceptions as the rule; confusing folk belief with reflective theology; abusing, ridiculing, and demonizing religious faith and holding it responsible for the great crimes against humanity." At some time or another, I had been guilty of all of these tactics. I had indeed thrown the baby out with the bathwater. Having seen how religion had been used to hurt people I loved— and how it spurred homophobia, misogyny, war, and hate—I had refused to believe that good things could come out of it.

Sack acknowledges this as well, going on to wisely offer, "Religion has done harm; I acknowledge that. But the cure for bad religion is good religion, not no religion, just as the cure for bad science is good science, not the abandonment of science."

Over and over, throughout my research for this book, I read the words of people who had learned to seek without contempt. I opened up with a willingness to admit that I knew very little and embarked on a journey for knowledge. I began to understand what the wise Swami Vivekananda meant when he quipped: "Religion, the great milk cow, has given many kicks... but never mind, it gives a great deal of milk."

My father, of course, saw the map for my journey before I even embarked on it. In the sermon he read on the day of my baptism, he announced:

> You see, I have found that an infant is quite helpless. Sarah's head wiggles from side to side. Until her neck muscles improve, we must support her head. She is helpless to support herself. I have found that an infant cannot be reasoned with. When Judy received a card with the feeding schedule it stated: 2:00, 6:00, 10:00, and "on demand." We did not quite know what "on demand" meant, but it didn't take long to find out. We realized that we could not reason with Sarah that it was 1:30 not 2:00. She was hungry; she knew it; and she demanded to be fed. We found out that Sarah is not too well-disciplined at her age of four weeks.
>
> So here is Sarah, our daughter, who cannot say "I believe." She is helpless, unable to reason, and undisciplined. That is the point of theology that intersects with baptism. It describes our condition before God. God chooses to be with us despite our helplessness. He does not require us to be always rational and reasonable. We do not have to say "I believe" before he will accept us. We do not have to be fully matured. We do not have to be great.

I doubt that my father thought it would take 44 years for me to be able to confidently state: "I believe." Likewise, he couldn't have known that it would finally happen through the typed words of his sermons. But don't press me too much to tell you exactly what I believe. I'm nowhere near being able to verbalize a nice, succinct statement or creed yet.

In his column for *Spirituality & Health* magazine, "Roadside Assistance for the Spiritual Traveler," Rabbi Rami Shapiro was asked this question by a reader: "I'm considering converting to [a new religion], but I'm afraid to leave [my current religion] because I might be damned to Hell for all eternity. What should I do?" It's a shame, really, that many people have been taught religious exclusivity; that questioning your religion, or practicing another one, will lead to damnation. Shapiro answers the question with a light, but wise, attitude: "I sympathize with your fear of damnation, but every religion claims to be true, so it is impossible to know which, if any, is actually true. My suggestion is for you to join a religion that supports your values, and if it turns out that your values send you to Hell, at least you'll be with like-minded people."

I love Rabbi Shapiro's humor, but I always find myself bristling when thinking about choosing just *one* religion. It is the same feeling I had when asked at the beginning of this project: "Well, are you a Christian?" And my answer kept coming out: "Yes and no." I wish I had known then Gandhi's brilliant answer when asked if he was a Hindu: "Yes, I am. I am also a Christian, a Muslim, a Buddhist, and a Jew."

One of Gandhi's contemporaries, Paramahansa Yogananda, suggested, "Religion is really nothing but the merging of our individuality in universality." And when I look around, I am pleased to see there is merging all around me. In fact, across town from my elementary school in Omaha, Nebraska (and where my father received his nickname "The Rev"), change is on the horizon. It's called the Tri-faith Initiative, and it is happening on a 38-acre plot where a Jewish country club used to be. The site will now house a church, synagogue, and mosque—all at a single location. Along with a shared location, the three faith communities share a single vision: "...to build bridges of respect, acceptance and trust, to challenge stereotypes, to learn from each other, and to counter the influence of fear and misunderstanding."

And this merging isn't restricted within the three Abrahamic traditions. Eastern teachings of God consciousness are increasingly merging with Western teachings about God. Baby boomers who were once criticized for their New Age fads have ushered in a rich tapestry of ancient wisdom to add to and complement their religions of birth. One of the most intriguing books I came across was *Jesus, Buddha, Krishna & Lao Tzu: The Parallel Sayings*. In it, author Richard Hooper laboriously combs the scriptures of Christianity, Buddhism, Hinduism, and Taoism to point out the overwhelming number of parallel sayings that appear, thus decreasing the perceived divide between Christianity and Eastern philosophies.

Even as religious intolerance screams at me from the television news, I read comforting stories of healing within and between denominations. For example, Catholics and Lutherans are planning a shared liturgy to mark the anniversary of the Reformation next year. Their joint report, "From Conflict to Communion," and their "Common Prayer" booklet emphasize the shared beliefs between the denominations, rather than the differences that split them apart five hundred years ago. The report passionately states, "We deeply regret the evil things that Catholics and Lutherans have mutually done to each other."

Increasingly, in my reading, I am coming across the concept of *perennial philosophy*. This term developed as early as the 1500s, but was popularized by the Transcendentalists of the early nineteenth century, and then by Aldous Huxley in his 1945 book *The Perennial Philosophy*. Perennialism, as summed up by Wikipedia, is the idea that there is a "perennial or mystic inner core to all religious or spiritual traditions, without the trappings, doctrinal literalism, sectarianism, and power structures that are associated with institutionalized religion ... each of the world's religious traditions sharing a single, universal truth on which foundation all religious knowledge and doctrine has grown."

Just over fifty years later, Wayne Teasdale ushered in what he called the "interspiritual age." In the book, *Community of Religions: Voices and Images of the Parliament of World Religions*, which in 1993 documented the hundredth anniversary of that groundbreaking event, Teasdale notes:

> *The rise of community among cultures and religious traditions brings with it a deeply fruitful openness to learning from one another. It makes possible what we can call "interspirituality": the assimilation of insights, values, and spiritual practices from the various religions and their application to one's own inner life and development. This phenomenon has truly revolutionary implications, especially for the real likelihood of a global culture and civilization forming that is unmistakably universal in more than a geographical sense.*

When I first came across interspirituality, I thought, "Aha!" I knew that although I had grown up in a religiously siloed community, my father had worked tirelessly on promoting "interfaith" dialogues and events— I was just too young to really understand it. I still had the black/white, either/or mentality of a child. But after reading ninety-eight books, attending ten college courses on Christianity and Judaism, watching numerous documentaries, meditating at a dozen weekend retreats, hiking countless hours to scriptures on audiobooks, and reading fifteen-hundred sermons, I finally get it.

I don't have to choose. This preacher's kid can have all religions. And each day, joyfully, with this vision, my spiritual journey continues, as my relationship with *That Which Makes Trees* grows deeper. The void I felt when detached from my faith is gone. And I know my journey is destined to continue—I just packed my bags for an interspiritual seminary.

Afterword:
Butterflies in my spirit

Thoughts from Amy Murdoch

> psyche ('sahy-kee)
> *noun*
> the human soul, spirit, or mind
> in Greek ψυχή ("psychí"), also meaning butterfly
> and "one who incites courage"
> —*dictionary.com*

I'm told as a child I was like a butterfly. Born a believer, a pure soul. Early mornings I would happily jump out of bed and proceed to wake-up the rest of the house, "Up Mom, up Dad, up Sis." I embodied bright life, joy, and happiness.

As the younger sister, I always wanted to play with the older girls. Being younger felt like a chip on my shoulder. I was determined to stand my ground and be part of the older "in" crowd. I, too, remember the butterfly ceremony Sarah mentioned in her opening chapter. However, in my version, I was upset I had to be the minister in black and white rather than one of the beautiful butterflies in pastels. I should have been happy to be included, but instead, I felt frustration.

This frustration also appeared when I tried to define my role and purpose in life. I remember hearing "Kids are to be seen, not heard" and "Respect your elders." I was confused about how to decipher these. I wanted to be heard, yet in certain situations, it seemed my voice didn't matter. And these messages didn't seem congruent with those I heard from my father.

I grew up trusting, thinking adults were infallible. And I believed when people "grew up" and became adults they would always try to "do the right thing." My naivety followed me through high school and college. Always in the back of my head, I heard two little voices—one continuously repeating forgiveness for people who hurt me and the second screaming "What about me?" I still struggle with wanting to please people and forgive people while also standing up for myself and being true to my spirit/soul.

Inwardly I felt like one person and outwardly, I felt like another. My internal persona was lonely, scared, and confused while my outward persona still exemplified the happy, joyous child. This internal void grew with time. The outward child still loved being me—climbing a tree in my carefully chosen ruffled tube top and jeans, carrying a matching purse. And in these moments, I still had carefree feelings of happiness.

I remember feeling horribly scared at night, although I was too scared to tell anyone. One evening after hours of rolling back and forth trying to sleep, I made up a prayer. After that evening, I said my prayer every night before nodding off to sleep:

> *Dear God,*
> *Thank you for this day and how it has gone.*
> *Please help me through this night and tomorrow safely and*
> *soundly without anything bad or painful happening to me.*
> *Please watch out for all those whom I love, especially those*
> *dearest to my heart.*
> *And please take me to the kingdom of heaven when I die.*
> *Thank you.*
> *Love Amy, Amen*

To this day, I still say this prayer, though later in life, I began alternating my prayer with the Lord's Prayer.

My early memories of church include volunteer babysitting during service, helping with post-service refreshments, and sneaking up into the balcony to watch weddings. My most cherished memory is my dad standing in the pulpit. I loved listening to him spin a story for the congregation about biblical times, current events, and life in general. He would keep you on the edge of your seat, yet also leave you thinking about the topic for days after. I felt a well-orchestrated feeling of calm and peace on Sunday mornings.

Sometimes, when Dad had a late counseling appointment, I would spend evenings at church. A typical evening included busying myself with homework in one of the preschool rooms. I knew the fastest routes through the church. Red exit lights illuminated the dark hallways—

making it an eerily on-point setting for a scary movie. Late night stillness in the church contradicted the comforting feelings of Sunday morning service, yet still, a sense of peace and warmth filled the quiet space.

In early 2004, I moved back to New York from California after my Dad's diagnosis (and before his passing). I felt compelled to head back East even though I dearly loved the West Coast. My Dad's diagnosis seemed mild to moderate, and I assumed he would persevere. I had rarely seen him sick growing up. One morning a month before his passing, I woke up feeling at peace yet with a large void. I felt horribly winded. I've always had extremely vivid dreams and frequently journal when I wake. In that dream:

> *I'm in a town with my father. We're traveling by car with the masses on roads, through tunnels, and then we come to stairs. Driving is no longer an option. Dad is weak. I help him. We try the stairs. The people are too busy to help. We walk down the cement steps by the side railing. I am holding him up. Helping. It is dangerous. He stumbles. We make it down and into a home. The home is beautiful. It's indoor/outdoor. Mini pools and gardens appear throughout the home with connecting bridges and gorgeous plants blooming everywhere. It's beautiful, yet I am still fearful. The ground begins to shake. I think it's impossible the massive, solid pillars of the home will topple. And then the impossible happens—the house starts to cave into the pools. I move to avoid the danger all around me. My father is no longer with me. The dust settles, and it is once again calm. I look around and notice the pools. What was once beautiful is still beautiful in a different way. It's quiet, calm, and peaceful. I swim slowly through the calm, cool water to the other side. There are others around me. I feel their presence. I am alone, yet I'm not alone, and I know this. I leave out the side door by myself, and I drive away.*

Through this dream, I think my dad was trying to tell me to be prepared that he would be leaving this world—yet peace would be possible after his passing. He was a pillar not only within our family but also in so many other facets of his life. It seemed impossible and implausible he would pass.

Maybe this is where my void hit home the most. How do I live a spiritually, morally directed life, yet also manage survival skills in today's world? I wear my vulnerability like a badge on my arm, which sometimes leads to learning some of life's lessons more than one time around. And maybe this also answers the question, "So... do preachers' kids have no religion?" We do have religion. Religion shaped my "little girl" and helped guide me towards being a "big girl."

Six years ago, my sister Sarah started talking to me about her project, and I was grateful that our father's work might continue through it. When I read Sarah's draft of this book, many things resonated although one thing truly stuck out. Dad's sermons didn't have a Disney ending. Often, as children, we grow up watching, hearing, and learning stories that end in perfect endings, but life doesn't always follow this pattern. Dad helped me make sense of how reality can be fulfilling, even when it is not perfect.

I thank God, my family, and my friends for their continued support on my journey. Today, my two little voices are beginning to balance, blend, and consequently "fill the void." Faith brings no guarantees, just opportunities. I'm learning to trust in my faith. My decisions are less flippant than before. My actions are more thoughtfully calculated. I've learned to ask for help. And accept help. And lastly, I'm happy— happy with life.

These sermons are a reminder we are all connected to a greater Source. Maybe the pure soul I felt as a child—that God created to come into this world—was a preview of what could be and will be when I exit this world. Maybe I'm finally emerging from my cocoon. Emerging into something more powerful and beautiful, created by a greater Source and strengthened with faith.

My sister and I are no longer struggling with our voids. We are no longer detached. We are attached to each other and to something greater than ourselves.

May the source be with you.
May its light shine upon you.

Amen.

An enormous thank you to...

Sean Bowen for tirelessly supporting my many writing sabbaticals. Without them, this book would still be in draft form.

Amy Murdoch for forgiving the mistakes of my ridiculous years and becoming my best friend.

Francine Glasser for saving my life. More than once.

Judy Murdoch who provided dates and locations where my memory or my sister Amy's were fuzzy, insisted that we both get As in English, and raised us in libraries.

Robert Bowen for participating in many long-winded theological conversations. Remember God loves every fabulous ounce of you.

The Reverend Dan Love for answering countless theological questions, even the irreverent ones.

The Reverend Eileen Fisher for encouraging me to expand and truly understanding me. Roadkill ministry here I come.

Paul Cohen for appearing in the right place at the right time to help publish this book. **Susan Piperato** for her stellar editing and for helping cure me of my italics addiction (*almost*).

Checko Miller for his eagle eyes and the wonderful edits that resulted from his hard work. Punctuation can indeed save lives. (To wit: That is a wrap. Let's eat friends!)

Pranjit Roy and his team for getting over six-hundred scans of typed sermons into a digital format I could work with. Without you, I would still be typing.

Kris Garnier, Meaghan Colligan, and my seminary mates who never stopped asking, "So, how is the book coming? Is it *done* yet?"

...and the many members of all of my father's churches, for helping guide me in this journey.

And to...

The Roxbury where much of this book was written. Some people have cabins or writing retreats, but I have The Roxbury. Just before you turn off the main road to get there, you must pass through Arkville, NY and its light-pole signs proclaiming "There's Noah place like Arkville." How auspicious that I would have to pass through a biblical reference every stay. I can't thank owners Greg and Joseph, as well as the entire staff, enough for providing me a silent, shimmering, sugar-filled sanctuary to research and write this book. I can think of no finer place to read, write, or relax. Plan your stay at theroxburymotel.com

Michigan State University Library for its quiet East Side. Eons ago when I attended MSU as a student, my diploma was delayed on account of unpaid overdue library fines that, luckily, my father stepped in to pay. Each year of this project, I traveled back to the library for research—using the same books my father had when he was minister of Peoples Church, located just across the street. Except now I avoided fines as well as the beckoning green floor lines. My father would be overjoyed at both.

Vassar College Library for giving me lending privileges, and for maintaining their stunning and inspiring stained-glass windows. I am blessed to have studied in view of a panel showing Lady Elena Lucretia Cornaro-Piscopia receiving a degree, after having been formerly denied the examination for the Doctor of Theology degree because she was a woman.

One Spirit Interfaith Seminary for saying yes, and teaching me how to do the same.

About
the contributors

Sarah Bowen

Sarah has been writing technical and marketing copy for over 20 years in order to finance her extensive travel addiction. To that end, she has traveled to every continent except Antarctica (but it's on the list!) and every state in the U.S. (except Montana, which is also on the list). The most interesting thing she'd ever done (prior to this book) was paraglide in the Himalayas with an Egyptian vulture named Bob.

Sean Bowen

Sean has been exhibiting his uniquely-styled paintings in New York City and the Hudson Valley for over 35 years. His work is generally full of strong color and form, but he graciously accepted the challenge to create divine line art illustrations in black & white for this book. (See more of his work at seanbowen.com). The author often holds him hostage in her projects since they married in 2010.

Amy Murdoch

Amy likewise often becomes a hostage in Sarah's projects. But this one she has been grateful to be part of, contributing the afterword. She's ecstatic to finally get a word in edgewise on her loquacious sister... for once.

Photos © Sean Bowen

CPSIA information can be obtained
at www.ICGtesting.com
Printed in the USA
FFOW03n0042230117
31587FF